Table of Contents

Table of Contents ....

Free Gift 15

Breakfast Instant Pot Recipes 16

    Ham and Egg Casserole 16

    Delicious Egg Bake 16

    Espresso Steel Cut Oats 17

    Chocolate Oatmeal 17

    Breakfast Meat Soufflé 18

    Tasty Quiche 18

    Peaches Oatmeal 19

    Apple Steel Cut Oats 19

    Mexican Breakfast 20

    French Toast 20

    Western Omelette 21

    Simple Frittata 21

    Simple Burrito Casserole 22

    Spanish Frittata 22

    French Eggs 23

    Eggs and Bacon Breakfast Risotto 23

    Fast Breakfast Oatmeal 24

    Simple Scotch Eggs 24

    Blueberry Breakfast Bowl 25

    Quinoa Bowls 25

    Quinoa Breakfast 26

    Tasty Breakfast Cake 26

    Cornmeal Porridge 27

    Breakfast Rice Pudding 27

    Pumpkin Oatmeal 28

    Buckwheat Porridge 28

    Breakfast Tortillas 29

    Special Pancake 29

    Squash Porridge 30

    Breakfast Banana Bread 30

    Millet and Oats Porridge 31

    Sweet Potato Hash 31

- Blueberry Breakfast Delight 32
- Breakfast Bacon Potatoes 32
- Potato and Spinach Hash 33
- Breakfast Banana Bread 33
- Veggie Breakfast Casserole 34
- Peach Breakfast 34
- Bread Pudding 35
- Egg Muffins 35
- Chocolate Bread Pudding 36
- Simple Fruit Cobbler 36
- Buckwheat Porridge 37
- Squash Porridge 37
- Espresso Oatmeal 38
- Breakfast Rice Pudding 38
- Apple Butter 39
- Veggie Quiche 39
- Strawberry Quinoa Bowl 40
- Cornmeal Porridge 40
- Breakfast Cobbler 41
- Tofu and Sweet Potato Mix 41
- Breakfast Apple Dish 42
- Brown Rice Mix 42
- Quinoa and Tomatoes Breakfast Mix 43
- Breakfast Rice and Chickpeas Medley 43
- Quinoa Salad 44
- Special Breakfast Beans 44
- Breakfast Arugula Salad 45
- Cranberry Beans Salad 45
- Wild Rice Breakfast Salad 46
- Rice and Black Beans Breakfast Dish 46
- Pineapple and Peas Breakfast Curry 47
- Brussels Sprouts and Potato Bowls 47
- Parsnip and Quinoa Breakfast Mix 48
- Simple Potato Salad 48
- Italian Eggplants Bowls 49
- Cauliflower and Barley Bowls 49
- Breakfast Egg Salad 50

- Strawberry Jam 50
- Celeriac Breakfast Mix 51
- Turkey Breast Breakfast Mix 51
- Fresh Peach Jam 52
- Breakfast Orange Marmalade 52
- Pomegranate Oatmeal 53
- Cheesy Cauliflower Bowls 53
- Rich Breakfast Potatoes 54
- Sweet Potatoes Casserole 54
- Swiss Chard Salad 55
- Beets Spread 55
- Millet Porridge 56
- Quinoa with Sausages 56
- Avocado Spread 57
- Pinto Beans Breakfast Salad 57
- Breakfast Chickpeas Spread 58
- Breakfast Cheese Spread 58
- Creamy Squash Bowl 59
- Italian Eggplant Breakfast Mix 59
- Easy Breakfast Butter 60
- Breakfast Apple Dumplings 60
- Carrot Breakfast Salad 61
- Tapioca Pudding 61
- Breakfast Chestnut Butter 62
- Breakfast Couscous Salad 62
- Couscous and Mint 63
- Simple Quince Jam 63
- Veggie and Couscous Breakfast 64
- Potato and Salmon Breakfast 64
- Rhubarb Breakfast Spread 65
- Strawberry and Rhubarb Breakfast Compote 65

Instant Pot Main Dish Recipes 66

- Chicken Curry 66
- Beef Stew 66
- Juicy Roast 67
- Easy Mac and Cheese 67
- Vegetarian Lentils Soup 68

Crispy Chicken	68
Delicious Ribs	69
Simple Chili	69
Rice and Beans	70
Tasty Turkey Meatballs	70
Simple Shredded Chicken	71
Beef Stew	71
Tasty Pho	72
Black Bean Soup	72
Pork Chops and Tomato Sauce	73
Comforting Chicken Dish	73
Chickpea Curry	74
Simple Beef Dish	74
Tasty Beef and Broccoli	75
Fast Salmon	75
Coconut Quinoa	76
Chicken Wrap	76
Steamed Tilapia	77
Lemon Pepper Salmon	77
Tasty Tikka Masala	78
Lemon and Olive Chicken	78
Fish Soup	79
Chili Mahi Mahi	79
Chicken and Tomatillo Salsa	80
Chicken with Dates	80
Cod and Orange Sauce	81
Simple Shrimp	81
Beef Curry	82
Beef and Artichokes	82
Shrimp Boil	83
Fast Shrimp Scampi	83
Pork Roast	84
Pork and Pineapple Delight	84
Delicious and Simple Octopus	85
Teriyaki Scallops	85
Squash and Apple Soup	86
Chicken and Veggie Soup	86

Mussels and White Wine Sauce	87
Beet Soup	87
Chicken and Kale Soup	88
Chicken and Fennel Soup	88
Onion Cream	89
Black Bean Soup	89
Delicious Onion Soup	90
Chicken and Red Cabbage Soup	90
Minestrone Soup	91
Swiss Chard Soup	91
Turkey Soup	92
Red Pepper Soup	92
Broccoli and Cheese Soup	93
Potato Soup	93
Potato Soup	94
Delicious Meatloaf	94
Cream of Spinach	95
Cantaloupe Soup	95
Bean Casserole	96
Flavored Pasta	96
Mussels Bowls	97
Artichokes and Citrus Sauce	97
Beans Chili	98
Pasta and Spinach	98
Chicken and Potatoes Mix	99
Cajun Sausage Mix	99
Pea and Ham Soup	100
Lamb Casserole	100
Easy Turkey Mix	101
Simple Chicken Fall Stew	101
Simple BBQ Ribs	102
Jambalaya	102
Pork and Lemon Sauce	103
Fennel Cream	103
Cod and Beer	104
Salmon with Lemon	104
Cauliflower Salad	105

Collard Greens Stew 105
Chinese Fish 106
Salmon and Risotto 106
Spicy Chicken Wings 107
Rich Chicken Salad 107
Salmon Casserole 108
Salmon and Chili Sauce 108
Calamari Stew 109
Simple Lamb Ribs and Sauce 109
Salmon and Veggies 110
Pasta with Salmon and Pesto 110
Chicken and Salsa 111
Green Beans Stew 111
Spicy Salmon 112
Mediterranean Cod 112
Spinach Pasta 113
Chickpeas Cakes 113
Fish and Orange Sauce 114
Tasty and Easy Shrimp 114
Pork Tenderloin and Pomegranate Sauce 115
Lemon Lamb Chops 115

Instant Pot Side Dish Recipes 116

Baked Sweet Potatoes 116
Broccoli Pasta 116
Tasty Carrots Mix 117
Minty Carrots 117
Simple Cauliflower Rice 118
Refried Beans 118
Tasty Carrots and Walnuts Salad 119
Sweet and Sour Side Salad 119
Sweet Brussels Sprouts 120
Simple Roasted Potatoes 120
Pearl Onions Side Dish 121
Haricots Verts Side Salad 121
Squash Risotto 122
Cabbage Side Dish 122
Green Beans and Cranberries Side Dish 123

Delicious Green Beans and Blue Cheese	123
Beans and Chorizo	124
Spanish Rice	124
Tasty Spinach and Salami	125
Creamy Spinach	125
Garlic Green Beans	126
Kale Sauté	126
Spaghetti Squash Delight	127
Artichokes Side Dish	127
Cabbage and Cream	128
Carrots and Kale	128
Braised Collard Greens	129
Collard Greens and Peas	129
Beets Side Dish	130
Sweet Potato Puree	130
Chinese Mustard Greens	131
Acorn Squash Side Dish	131
Beet and Cabbage Mix	132
Broccoli and Garlic	132
Tasty Maple Acorn Squash Dish	133
Red Onions and Apples Mix	133
Creamy Corn	134
Tasty Rice and Quinoa	134
Tasty Mushrooms and Rosemary	135
Chestnut Mushrooms	135
Delicious Mushrooms Side Dish	136
Mashed Potatoes	136
Delicious Shiitake Mushrooms Mix	137
Brussels Sprouts Side Salad	137
Mushrooms and Asparagus	138
Onion, Celery and Bread Side Dish	138
Cauliflower and Grapes	139
Brussels Sprouts and Chestnuts	139
Cranberry Side Dish	140
Green Beans and Bacon	140
Tasty Vidalia Onions Mix	141
Parmesan Zucchini Fries	141

Beans and Avocado Salsa	142
Spicy Zucchini	142
Flavored Parmesan Mushrooms	143
Simple Buttery Potatoes	143
Mexican Zucchini Side Dish	144
Zucchini and Mushrooms	144
Green Beans Fries	145
Mixed Veggies	145
Yellow Squash and Zucchini	146
Bell Peppers Stir Fry	146
Simple Corn Side Dish	147
Tomatoes Side Salad	147
Bell Peppers and Sausages	148
Mixed Veggies Side Dish	148
Tomatoes and Corn Side Salad	149
Sweet Pearl Onion Mix	149
Braised Endives	150
Simple Bok Choy Side Dish	150
Tomatoes and Burrata Side Salad	151
Arborio Rice Side Salad	151
Bok Choy and Rice	152
Collard Greens and Bacon	152
Simple Spinach Side Dish	153
Squash and Apple Mash	153
Simple Collard Greens Side Dish	154
Spicy Collard Greens	154
Brown Rice Salad	155
Kidney Beans and Corn Side Dish	155
Eggplant and Cashews Mix	156
Green Cabbage and Tomatoes Side Dish	156
Rice and Edamame	157
Poached Fennel	157
Fennel and Shallots	158
Pea Rice	158
Radishes Side Salad	159
Turnip Mash	159
Garlic Beets Salad	160

- Mango Side Salad 160
- Rice with Fennel 161
- Coconut Cabbage 161
- Sweet Potato Side Salad 162
- Sweet Potatoes Mash 162
- Corn on the Cob 163
- Steamed Leeks 163
- Turnips and Chili Pepper Side Dish 164
- Spinach and Squash Mix 164
- Sautéed Escarole 165
- Stir Fried Okra 165

Instant Pot Snack and Appetizer Recipes 166
- Fish Balls 166
- Baby Carrots Snack 166
- Beef Dip 167
- Potato Wedges 167
- Greek Meatballs 168
- Cocktail Boiled Peanuts 168
- BBQ Chicken Wings 169
- Beef Meatballs 169
- Chinese Style Peanuts 170
- Southern Peanuts 170
- Stuffed Chicken Breasts 171
- Baby Back Ribs Appetizer 171
- Simple Red Pepper Hummus 172
- Asian Wings 172
- Crispy Chicken 173
- Boiled Peanuts 173
- Mexican Corn on the Cob 174
- BBQ Square Ribs 174
- Roasted Hummus 175
- Pasta Appetizer Salad 175
- Grated Carrot Appetizer Salad 176
- Green Beans Salad 176
- Honey Chicken Appetizer 177
- Hot Wings 177
- Watercress Appetizer Salad 178

Ham and Cheese Dip	178
Italian Dip	179
Mussels Appetizer	179
Scallion Spread	180
Crab Spread	180
Italian Mussels	181
Clams Appetizer	181
Tasty Black Bean Salsa	182
Special Ranch Spread	182
Beet Appetizer Salad	183
Onion Dip	183
Chicken Dip	184
Blue Cheese Dip	184
Chili Dip	185
Corn Dip	185
Chunky Warm Salsa	186
Cumin Dip	186
Cabbage Rolls	187
Tofu Appetizer	187
Pinto Bean Dip	188
Light Lemon Dip	188
Lentils Patties	189
Black Beans Patties	189
Green Olive Pate	190
Shrimp and Tomatoes Appetizer Mix	190
Chickpeas Appetizer	191
Mushroom Cakes	191
Tomatoes Appetizer Salad	192
Kale and Carrots Salad	192
Beets Cakes	193
Mango Salsa	193
Kale and Wild Rice Appetizer Salad	194
Minty Kale Salad	194
Mushroom Dip	195
Cauliflower Dip	195
Broccoli Appetizer Salad	196
Creamy Broccoli Appetizer	196

Red Pepper Dip 197
Artichokes Spread 197
Broccoli and Bacon Appetizer Salad 198
Cheesy Broccoli Appetizer Salad 198
Easy Tortillas 199
White Beans Dip 199
Brussels Sprouts and Broccoli Appetizer Salad 200
Crunchy Brussels Sprouts Salad 200
Chicken Appetizer Salad 201
Octopus Appetizer 201
Brussels Sprouts and Apples Appetizer 202
Sweet Brussels Sprouts Appetizer 202
Orange and Beet Appetizer 203
Hulled Barley Appetizer 203
Appetizer Egg Spread 204
Potatoes and Shrimp Appetizer Salad 204
Wheat Berries Appetizer 205
Veggies and Wheat Appetizer Salad 205
Stuffed Bell Peppers Appetizer 206
Brussels Sprouts and Potatoes Appetizer Salad 206
Fresh Bulgur Appetizer 207
Summer Lentils Appetizer 207
Veggie Dumplings 208
Tomatoes and Garlic Dip 208
Pork Burritos 209
Beef Sandwiches 209
Cashew Spread 210
Mushroom Appetizer Salad 210
Turnips Spread 211
Calamari Salad 211
Lemony Endives Appetizer 212
Easy Endives Platter 212
Cauliflower Salad 213
Chicken Sandwiches 213
Creamy Endives Appetizer Salad 214
Zucchini Spread 214
Lamb Ribs 215

  Pork Cakes 215
Instant Pot Dessert Recipes 216
  Cranberries Dessert Bowl 216
  Banana Cake 216
  Simple Pumpkin and Yogurt Cake 217
  Apple Bread 217
  Apple Cobbler 218
  Pumpkin Granola 218
  Easy Sweet Soufflé 219
  Tasty Blackberry Pie 219
  Rice Pudding 220
  Black Rice Pudding 220
  Millet Pudding 220
  Peanut Butter Cups 221
  Simple Cake Bars 221
  Sweet Chia Pudding 222
  Lemon Marmalade 222
  White Chocolate Mousse 223
  Easy Lemon Pie 223
  Pumpkin Cake 224
  Apple Cake 224
  Special Cookies 225
  Delicious Berry Cobbler 225
  Chocolate Cake 226
  Easy Apples and Wine 226
  Simple Ricotta Mousse 227
  Baked Custard 227
  Apricots and Cranberries Pudding 228
  Beans Cake 228
  Rhubarb and Strawberries Mix 229
  Cherry Pie 229
  Orange Cream 230
  Pears with Garlic and Jelly 230
  Stuffed Strawberries 231
  Glazed Fruits 231
  Classic Ricotta Cake 232
  Spicy Tomato Jam 232

Peach Jam	232
Lemon Cookies	233
Chocolate Cake	233
Lime Pie	234
Peach Compote	234
Apples and Wine Sauce	235
Cream and Cinnamon Puddings	235
Carrot Cake	236
Cheesecake	236
Poached Pears	237
Flavored Pears	237
Chocolate Pudding	238
Carrot Pudding and Rum Sauce	238
Dates and Ricotta Cake	239
Lemon and Orange Jam	239
Lemon Pudding	240
Sweet Corn Pudding	240
Ginger and Peach Marmalade	241
Winter Cherry Mix	241
Apricot Jam	242
Blueberry Jam	242
Peach and Cinnamon Compote	243
Ginger Cookies Cheesecake	243
Bread Pudding	244
Cranberry Bread Pudding	244
Strawberry and Chia Marmalade	245
Lemon and Maple Syrup Pudding	245
Apples and Pears Salad	246
Apples and Red Grape Juice	246
Simple Banana Cake	247
Pineapple Pudding	247
Strawberry Shortcakes	248
Caramel Pudding	248
Coconut Cream and Cinnamon Pudding	249
Coconut Pancake	249
Black Tea Cake	250
Green Tea Pudding	250

Easy Plum Jam	251
Blueberry and Coconut Sweet Bowls	251
Lemon Curd	252
Apples and Honey	252
Strawberries Dessert	252
Coconut and Avocado Pudding	253
Cocoa and Milk Pudding	253
Peaches and Cream	254
Stuffed Peaches	254
Cocoa and Walnuts Sweet Cream	255
Cream Cheese Pudding	255
Cranberry and Pear Cake	256
Chocolate Fondue	256
Egg and Coconut Cream	257
Blueberries and Strawberries Compote	257
Pear and Maple Dessert	258
Cherry Bowls	258
Sweet Zucchini Bread	259
Poached Figs	259
Cold Pineapple and Cherries Mix	260
Fall Plums Mix	260
Sweet Blueberry Butter	261
Sweet Quinoa Dessert	261
Sweet Baked Plums	261
Pumpkin and Coconut Sweet Mix	262
Apricot Marmalade	262
Milk and Cream Pudding	263
Fall Pear Cake	263
Recipe Index	264

Free Gift

Up to 1000 delicious and healthy recipes from cooking traditions all around the world.

Please follow this link to get instant access to your Free Cookbook:
http://bookretailseller.pro/

Breakfast Instant Pot Recipes

Ham and Egg Casserole

Preparation time: 10 minutes
Cooking time: 25 minutes
Servings: 2

Ingredients:
- 6 eggs
- ½ yellow onion, chopped
- 1 cup ham, chopped
- 1 cup cheddar cheese, shredded
- 4 red potatoes, cubed
- 1 cup milk
- Cooking spray
- 2 cups water
- A pinch of salt and black pepper

Directions:
In a bowl, mix eggs with milk, salt, pepper, potatoes, ham, onion and cheese, whisk and pour into a cooking pan sprayed with cooking oil. Put the water in your instant pot, add the steamer basket inside, add the pan with the eggs mix, cover and cook on Manual for 25 minutes. Leave your casserole to cool down a bit, slice, divide between 2 plates and serve for breakfast. Enjoy!

Nutrition: calories 210, fat 2, fiber 3, carbs 5, protein 7

Delicious Egg Bake

Preparation time: 10 minutes
Cooking time: 20 minutes
Servings: 2

Ingredients:
- 3 bacon slices, chopped
- 2 tablespoons milk
- 1 cup hash browns
- ¼ cup cheddar cheese, shredded
- A pinch of salt and black pepper
- 3 eggs
- 1 and ½ cups water
- 1 small red bell pepper, chopped
- 2 mushrooms, chopped

Directions:
Set your instant pot on Sauté mode, add bacon, stir and cook for a couple of minutes. Add mushrooms and bell pepper, stir and cook for 3 minutes more. Add hash browns, stir, cook for 2 minutes more, transfer everything to a bowl and clean your instant pot. Add eggs, milk, salt, pepper and cheese to the bowl with the veggies and the ham, whisk everything and transfer to a greased heatproof dish. Add the water to your instant pot, add the steamer basket, place the heatproof dish inside, cover and cook on High for 10 minutes. Leave casserole to cool down a bit, slice and serve for breakfast. Enjoy!

Nutrition: calories 231, fat 4, fiber 1, carbs 4, protein 7

Espresso Steel Cut Oats

Preparation time: 10 minutes
Cooking time: 10 minutes
Servings: 4

Ingredients:
- 2 and ½ cups water
- 1 cup milk
- 1 cup steel cut oats
- 2 tablespoons sugar
- 1 teaspoon espresso powder

Directions:
In your instant pot, mix water with milk, oats, sugar and espresso powder, stir a bit, cover and cook on High for 10 minutes. Stir your oatmeal again, divide into bowls and serve for breakfast. Enjoy!

Nutrition: calories 120, fat 2, fiber 4, carbs 10, protein 5

Chocolate Oatmeal

Preparation time: 10 minutes
Cooking time: 10 minutes
Servings: 6

Ingredients:
- 1 cup milk
- 2 cups oatmeal
- 6 cups water
- 2 and ½ tablespoons cocoa powder
- 1 teaspoon cinnamon powder

Directions:
In your instant pot, mix water with milk, oatmeal, cocoa powder and cinnamon, stir, cover and cook on High for 10 minutes. Stir oatmeal again, divide into bowls and serve. Enjoy!

Nutrition: calories 110, fat 4, fiber 5, carbs 8, protein 5

Breakfast Meat Soufflé

Preparation time: 10 minutes
Cooking time: 30 minutes
Servings: 2

Ingredients:
- 3 eggs, whisked
- A pinch of salt and black pepper
- ¼ cup milk
- 2 bacon slices, cooked and crumbled
- ½ cup sausage, cooked and ground
- ¼ cup ham, chopped
- ½ cup cheddar cheese, shredded
- 1 green onion, chopped
- 1 cup water

Directions:
In a bowl, mix eggs with milk, salt, pepper, sausage, bacon, green onion, ham and cheese, stir and pour into a soufflé dish. Put the water in your instant pot, add the steamer basket, add the soufflé dish, cover the dish with some tin foil, cover pot and cook on High for 30 minutes. Serve hot for breakfast. Enjoy!

Nutrition: calories 212, fat 2, fiber 4, carbs 6, protein 10

Tasty Quiche

Preparation time: 10 minutes
Cooking time: 30 minutes
Servings: 2

Ingredients:
- 1 cup water
- 3 eggs
- ¼ cup milk
- A pinch of salt and black pepper
- 1 tablespoon chives, chopped
- ½ cup cheddar cheese, shredded
- Cooking spray

Directions:
IN a bowl, mix eggs with salt, pepper, chives and milk and whisk well. Wrap a cake pan with tin foil, grease with cooking spray and add the cheese into the pan. Pour eggs mixture over cheese and spread evenly. Add the water to your instant pot, add the steamer basket inside, add the cake pan, cover and cook on High for 30 minutes. Divide between 2 plates and serve for breakfast. Enjoy!

Nutrition: calories 214, fat 4, fiber 2, carbs 7, protein 8

Peaches Oatmeal

Preparation time: 10 minutes
Cooking time: 10 minutes
Servings: 8

Ingredients:
- 4 cups rolled oats
- 3 and ½ cups milk
- 3 and ½ cups water
- 1/3 cup sugar
- 4 peaches, stones removed and chopped

Directions:
In your instant pot, mix water with milk, oats, sugar and peaches, stir, cover and cook on High for 10 minutes. Stir oatmeal a bit more, divide into bowls and serve. Enjoy!

Nutrition: calories 152, fat 4, fiber 7, carbs 8, protein 4

Apple Steel Cut Oats

Preparation time: 10 minutes
Cooking time: 4 minutes
Servings: 4

Ingredients:
- 1 and ½ cups water
- 2 apples, peeled, cored and chopped
- ½ cup Greek yogurt
- 1 cup steel cut oats
- ¼ cup maple syrup

Directions:
In your instant pot, mix water with apples, oats and maple syrup, stir, cover and cook on Manual for 4 minutes. Stir oatmeal again, divide into bowls, top with yogurt and serve. Enjoy!

Nutrition: calories 142, fat 4, fiber 6, carbs 6, protein 4

Mexican Breakfast

Preparation time: 10 minutes
Cooking time: 26 minutes
Servings: 2

Ingredients:
- 2 eggs, whisked
- 1 small red onion, chopped
- ¼ pound sausage, ground
- 1 small red bell pepper, chopped
- 2 ounces black beans
- 2 green onions, chopped
- 2 tablespoons flour
- ¼ cup cotija cheese, shredded
- ¼ cup mozzarella cheese, shredded
- 1 tablespoon cilantro, chopped

Directions:
Set your instant pot on sauté mode, add red onion and sausage, stir and cook for 6 minutes. In a bowl, mix eggs with flour and whisk well. Add eggs to the pot and stir. Also, add beans, red bell pepper, green onion, cotija and mozzarella cheese, stir a bit, cover and cook on High for 20 minutes. Divide your Mexican breakfast between 2 plates, sprinkle cilantro on top and serve for breakfast. Enjoy!

Nutrition: calories 254, fat 5, fiber 3, carbs 7, protein 10

French Toast

Preparation time: 10 minutes
Cooking time: 25 minutes
Servings: 2

Ingredients:
- 3 French bread slices, cubed
- 1 tablespoon brown sugar
- 2 bananas, sliced
- 2 eggs
- 1 tablespoon cream cheese
- ¼ cup milk
- ½ tablespoon white sugar
- 1 tablespoon butter
- A pinch of cinnamon powder
- ½ teaspoon vanilla extract
- 2 tablespoons pecans, chopped
- Cooking spray
- ¾ cup water

Directions:
Grease a heatproof dish with cooking spray and add a layer of bread cubes on the bottom. Add a layer of banana slices and sprinkle the brown sugar all over. Add melted cream cheese and spread evenly. Add the rest of the bread cubes and banana slices, butter and sprinkle half of the pecans all over. In a bowl, mix eggs with white sugar, milk, cinnamon and vanilla, whisk well and pour this over bread and banana mix. Add the water to your instant pot, add the trivet inside, add the heatproof dish, cover and cook on High for 25 minutes. Divide this mix into 2 plates, sprinkle the rest of the pecans on top and serve. Enjoy!

Nutrition: calories 200, fat 3, fiber 3, carbs 5, protein 8

Western Omelette

Preparation time: 10 minutes
Cooking time: 30 minutes
Servings: 4

Ingredients:
- 6 eggs, whisked
- 8 ounces bacon, chopped
- ½ cup half and half
- A pinch of salt
- 4 spring onions, chopped
- 1 and ½ cups water, for the instant pot

Directions:
In a bowl, mix eggs with half-and-half, bacon, spring onions and salt, whisk well and pour into a soufflé dish. Add water to your instant pot, add steamer basket, add soufflé dish inside, cover and cook on High for 30 minutes. Leave omelet to cool down a bit, slice, divide between plates and serve for breakfast. Enjoy!

Nutrition: calories 200, fat 6, fiber 5, carbs 12, protein 6

Simple Frittata

Preparation time: 10 minutes
Cooking time: 5 minutes
Servings: 6

Ingredients:
- 1 tablespoon almond milk
- 5 eggs, whisked
- A pinch of salt
- 2 tablespoons cheddar cheese, grated
- 1 red bell pepper, chopped
- 1 and ½ cups water, for the instant pot

Directions:
In a bowl, mix eggs with almond milk, salt, cheese and red bell pepper, whisk well and pour into 6 baking molds. Add water to your instant pot, add steamer basket, add baking molds inside, cover and cook on High for 5 minutes. Serve your frittatas hot. Enjoy!

Nutrition: calories 200, fat 4, fiber 5, carbs 7, protein 6

Simple Burrito Casserole

Preparation time: 10 minutes
Cooking time: 13 minutes
Servings: 2

Ingredients:
- 2 eggs
- ½ pound red potatoes, cubed
- A pinch of salt and black pepper
- 1 small yellow onion, chopped
- 1 small jalapeno, chopped
- 2 ounces ham, cubed
- A pinch of mesquite seasoning
- A pinch of chili powder
- A pinch of taco seasoning
- 1 small avocado, pitted, peeled and chopped
- Salsa for serving
- 2 tortillas
- 1 cup water+ 1 tablespoon

Directions:
In a bowl, mix eggs with salt, pepper, mesquite seasoning, chili powder, 1 tablespoon water and taco seasoning and whisk well. Add ham, potatoes, onion and jalapeno, stir and pour everything into a heatproof dish. Add 1 cup water to your instant pot, add the trivet, and the heatproof dish inside, cover and cook on Manual for 13 minutes. Divide this into 2 tortillas, divide avocado, spread salsa, roll burritos and serve them for breakfast. Enjoy!

Nutrition: calories 253, fat 4, fiber 4, carbs 6, protein 8

Spanish Frittata

Preparation time: 10 minutes
Cooking time: 18 minutes
Servings: 2

Ingredients:
- 3 eggs
- 2 ounces hash browns
- ½ tablespoon butter, melted
- 2 tablespoons scallions, chopped
- A pinch of salt and black pepper
- 1 small garlic clove, minced
- 1 tablespoon Bisquick
- 2 tablespoons milk
- ½ teaspoon tomato paste
- 1 and ½ cups water
- 2 ounces cheddar cheese, grated

Directions:
In a bowl, mix bisquick with milk and tomato paste and stir. In another bowl, mix eggs with garlic, scallions, salt, pepper and milk mix and whisk everything. Spread hash browns into a greased baking dish, add melted butter and pour eggs mix all over. Spread eggs and top with cheese. Put the water in your instant pot, add the trivet, add casserole inside, cover and cook on High for 20 minutes. Divide frittata between 2 plates and serve. Enjoy!

Nutrition: calories 215, fat 4, fiber 3, carbs 6, protein 8

French Eggs

Preparation time: 10 minutes
Cooking time: 8 minutes
Servings: 4

Ingredients:
- 4 slices bacon
- 4 eggs
- 4 tablespoons chives, chopped
- A drizzle of olive oil
- A pinch of salt
- 1 cup water, for the instant pot

Directions:
Grease 4 ramekins with a drizzle of oil, crack an egg in each, add a bacon slice on top, season with a pinch of salt and top each with chives. Add water to your instant pot, add steamer basket, add ramekins inside, cover and cook on High for 8 minutes. Serve your baked eggs right away. Enjoy!

Nutrition: calories 182, fat 5, fiber 4, carbs 10, protein 5

Eggs and Bacon Breakfast Risotto

Preparation time: 10 minutes
Cooking time: 10 minutes
Servings: 2

Ingredients:
- ¾ cup Arborio rice
- 2 eggs, poached.
- 3 bacon slices, chopped
- 1 and ½ cups chicken stock
- 2 tablespoons parmesan, grated

Directions:
Set your instant pot on sauté mode, add bacon, stir and cook for 5 minutes. Add rice, stir and cook for 1 minute. Add stock, stir, cover and cook on Manual for 5 minutes. Add parmesan, stir and divide risotto between plates. Add eggs on the side and serve for breakfast. Enjoy!

Nutrition: calories 214, fat 5, fiber 6, carbs 12, protein 5

Fast Breakfast Oatmeal

Preparation time: 10 minutes
Cooking time: 3 minutes
Servings: 2

Ingredients:
- ½ cup steel cut oats
- 1 and ½ cups water
- 1 teaspoon vanilla extract

Directions:
Put the water in your instant pot, add vanilla extract and oats, stir a bit, cover and cook on High for 3 minutes. Divide into 2 bowls and serve for breakfast. Enjoy!

Nutrition: calories 142, fat 1, fiber 1, carbs 2, protein 2

Simple Scotch Eggs

Preparation time: 10 minutes
Cooking time: 12 minutes
Servings: 2

Ingredients:
- 2 eggs
- ½ pound sausage, ground
- 1 tablespoon olive oil
- A pinch of chili powder
- Black pepper to the taste
- 2 cups water

Directions:
Put 1 cup water in your instant pot, add the steamer basket, place eggs inside, cover, cook on High for 6 minutes, transfer eggs to a bowl filled with ice water, cool them down and peel them quickly. In a bowl, mix sausage meat with black pepper and chili powder and stir well. Divide sausage meat into 2 pieces, flatten each on a working surface, add eggs in the middle, wrap them in meat and shape 2 meatballs. Set your instant pot on Sauté mode, add the oil, heat it up, add scotch eggs, brown them on all sides and transfer to a plate. Clean your instant pot, add the rest of the water, add the steamer basket, place eggs inside, cover and cook on High for 6 minutes more. Divide eggs between 2 plates and serve them for breakfast with a tasty side salad. Enjoy!

Nutrition: calories 174, fat 4, fiber 1, carbs 6, protein 10

Blueberry Breakfast Bowl

Preparation time: 1 hour and 10 minutes
Cooking time: 1 minute
Servings: 4

Ingredients:
- 1 and ½ cups water
- 1 and ½ cups quinoa
- 1 tablespoon honey
- 3 tablespoons blueberries
- 1 cup apple juice

Directions:
In your instant pot, mix water with quinoa, stir, cover, cook on High for 1 minute, stir a bit and leave aside for 10 minutes. Divide quinoa into bowls, add honey, apple juice and blueberries, toss a bit and serve for breakfast. Enjoy!

Nutrition: calories 172, fat 5, fiber 4, carbs 5, protein 6

Quinoa Bowls

Preparation time: 10 minutes
Cooking time: 1 minute
Servings: 4

Ingredients:
- 1 and ½ cups quinoa
- 2 tablespoons honey
- 2 and ¼ cups water
- ¼ teaspoon pumpkin pie spice
- 2 cups strawberries, chopped

Directions:
In your instant pot, mix quinoa with honey, water, spice and strawberries, stir, cover and cook on High for 1 minute. Leave quinoa aside for 10 minutes, stir a bit, divide everything into bowls and serve. Enjoy!

Nutrition: calories 162, fat 3, fiber 3, carbs 6, protein 3

Quinoa Breakfast

Preparation time: 10 minutes
Cooking time: 1 minute
Servings: 2

Ingredients:
- 1 cup quinoa
- 2 cups water
- 1 tablespoon maple syrup
- ¼ teaspoon vanilla extract
- A pinch of cinnamon powder
- ¼ cup fresh berries

Directions:
Put quinoa in your instant pot, add cinnamon, vanilla, water and maple syrup, stir, cover and cook on High for 1 minute. Leave quinoa aside for 10 minutes, fluff with a fork, divide into 2 bowls, top each with fresh berries and serve for breakfast. Enjoy!

Nutrition: calories 173, fat 1, fiber 2, carbs 2, protein 3

Tasty Breakfast Cake

Preparation time: 10 minutes
Cooking time: 25 minutes
Servings: 2

Ingredients:
- 1 cup water
- 3 eggs
- 2 tablespoons sugar
- 1 tablespoon butter, melted
- 5 tablespoons ricotta cheese
- 5 tablespoons yogurt
- 1 teaspoon vanilla extract
- ½ cup whole wheat flour
- 1 teaspoon baking powder
- ½ cup berry compote
- Cooking spray

Directions:
In a bowl, mix eggs with sugar and whisk until it dissolves. Add ricotta cheese, butter, vanilla and yogurt and whisk well again. In another bowl, mix baking powder with flour, stir and add this to eggs mix. Stir well, pour this into a cake pan greased with cooking spray and spread evenly. Drop spoonfuls of berry compote over cake mix and swirl with a knife. Add the water to your instant pot, add the trivet inside, add cake pan, cover pot and cook on High for 25 minutes. Divide cake between 2 plates and serve for breakfast. Enjoy!

Nutrition: calories 251, fat 1, fiber 2, carbs 4, protein 7

Cornmeal Porridge

Preparation time: 10 minutes
Cooking time: 20 minutes
Servings: 4

Ingredients:
- 1 cup cornmeal
- 1 cup milk
- 4 cups water
- ½ teaspoon nutmeg, ground
- ½ cup sweetened condensed milk

Directions:
In a bowl, mix 1 cup water with cornmeal and stir well. In your instant pot, mix the rest of the water with milk and cornmeal mix and stir. Also add nutmeg, stir, cover and cook on High for 6 minutes. Add condensed milk, stir, divide into bowls and serve. Enjoy!

Nutrition: calories 241, fat 4, fiber 6, carbs 12, protein 6

Breakfast Rice Pudding

Preparation time: 10 minutes
Cooking time: 20 minutes
Servings: 6

Ingredients:
- 2 cups nut milk
- 1 and ¼ cups water
- 1 cup basmati rice
- 1 cup coconut cream
- ¼ cup maple syrup

Directions:
In your instant pot, mix nut milk with water, rice, cream and maple syrup, stir well, cover and cook on High for 20 minutes. Stir pudding again, divide into bowls and serve. Enjoy!

Nutrition: calories 251, fat 5, fiber 3, carbs 6, protein 5

Pumpkin Oatmeal

Preparation time: 10 minutes
Cooking time: 3 minutes
Servings: 2

Ingredients:
- 2 cups water
- ½ cup steel cut oats
- ½ cup pumpkin puree
- ½ teaspoon cinnamon powder
- ½ teaspoon allspice
- ½ teaspoon vanilla extract

For the topping:
- 2 tablespoons pecans, chopped
- 3 tablespoons brown sugar
- ½ tablespoon cinnamon powder

Directions:
In your instant pot, mix water with steel cut oats, pumpkin puree, ½ teaspoon cinnamon, allspice and vanilla, stir, cover and cook on High for 3 minutes. Meanwhile, in a bowl, mix pecans with brown sugar and ½ tablespoon cinnamon powder and stir well. Divide pumpkin oatmeal into 2 bowls, spread some of the pecans topping and serve. Enjoy!

Nutrition: calories 132, fat 1, fiber 2, carbs 2, protein 4

Buckwheat Porridge

Preparation time: 10 minutes
Cooking time: 6 minutes
Servings: 2

Ingredients:
- 1 cup buckwheat groats, rinsed
- ¼ cup raisins
- 3 cups rice milk
- 1 banana, peeled and sliced
- ½ teaspoon vanilla extract

Directions:
Put buckwheat in your instant pot, add raisins, milk, banana and vanilla, stir a bit, cover and cook on High for 6 minutes. Divide buckwheat porridge into 2 bowls and serve for breakfast. Enjoy!

Nutrition: calories 162, fat 1, fiber 2, carbs 2, protein 5

Breakfast Tortillas

Preparation time: 10 minutes
Cooking time: 13 minutes
Servings: 6

Ingredients:
- 2 pound red potatoes, cubed
- 4 eggs, whisked
- 6 ounces ham, cubed
- 6 tortillas, for serving
- ¼ cup yellow onion, chopped
- 1 cup water, for the instant pot

Directions:
In a bowl, mix eggs with ham, onion and potatoes and whisk well. Add this to a baking dish and spread. Add water to your instant pot, add trivet, add baking dish inside, cover and cook on High for 13 minutes. Arrange tortillas on a working surface, divide eggs mix on each, wrap and serve for breakfast. Enjoy!

Nutrition: calories 212, fat 3, fiber 7, carbs 9, protein 12

Special Pancake

Preparation time: 10 minutes
Cooking time: 45 minutes
Servings: 4

Ingredients:
- 2 cups white flour
- 2 eggs
- 1 and ½ cups milk
- 2 tablespoons sugar
- 2 and ½ teaspoons baking powder

Directions:
In a bowl, mix flour with eggs, milk, sugar and baking powder and whisk really well. Add this to your instant pot, spread, cover and cook on Manual for 45 minutes. Leave your pancake to cool down, slice, divide between plates and serve. Enjoy!

Nutrition: calories 251, fat 5, fiber 2, carbs 6, protein 3

Squash Porridge

Preparation time: 10 minutes
Cooking time: 8 minutes
Servings: 2

Ingredients:
- 3 small apples cored
- 1 small delicata squash
- 1 and ½ tablespoon gelatin
- 2 tablespoon slippery elm
- ½ cup water
- 1 and ½ tablespoons maple syrup
- A pinch of cinnamon powder
- A pinch of ginger powder
- A pinch of cloves, ground

Directions:
Put the squash and apples in your instant pot, add water, cinnamon, ginger and cloves, cover and cook on Manual for 8 minutes. Leave squash to cool down, transfer to a cutting board, halve, deseed and transfer to your blender. Add apples, water and spices as well and pulse really well. Add slippery elm, maple syrup and gelatin, blend well, divide into 2 big bowls and serve for breakfast. Enjoy!

Nutrition: calories 174, fat 2, fiber 1, carbs 3, protein 4

Breakfast Banana Bread

Preparation time: 10 minutes
Cooking time: 50 minutes
Servings: 2

Ingredients:
- 2 bananas, peeled and mashed
- ½ tablespoon vanilla
- ½ stick butter, soft
- ¼ cup sugar
- 1 cup flour
- 1 egg
- ½ teaspoon baking powder
- 1 cup water
- Cooking spray

Directions:
In a bowl, mix banana puree with vanilla, butter, sugar, flour, egg and baking powder and stir well until you obtain a bread batter. Grease a loaf pan with cooking spray and pour bread mixture into it. Add the water to your instant pot, add the trivet, and loaf pan inside, cover and cook on High for 50 minutes. Divide breakfast bread into 2 plates and serve for breakfast. Enjoy!

Nutrition: calories 261, fat 3, fiber 3, carbs 6, protein 7

Millet and Oats Porridge

Preparation time: 10 minutes
Cooking time: 13 minutes
Servings: 8

Ingredients:
- 1 cup millet
- ½ cup rolled oats
- 3 cups water
- ½ teaspoon ginger powder
- 2 apples, cored and chopped

Directions:
Set your instant pot on sauté mode, add millet, stir and toast for 3 minutes. Add oats, water, ginger and apples, stir, cover and cook on High for 10 minutes. Stir porridge again, divide into bowls and serve. Enjoy!

Nutrition: calories 200, fat 2, fiber 3, carbs 4, protein 5

Sweet Potato Hash

Preparation time: 10 minutes
Cooking time: 10 minutes
Servings: 4

Ingredients:
- 1 tablespoon Italian seasoning
- 6 eggs
- 1 sweet potato, cubed
- ½ pound pork sausage, ground
- 1 yellow onion, chopped
- 2 cups water, for the instant pot

Directions:
Set your instant pot on sauté mode, add onion, sausage meat and sweet potato, stir, cook for 5 minutes and transfer to a baking dish. In a bowl, mix eggs with Italian seasoning, whisk well and pour over sausage mixture. Add the water to your instant pot, add trivet, add baking dish inside, cover and cook on High for 5 minutes. Leave hash to cool down a bit, divide between plates and serve. Enjoy!

Nutrition: calories 216, fat 6, fiber 3, carbs 12, protein 5

Blueberry Breakfast Delight

Preparation time: 5 minutes
Cooking time: 6 minutes
Servings: 2

Ingredients:
- 2/3 cup old fashioned oats
- 2/3 cup Greek yogurt
- 2/3 cup almond milk
- 2/3 cup blueberries
- 2 tablespoons chia seeds
- 1 teaspoon sugar
- A pinch of cinnamon powder
- ½ teaspoon vanilla
- 1 and ½ cups water

Directions:
In a heatproof bowl, mix oats with milk, yogurt, blueberries, chia seeds, sugar, cinnamon and vanilla and stir. Put the water in your instant pot, add the trivet, add the bowl inside, cover and cook on High for 6 minutes. Stir blueberries mix again, divide into 2 bowls and serve. Enjoy!

Nutrition: calories 154, fat 2, fiber 1, carbs 2, protein 3

Breakfast Bacon Potatoes

Preparation time: 10 minutes
Cooking time: 7 minutes
Servings: 2

Ingredients:
- ½ pound red potatoes, cubed
- 1 bacon strip, chopped
- 1 teaspoon parsley, dried
- A pinch of salt and black pepper
- ½ teaspoon garlic powder
- 1.5-ounce cheddar cheese, grated
- 1 ounce ranch dressing
- 1 tablespoon water

Directions:
In your instant pot with potatoes with bacon, parsley, salt, pepper, garlic powder and water, stir a bit, cover and cook on Manual for 7 minutes. Add cheese and dressing, toss, divide between 2 plates and serve for breakfast. Enjoy!

Nutrition: calories 258, fat 2, fiber 6, carbs 9, protein 12

Potato and Spinach Hash

Preparation time: 10 minutes
Cooking time: 10 minutes
Servings: 4

Ingredients:
- 3 sweet potatoes, baked, peeled and cubed
- 12 ounces chorizo, chopped
- 11 ounces baby spinach
- A pinch of salt
- 1 small yellow onion, chopped

Directions:
Set your instant pot on sauté mode, add chorizo and onion, stir and cook for 2-3 minutes. Add potato cubes, baby spinach and salt, toss a bit, cover and cook on High for 7 minutes. Divide between plates and serve for breakfast. Enjoy!

Nutrition: calories 192, fat 4, fiber 7, carbs 6, protein 2

Breakfast Banana Bread

Preparation time: 10 minutes
Cooking time: 1 hour
Servings: 8

Ingredients:
- 1 and ½ cups water, for the instant pot
- 1 and ½ cups steel cut oats
- 2 bananas, peeled and chopped
- 4 eggs, whisked
- 1/3 cup honey
- ½ teaspoon baking soda

Directions:
In your blender, mix oats with bananas, eggs, honey and baking soda, pulse well and pour into a loaf pan. Add water to your instant pot, add trivet, add pan inside, cover and cook on High for 1 hour. Slice, divide between plates and serve for breakfast. Enjoy!

Nutrition: calories 192, fat 5, fiber 5, carbs 6, protein 2

Veggie Breakfast Casserole

Preparation time: 10 minutes
Cooking time: 30 minutes
Servings: 2

Ingredients:
- 3 eggs
- 3 tablespoons milk
- 3 tablespoons white flour
- A pinch of salt and black pepper
- 1 small red bell pepper, chopped
- ½ cup tomatoes, chopped
- 1 green onion, chopped
- ½ cup cheddar cheese, shredded
- 1 small zucchini, chopped
- 1 cup water

Directions:
In a bowl, mix eggs with flour, milk, salt, pepper, bell pepper, tomatoes, onion, zucchini and half of the cheese and stir well. Pour this into a heatproof dish and cover with some tin foil. Put the water in your instant pot, add the trivet, and the dish with the veggies mix, cover pot and cook on High for 30 minutes. Uncover dish, sprinkle the rest of the cheese all over, divide between 2 plates and serve. Enjoy!

Nutrition: calories 200, fat 1, fiber 2, carbs 3, protein 8

Peach Breakfast

Preparation time: 10 minutes
Cooking time: 3 minutes
Servings: 2

Ingredients:
- 1 cup rolled oats
- ½ peach, chopped
- 2 cups water
- ½ teaspoon vanilla extract
- 1 tablespoon flax meal
- 3 tablespoons almonds, chopped
- Maple syrup to the taste

Directions:
In your instant pot, mix oats with peach, water and vanilla extract, stir a bit, cover and cook on High for 3 minutes. Stir you oatmeal again, divide into 2 bowls, top with flax meal, almonds and maple syrup and serve for breakfast. Enjoy!

Nutrition: calories 143, fat 3, fiber 1, carbs 4, protein 6

Bread Pudding

Preparation time: 10 minutes
Cooking time: 15 minutes
Servings: 10

Ingredients:
- 1 bread loaf, cubed
- 2 cups coconut milk
- 4 eggs
- ½ cup butter
- ½ cup maple syrup
- 2 cups water, for your instant pot

Directions:
In a blender, mix coconut milk with eggs, butter and maple syrup and pulse well. Transfer this to a pudding pan, add bread cubes, toss well and cover pan with tin foil. Add the water to your instant pot, add trivet, add pudding pan, cover and cook on High for 15 minutes. Divide between plates and serve for breakfast. Enjoy!

Nutrition: calories 271, fat 4, fiber 6, carbs 12, protein 10

Egg Muffins

Preparation time: 10 minutes
Cooking time: 8 minutes
Servings: 4

Ingredients:
- 1 and ½ cups water, for the instant pot
- 4 eggs
- 4 tablespoons cheddar cheese, shredded
- 4 bacon slices, cooked and crumbled
- 1 green onion, chopped
- A pinch of salt

Directions:
In a bowl, mix eggs with cheese, bacon, onion and salt, whisk well and divide into muffin cups. Add the water to your instant pot, add steamer basket, add muffin cups inside, cover and cook on High for 8 minutes. Divide muffins between plates and serve them for breakfast. Enjoy!

Nutrition: calories 182, fat 7, fiber 4, carbs 8, protein 12

Chocolate Bread Pudding

Preparation time: 10 minutes
Cooking time: 11 minutes
Servings: 2

Ingredients:
- 1 egg
- ¼ cup milk
- 2 cups challah bread, cubed
- ½ teaspoon cinnamon powder
- ¼ cup condensed milk
- 1/3 cup chocolate, cut into medium chunks
- 1 cup water

Directions:
In a bowl, mix egg with milk, condensed milk and cinnamon and stir. Add bread cubes and chocolate, stir gently and divide this into 2 ramekins. Put the water in your instant pot, add the trivet, add ramekins inside, cover and cook on High for 11 minutes. Serve your puddings hot. Enjoy!

Nutrition: calories 164, fat 3, fiber 1, carbs 3, protein 3

Simple Fruit Cobbler

Preparation time: 10 minutes
Cooking time: 10 minutes
Servings: 2

Ingredients:
- 1 plum, stone removed and chopped
- 1 apple, cored and chopped
- 1 pear, cored and chopped
- 3 tablespoons coconut oil
- 2 tablespoons honey
- ½ teaspoon cinnamon powder
- ¼ cup coconut, shredded and unsweetened
- 2 tablespoons sunflower seeds, roasted
- ¼ cup pecans, chopped

Directions:
In the steel bowl of your instant pot, mix plum with apple, pear, oil, honey and cinnamon, stir, cover, steam for 10 minutes and transfer to a bowl. Put pecans, sunflower seeds and coconut in your instant pot bowl, set on Sauté mode, cook for 5 minutes and sprinkle all over fruits mix. Divide into 2 bowls and serve for breakfast. Enjoy!

Nutrition: calories 132, fat 2, fiber 3, carbs 4, protein 4

Buckwheat Porridge

Preparation time: 10 minutes
Cooking time: 6 minutes
Servings: 4

Ingredients:
- 1 cup buckwheat
- 1 banana, peeled and sliced
- 3 cups rice milk
- 1 teaspoon cinnamon powder
- ¼ cup raisins

Directions:
In your instant pot, mix buckwheat with banana, milk, cinnamon and raisins, stir, cover and cook on High for 6 minutes. Stir porridge, divide into bowls and serve. Enjoy!

Nutrition: calories 182, fat 4, fiber 3, carbs 6, protein 7

Squash Porridge

Preparation time: 10 minutes
Cooking time: 8 minutes
Servings: 4

Ingredients:
- 4 small apples, cored and chopped
- 1 squash, peeled and chopped
- 2 tablespoons cinnamon powder
- 2 tablespoons maple syrup
- ½ cup water

Directions:
In your instant pot, mix apples with squash, cinnamon, maple syrup and water, stir, cover and cook on High for 8 minutes. Stir porridge one more time, divide into bowls and serve. Enjoy!

Nutrition: calories 162, fat 5, fiber 6, carbs 8, protein 2

Espresso Oatmeal

Preparation time: 10 minutes
Cooking time: 10 minutes
Servings: 2

Ingredients:
- 1 and ¼ cups water
- 1 tablespoon white sugar
- ½ cup steel cut oats
- ½ cup milk
- ½ teaspoon espresso powder
- 1 teaspoon vanilla extract
- A pinch of salt
- Grated chocolate for serving
- Whipped cream for serving

Directions:
In your instant pot, mix water with oats, milk, sugar, salt and espresso powder, stir, cover and cook on High for 10 minutes. Add vanilla extract, stir, cover pot, leave everything aside for 5 minutes and divide into bowls. Top with grated chocolate and whipped cream and serve. Enjoy!

Nutrition: calories 200, fat 2, fiber 1, carbs 3, protein 4

Breakfast Rice Pudding

Preparation time: 10 minutes
Cooking time: 20 minutes
Servings: 2

Ingredients:
- 1 cup milk
- 1 cup water
- 1 cup basmati rice
- 4 tablespoons heavy cream
- 2 tablespoons maple syrup
- ½ teaspoon vanilla extract
- A pinch of salt

Directions:
In your instant pot, mix milk with water, rice, salt and maple syrup, stir, cover and cook on High for 20 minutes. Add cream and vanilla extract, stir, divide into 2 bowls and serve for breakfast. Enjoy!

Nutrition: calories 193, fat 3, fiber 1, carbs 3, protein 4

Apple Butter

Preparation time: 10 minutes
Cooking time: 10 minutes
Servings: 6

Ingredients:
- 30 ounces pumpkin puree
- 4 apples, cored, peeled and cubed
- 12 ounces apple cider
- 1 cup sugar
- 1 tablespoon pumpkin pie spice

Directions:
In your instant pot, mix pumpkin puree with apples, cider, sugar and spice, stir, cover and cook on High for 10 minutes. Stir butter again, divide into small jars and serve cold for breakfast. Enjoy!

Nutrition: calories 182, fat 6, fiber 7, carbs 8, protein 2

Veggie Quiche

Preparation time: 10 minutes
Cooking time: 30 minutes
Servings: 6

Ingredients:
- ½ cup milk
- 8 eggs, whisked
- 1 red bell pepper, chopped
- 2 green onions, chopped
- Salt to the taste
- 1 cup water, for the instant pot

Directions:
In a bowl, mix eggs with milk, bell pepper, onions and salt, whisk well and pour into a pan. Add the water to your instant pot, add trivet inside, add pan, cover it with tin foil, cover pot and cook on High for 30 minutes. Slice quiche, divide between plates and serve for breakfast. Enjoy!

Nutrition: calories 200, fat 3, fiber 4, carbs 7, protein 6

Strawberry Quinoa Bowl

Preparation time: 10 minutes
Cooking time: 1 minute:
Servings: 2

Ingredients:
- 1 cup quinoa
- 1 tablespoon honey
- 1 and ½ cups water
- ½ teaspoon vanilla
- A pinch of pumpkin pie spice
- 1 cup strawberries, sliced
- ½ cup vanilla yogurt

Directions:
In your instant pot, mix quinoa with water, honey, vanilla, pumpkin pie spice, yogurt and strawberries, stir a bit, cover and cook on High for 1 minute. Leave quinoa mix aside for 10 minutes, fluff with a fork, divide into 2 bowls and serve for breakfast. Enjoy!

Nutrition: calories 173, fat 2, fiber 2, carbs 3, protein 7

Cornmeal Porridge

Preparation time: 10 minutes
Cooking time: 20 minutes
Servings: 2

Ingredients:
- 2 cups water
- ½ cup milk
- ½ cup cornmeal
- 1 cinnamon stick
- 2 pimiento berries
- ½ teaspoon vanilla extract
- A pinch of nutmeg, ground
- 1/3 cup condensed milk

Directions:
In your instant pot, mix water with milk and cornmeal and stir really well. Add cinnamon, berries, nutmeg, vanilla extract and condensed milk, stir, cover and cook on High for 6 minutes. Divide into 2 bowls and serve for breakfast. Enjoy!

Nutrition: calories 200, fat 1, fiber 3, carbs 3, protein 8

Breakfast Cobbler

Preparation time: 10 minutes
Cooking time: 15 minutes
Servings: 2

Ingredients:
- 1 plum, stone removed and chopped
- 1 apple, cored and chopped
- 3 tablespoons coconut oil
- 2 tablespoons honey
- ¼ cup coconut, shredded

Directions:
In your instant pot, mix plum with apple, half of the oil and honey, stir, cover and cook on Manual for 10 minutes. Transfer this to bowls and clean your instant pot. Set the pot on sauté mode, add the rest of the oil, heat it up, add coconut, stir and toast for 5 minutes. Sprinkle this over fruit mixture and serve. Enjoy!

Nutrition: calories 172, fat 7, fiber 3, carbs 6, protein 2

Tofu and Sweet Potato Mix

Preparation time: 10 minutes
Cooking time: 10 minutes
Servings: 4

Ingredients:
- 1 pound extra firm tofu, cubed
- 1 cup sweet potato, chopped
- 2 teaspoons sesame seed oil
- 1/3 cup veggie stock
- 2 tablespoons red pepper sauce

Directions:
Set your instant pot on sauté mode, add oil, heat it up, add sweet potato, stir and cook for 2 minutes. Add tofu and stock, stir, cook for 2 minutes more, cover pot and cook on High for 3 minutes. Add pepper sauce, toss, divide into bowls and serve for breakfast. Enjoy!

Nutrition: calories 172, fat 7, fiber 1, carbs 20, protein 6

Breakfast Apple Dish

Preparation time: 10 minutes
Cooking time: 8 minutes
Servings: 2

Ingredients:
- 1 teaspoon cinnamon powder
- 2 apples, cored, peeled and cut into medium chunks
- A pinch of nutmeg, ground
- ½ cup water
- ½ tablespoon maple syrup
- 2 tablespoons butter
- 2/3 cup old fashioned rolled oats
- 2 tablespoons flour
- 2 tablespoons brown sugar

Directions:
Put apples in your instant pot, sprinkle cinnamon and nutmeg and add water and maple syrup over them. In a bowl, mix butter with oats, flour and sugar and stir. Drop spoonfuls of this mix over apples, cover and cook on High for 8 minutes. Divide between 2 plates and serve. Enjoy!

Nutrition: calories 183, fat 3, fiber 1, carbs 3, protein 6

Brown Rice Mix

Preparation time: 10 minutes
Cooking time: 40 minutes
Servings: 2

Ingredients:
- 1/3 cup brown rice
- 2 cups mushroom stock
- 1 cup bok choy, chopped
- 1 tablespoon ginger, grated
- 1 cup shiitake mushrooms, chopped
- 1 garlic clove, minced
- ½ cup water
- 1 tablespoon scallions, chopped
- A drizzle of soy sauce

Directions:
In your instant pot, mix rice with mushroom stock, bok choy, ginger, mushrooms, garlic and water, stir, cover and cook on Manual for 40 minutes. Divide into bowls, sprinkle scallions on top, drizzle soy sauce all over and serve for breakfast. Enjoy!

Nutrition: calories 193, fat 3, fiber 1, carbs 2, protein 4

Quinoa and Tomatoes Breakfast Mix

Preparation time: 10 minutes
Cooking time: 12 minutes
Servings: 6

Ingredients:
- 1 small yellow onion, chopped
- 28 ounces canned tomatoes, chopped
- 14 ounces coconut milk
- ¼ cup quinoa
- 1 tablespoon ginger, grated

Directions:
In your instant pot, mix onion with quinoa, tomatoes, milk and ginger, stir, cover and cook on High for 12 minutes. Stir one more time, divide into bowls and serve for breakfast. Enjoy!

Nutrition: calories 260, fat 9, fiber 11, carbs 30, protein 7

Breakfast Rice and Chickpeas Medley

Preparation time: 10 minutes
Cooking time: 27 minutes
Servings: 4

Ingredients:
- 1 tablespoon olive oil
- 1 red onion, chopped
- 1 cup chickpeas
- 14 ounces tomatoes, chopped
- 1 and ½ cups brown rice

Directions:
Set your instant pot on sauté mode, add the oil, heat it up, add onion, stir and cook for 7 minutes. Add tomatoes, chickpeas and rice, stir, cover and cook on High for 20 minutes. Stir one more time, divide into bowls and serve for breakfast. Enjoy!

Nutrition: calories 253, fat 4, fiber 3, carbs 9, protein 7

Quinoa Salad

Preparation time: 10 minutes
Cooking time: 5 minutes
Servings: 2

Ingredients:
- ½ cup quinoa
- 1 cup strawberries, sliced
- 1 cup water
- 1 cup pecans, chopped
- 2 green onion, chopped
- ½ cup broccoli, chopped

For the dressing:
- A pinch of garlic powder
- A drizzle of olive oil
- 1 tablespoon balsamic vinegar
- ½ tablespoon basil, chopped

Directions:
Put water and quinoa in your instant pot, cover, cook on High for 5 minutes, leave aside for 10 more minutes, fluff with a fork and transfer to a bowl. Add strawberries, pecans, onion and broccoli and toss. In a separate bowl, mix garlic powder with oil, basil and vinegar and whisk really well. Add this to quinoa salad, toss, divide between 2 plates and serve for breakfast. Enjoy!

Nutrition: calories 124, fat 2, fiber 1, carbs 3, protein 4

Special Breakfast Beans

Preparation time: 10 minutes
Cooking time: 15 minutes
Servings: 2

Ingredients:
- ½ cup anasazi beans, soaked overnight and drained
- 1 cup onion, sliced
- ½ tablespoon olive oil
- 1/3 cup mushrooms, sliced
- A pinch of sugar
- ¼ teaspoon liquid smoke
- 1 cup beef stock
- ½ teaspoon smoked paprika
- 1 teaspoon red miso
- 1/3 cup water
- ½ teaspoon tamari

Directions:
Put the oil in your instant pot, set on sauté mode, heat it up, add sugar and onion, stir and sauté for 10 minutes. Add beans, mushrooms, smoke, beef stock, water, paprika, miso and tamari, stir, cover and cook on High for 5 minutes. Divide between 2 plates and serve for breakfast. Enjoy!

Nutrition: calories 193, fat 4, fiber 4, carbs 6, protein 8

Breakfast Arugula Salad

Preparation time: 10 minutes
Cooking time: 15 minutes
Servings: 6

Ingredients:
- 2 cups water
- 1 cup kamut grains, soaked for 12 hours
- 1 teaspoon sunflower oil
- 4 ounces arugula
- 2 blood oranges, peeled and cut into medium segments

Directions:
In your instant pot, mix kamut grains with sunflower oil and the water, stir, cover and cook on High for 15 minutes. Drain kamut, transfer to a bowl, add arugula and orange segments, toss well and serve for breakfast. Enjoy!

Nutrition: calories 163, fat 6, fiber 2, carbs 7, protein 3

Cranberry Beans Salad

Preparation time: 10 minutes
Cooking time: 15 minutes
Servings: 4

Ingredients:
- 1 cup cranberry beans, soaked and drained
- 1 and ½ cups green beans
- ½ red onion, chopped
- 5 tablespoons apple cider vinegar
- 4 tablespoons olive oil
- 1 cup water, for the instant pot

Directions:
Put the water in your instant pot, add steamer basket, add cranberry and green beans inside, cover and cook on High for 15 minutes. Drain all beans, transfer them to a salad bowl, add onion, vinegar and oil, toss and serve for breakfast. Enjoy!

Nutrition: calories 170, fat 4, fiber 7, carbs 15, protein 6

Wild Rice Breakfast Salad

Preparation time: 10 minutes
Cooking time: 30 minutes
Servings: 2

Ingredients:
- 1 garlic clove, minced
- ½ shallot, chopped
- ½ teaspoon rosemary, dried
- 1 and ½ cups veggie stock
- ½ cup wild rice
- Juice from 1 orange
- 1/3 cup cranberries, dried
- 1 tablespoon maple syrup
- ½ tablespoon mustard
- ½ tablespoon tamari
- 1/3 cup pecans, chopped

Directions:
Set your instant pot on sauté mode, add half of the stock, shallot and garlic, stir and sauté for 5 minutes. Add rosemary, rice, the rest of the stock, cranberries and orange juice, stir, cover and cook on Manual for 25 minutes. Add maple syrup, tamari, mustard and pecans, stir, divide between 2 plates and serve for breakfast. Enjoy!

Nutrition: calories 254, fat 1, fiber 4, carbs 10, protein 5

Rice and Black Beans Breakfast Dish

Preparation time: 10 minutes
Cooking time: 28 minutes
Servings: 2

Ingredients:
- ½ cup onion, chopped
- 2 garlic cloves, minced
- 1 cup brown rice
- 1 cup black beans
- 4 and ½ cups water
- A pinch of salt
- 1 lime, cut into wedges
- 1 avocado, pitted, peeled and sliced

Directions:
In your instant pot, mix rice with beans, water, salt, garlic and onion, stir, cover and cook on Manual for 28 minutes. Divide into 2 bowls, top with avocado pieces and serve for breakfast with lime wedges on the side. Enjoy!

Nutrition: calories 200, fat 4, fiber 5, carbs 10, protein 8

Pineapple and Peas Breakfast Curry

Preparation time: 10 minutes
Cooking time: 20 minutes
Servings: 4

Ingredients:
- 1 cup peas, soaked and drained
- 4 cups water
- 1 teaspoon curry powder
- 1 cup canned pineapple, cut into medium chunks
- ¼ cup cashew butter

Directions
In your instant pot, mix peas with water, cover and cook on High for 16 minutes. Drain peas, transfer to a bowl, clean the pot and set it in sauté mode. Add peas, curry powder, pineapple and cashew butter, toss well, cook for 1 minute, cover pot, cook on High for 2 minutes, divide into bowls and serve for breakfast. Enjoy!

Nutrition: calories 181, fat 6, fiber 6, carbs 15, protein 8

Brussels Sprouts and Potato Bowls

Preparation time: 10 minutes
Cooking time: 7 minutes
Servings: 4

Ingredients:
- 1 and ½ pounds Brussels sprouts, trimmed
- 1 cup small potatoes, roughly chopped
- 1 and ½ tablespoons olive oil
- ½ cup veggie stock
- Salt to the taste

Directions:
In your instant pot, mix sprouts with potatoes, stock and salt, stir a bit, cover and cook on High for 5 minutes. Set the pot on sauté mode, add oil, toss a bit, cook for 1-2 minutes, divide into bowls and serve right away for breakfast Enjoy!

Nutrition: calories 121, fat 4, fiber 7, carbs 14, protein 5

Parsnip and Quinoa Breakfast Mix

Preparation time: 10 minutes
Cooking time: 30 minutes
Servings: 2

Ingredients:
- 1 pound parsnips, peeled and roughly chopped
- 1 and ½ tablespoon balsamic vinegar
- 2 tablespoons veggie stock
- 1 tablespoon maple syrup
- A pinch of salt and black pepper
- ½ cup quinoa, already cooked
- 1 avocado, pitted, peeled and chopped
- 3 tablespoons cashews, roasted
- Juice from ½ lemon

Directions:
In your instant pot, mix parsnips with vinegar and stock, stir, cover, cook on High for 3 minutes, transfer to a bowl, mix with maple syrup, a pinch of salt and pepper and toss. In a large bowl, mix quinoa with cashews and avocado and toss. Add parsnips, toss again, divide into 2 bowls and serve with lemon juice on top. Enjoy!

Nutrition: calories 200, fat 4, fiber 1, carbs 3, protein 4

Simple Potato Salad

Preparation time: 10 minutes
Cooking time: 4 minutes
Servings: 2

Ingredients:
- 2 potatoes, peeled and cubed
- 2 eggs
- 1 and ½ cups water
- 1 small yellow onion, chopped
- ¼ cup mayonnaise
- 1 tablespoon parsley, chopped
- 1 tablespoon mustard
- A pinch of salt and black pepper

Directions:
Put the water in your instant pot, add the steamer basket, add eggs and potatoes, cover and cook on High for 4 minutes. Drain potatoes and eggs, peel everything, chop and transfer to a bowl. Add onion, parsley, salt and pepper and toss. Add mustard and mayo, toss again, divide into 2 bowls and serve for breakfast. Enjoy!

Nutrition: calories 194, fat 4, fiber 2, carbs 5, protein 8

Italian Eggplants Bowls

Preparation time: 10 minutes
Cooking time: 9 minutes
Servings: 3

Ingredients:
- 4 cups eggplant, cubed
- 1 tablespoon olive oil
- 1 tablespoon garlic powder
- 3 garlic cloves, minced
- 1 cup tomato sauce

Directions:
Set your instant pot on Sauté mode, add oil, heat it up, add garlic, stir and cook for a couple of minutes. Add eggplant, garlic powder and tomato sauce, stir, cover and cook on High for 7 minutes. Divide into bowls and serve for breakfast. Enjoy!

Nutrition: calories 172, fat 4, fiber 5, carbs 7, protein 4

Cauliflower and Barley Bowls

Preparation time: 10 minutes
Cooking time: 34 minutes
Servings: 4

Ingredients:
- 4 tablespoons extra virgin olive oil
- 1 cauliflower head, florets separated
- ½ cup parmesan, grated
- 1 cup pearl barley
- 3 cups chicken stock

Directions:
Set your instant pot on Sauté mode, add 3 tablespoons oil, heat it up, add cauliflower, some salt and pepper, stir and sauté for 10 minutes. Add half of the parmesan, stir and cook for 3-4 minutes more. Add the rest of the oil, barley and stock, stir, cover and cook on High for 20 minutes. Add the rest of the parmesan, toss, divide into bowls and serve for breakfast. Enjoy!

Nutrition: calories 252, fat 4, fiber 6, carbs 20, protein 6

Breakfast Egg Salad

Preparation time: 10 minutes
Cooking time: 5 minutes
Servings: 2

Ingredients:
- 4 eggs
- 2 tablespoons mayonnaise
- A pinch of salt and black pepper
- A drizzle of olive oil
- 1 cup water

Directions:
Grease a baking dish with a drizzle of oil and crack eggs into the dish. Put the water in your instant pot, add the trivet, add the baking dish inside, cover and cook on High for 5 minutes. Leave eggs to cool down, mash them with a potato masher, transfer to a bowl, mix with salt, pepper and mayo, stir well and serve for breakfast. Enjoy!

Nutrition: calories 193, fat 2, fiber 1, carbs 2, protein 4

Strawberry Jam

Preparation time: 20 minutes
Cooking time: 4 minutes
Servings: 2

Ingredients:
- 2 pounds strawberries, halved
- ¼ cup sugar
- Juice from ½ orange

Directions:
In your instant pot, mix strawberries with orange juice and sugar, stir and leave them aside for 20 minutes. Cover pot, cook your jam on Manual for 4 minutes, blend everything using an immersion blender and serve for breakfast. Enjoy!

Nutrition: calories 164, fat 4, fiber 2, carbs 5, protein 3

Celeriac Breakfast Mix

Preparation time: 10 minutes
Cooking time: 8 minutes
Servings: 6

Ingredients:
- 2 teaspoons parsley, dried
- 3 bacon strips
- 2 pounds celeriac, peeled and cubed
- 4 ounces cheddar cheese, shredded
- 2 tablespoons chicken stock

Directions:
Set your instant pot on sauté mode, add bacon, stir and cook for a couple of minutes. Add parsley, celeriac and stock, stir, cover and cook on High for 6 minutes. Add cheese, toss, divide between plates and serve for breakfast. Enjoy!

Nutrition: calories 164, fat 3, fiber 2, carbs 6, protein 7

Turkey Breast Breakfast Mix

Preparation time: 10 minutes
Cooking time: 7 minutes
Servings: 4

Ingredients:
- 4 avocado slices
- 4 turkey breast slices, already cooked
- 2 tablespoons olive oil
- 4 eggs, whisked
- 2 tablespoons veggie stock

Directions:
Set your instant pot on sauté mode, oil, heat it up, add turkey, brown for a couple of minutes and divide between plates. Heat up the pot again, add eggs and veggie stock, stir, cover and cook on High for 5 minutes. Divide eggs and avocado slices next to turkey breast slices and serve for breakfast. Enjoy!

Nutrition: calories 185, fat 2, fiber 2, carbs 16, protein 6

Fresh Peach Jam

Preparation time: 10 minutes
Cooking time: 16 minutes
Servings: 2

Ingredients:
- 2 cups peaches, stones removed and roughly chopped
- Juice from 1/3 lemon
- ¼ cup honey
- ½ tablespoon vanilla extract

Directions:
In your instant pot, mix peaches with lemon juice, honey and vanilla, stir, cover and cook on High for 1 minute, Turn instant pot to Sauté mode, cook your jam for 15 minutes more, blend using an immersion blender and serve for breakfast. Enjoy!

Nutrition: calories 164, fat 2, fiber 1, carbs 2, protein 3

Breakfast Orange Marmalade

Preparation time: 10 minutes
Cooking time: 10 minutes
Servings: 2

Ingredients:
- ½ pound oranges, thinly sliced
- ½ cup water
- 1 cup sugar

Directions:
In your instant pot, mix oranges with water and sugar, stir, cover and cook on High for 10 minutes. Serve this for breakfast the next day! Enjoy!

Nutrition: calories 153, fat 3, fiber 2, carbs 3, protein 6

Pomegranate Oatmeal

Preparation time: 5 minutes
Cooking time: 3 minutes
Servings: 4

Ingredients:
- 2 cups coconut, shredded
- 2 cup water
- 1 cup pomegranate juice
- Seeds of 2 pomegranates
- 2 tablespoon sugar

Directions:
In your instant pot, mix coconut with water and pomegranate juice, stir, cover and cook on High for 3 minutes. Add pomegranate seeds and sugar, stir, divide into bowls and serve for breakfast. Enjoy!

Nutrition: calories 153, fat 3, fiber 5, carbs 10, protein 4

Cheesy Cauliflower Bowls

Preparation time: 10 minutes
Cooking time: 4 minutes
Servings: 6

Ingredients:
- 1 cauliflower head, florets separated
- ½ cup veggie stock
- 1/3 cup parmesan, grated
- 1 tablespoon parsley, chopped
- 3 tablespoons olive oil

Directions:
In a bowl, mix oil with cauliflower florets, toss and transfer to your instant pot. Add stock, cover pot and cook on High for 4 minutes. Add parsley and parmesan, toss, divide into bowls and serve for breakfast. Enjoy!

Nutrition: calories 120, fat 2, fiber 3, carbs 5, protein 3

Rich Breakfast Potatoes

Preparation time: 10 minutes
Cooking time: 25 minutes
Servings: 2

Ingredients:
- 2 gold potatoes
- 4 cups water
- ½ red bell pepper, chopped
- ½ pound pork sausage
- 1 small yellow onion, chopped
- ½ yellow onion, chopped
- A pinch of potato seasoning
- A pinch of garlic powder
- A pinch of salt and black pepper
- 1 tablespoon green onions, chopped
- Hot sauce to the taste
- Cooking spray
- 2 eggs
- 2 tablespoons apple cider vinegar

Directions:
Put the water in your instant pot, add the steamer basket, add potatoes inside, cover and cook on High for 20 minutes. Meanwhile, grease a pan with cooking spray, heat it up over medium heat, add yellow onion, stir and cook for 2 minutes. Add seasoning, sausage, salt, pepper, garlic powder, orange and red pepper, stir and cook for 2 minutes. Drain potatoes, split them a bit, scrape sides, leave skins aside and transfer potato pulp to a bowl. Add onion and sausage mix, stir well and stuff potatoes with this mix. Put some water in a pot, add the vinegar, bring to a boil over medium heat, crack eggs, poach them for 5 minutes and divide them on top of potatoes. Sprinkle green onions, drizzle hot sauce all over and serve them for breakfast. Enjoy!

Nutrition: calories 214, fat 3, fiber 1, carbs 2, protein 4

Sweet Potatoes Casserole

Preparation time: 10 minutes
Cooking time: 30 minutes
Servings: 2

Ingredients:
- 1 and ½ cups water
- 1 tablespoon olive oil
- 1 teaspoon garlic, minced
- ½ cup leeks, chopped
- ½ cup kale, chopped
- 3 eggs
- 4 tablespoons sweet potato, grated
- ½ cup sausage, cooked

Directions:
Put the oil in your instant pot, set it on sauté mode, heat it up, add garlic, leeks and kale, stir, cook for 2 minutes, transfer them to a bowl and clean the pot. Add sweet potato, sausage and eggs to the bowl with the veggies, whisk everything and pour into a greased heatproof dish. Add the water to your instant pot, add the trivet, add the dish inside, cover with a tin foil, cover the pot as well and cook on Manual for 25 minutes. Divide between 2 plates and serve for breakfast. Enjoy!

Nutrition: calories 200, fat 1, fiber 3, carbs 6, protein 9

Swiss Chard Salad

Preparation time: 10 minutes
Cooking time: 5 minutes
Servings: 4

Ingredients:
- 1 bunch Swiss chard, cut into strips
- 2 tablespoons olive oil
- 1 tablespoon balsamic vinegar
- ¼ teaspoon red pepper flakes
- ¼ cup pine nuts, toasted

Directions:
Set your instant pot on sauté mode, add oil, heat it up, add chard, stir and cook for 2 minutes. Add pepper flakes and vinegar, stir, cover and cook on High for 3 minutes. Add pine nuts, toss, divide into bowls and serve for breakfast. Enjoy!

Nutrition: calories 110, fat 2, fiber 1, carbs 6, protein 4

Beets Spread

Preparation time: 10 minutes
Cooking time: 12 minutes
Servings: 6

Ingredients:
- 8 carrots, chopped
- 4 beets, peeled and chopped
- 1 cup veggie stock
- ¼ cup lemon juice
- 1 bunch basil, chopped

Directions:
In your instant pot, mix beets with stock and carrots, stir, cover and cook on High for 12 minutes. Blend using an immersion blender, add lemon juice and basil, stir, divide into bowls and serve for breakfast. Enjoy!

Nutrition: calories 100, fat 1, fiber 6, carbs 10, protein 3

Millet Porridge

Preparation time: 10 minutes
Cooking time: 10 minutes
Servings: 2

Ingredients:
- 3 tablespoons millet
- 1 cup water
- 1 small apple, cored and chopped
- 2 tablespoons rolled oats
- ¼ teaspoon cinnamon powder
- ¼ teaspoon ginger powder
- A pinch of salt

Directions:
In your instant pot, mix millet with oats, water, apple, cinnamon, ginger and salt, stir, cover and cook on High for 10 minutes. Divide into 2 bowls and serve. Enjoy!

Nutrition: calories 132, fat 1, fiber 2, carbs 2, protein 3

Quinoa with Sausages

Preparation time: 10 minutes
Cooking time: 6 minutes
Servings: 2

Ingredients:
- ½ pound sausage meat, casings removed
- 1 tablespoon olive oil
- 1 small yellow onion, chopped
- ½ teaspoon sweet paprika
- A pinch of turmeric powder
- 1 cup quinoa
- 1 cup chicken stock
- 1 red bell pepper, chopped
- ½ small broccoli head, florets separated
- 1 ounce Bella mushrooms, halved

Directions:
Put the oil in your instant pot, set on sauté mode, heat it up, add sausage and onion, stir and brown for a few minutes. Add turmeric and paprika and stir. Add stock, quinoa, bell pepper, mushrooms and bell pepper, stir, cover and cook on High for 1 minute. Leave instant pot aside covered for 10 minutes, fluff quinoa with a fork, divide into 2 bowls and serve. Enjoy!

Nutrition: calories 174, fat 2, fiber 1, carbs 3, protein 4

Avocado Spread

Preparation time: 10 minutes
Cooking time: 2 minutes
Servings: 4

Ingredients:
- ½ cup cilantro, chopped
- 2 avocados, pitted, peeled and halved
- ¼ teaspoon stevia
- Juice of 2 limes
- 1 cup coconut milk
- 1 cup water, for the instant pot

Directions:
Add the water to your instant pot, add the steamer basket, add avocados, cover and cook on High for 2 minutes. Transfer to your blender, add cilantro, stevia, lime juice and coconut milk, blend well, divide into small bowls and serve for breakfast. Enjoy!

Nutrition: calories 190, fat 6, fiber 4, carbs 10, protein 4

Pinto Beans Breakfast Salad

Preparation time: 10 minutes
Cooking time: 30 minutes
Servings: 2

Ingredients:
- ½ pound pinto beans, soaked and drained
- 1 tablespoon olive oil
- ½ yellow onion, chopped
- 1 and ½ cups veggie stock
- 1 red bell pepper, roughly chopped

Directions:
In your instant pot, mix beans with stock, stir, cover and cook on High for 30 minutes. Drain beans, transfer them to a bowl, add onion, bell pepper and oil, toss, divide into bowls and serve for breakfast. Enjoy!

Nutrition: calories 201, fat 5, fiber 7, carbs 16, protein 5

Breakfast Chickpeas Spread

Preparation time: 10 minutes
Cooking time: 18 minutes
Servings: 2

Ingredients:
- 1/3 cup chickpeas
- 2 garlic cloves
- 1 bay leaf
- ½ tablespoon tahini
- Juice from 1/3 lemon
- A pinch of cumin, ground
- A pinch of sea salt and white pepper
- 1 tablespoon parsley
- A drizzle of olive oil
- A pinch of sweet paprika
- 2 cups water

Directions:
In your instant pot, mix chickpeas with bay leaf, salt, pepper and water, stir, cover and cook on High for 18 minutes. Drain chickpeas, transfer them to your blender, add garlic, tahini, lemon juice, cumin and pulse really well. Transfer to a bowl, sprinkle parsley and paprika, drizzle oil all over and serve for breakfast. Enjoy!

Nutrition: calories 194, fat 2, fiber 1, carbs 2, protein 4

Breakfast Cheese Spread

Preparation time: 10 minutes
Cooking time: 20 minutes
Servings: 2

Ingredients:
- 1/3 pound American cheese
- 1/3 tablespoon butter
- 1/3 cup queso, shredded
- 2 ounces cream cheese
- 1/3 tablespoon garlic, minced
- 1/3 tablespoon milk
- ¼ teaspoon oregano, dried
- 1 cup water

Directions:
In a heatproof bowl, mix American cheese with queso, cream cheese, butter, garlic, oregano and milk and whisk well. Add the water to you instant pot, add the trivet on the bottom, cover the heatproof dish with tin foil, add it to the pot, cover and cook on High for 18 minutes. Stir spread again and serve for breakfast. Enjoy!

Nutrition: calories 183, fat 2, fiber 3, carbs 2, protein 4

Creamy Squash Bowl

Preparation time: 10 minutes
Cooking time: 10 minutes
Servings: 3

Ingredients:
- ½ tablespoon olive oil
- 1 small yellow onion, chopped
- 1 big yellow squash, peeled and roughly chopped
- 3 tablespoons chicken stock
- ½ tablespoon sour cream

Directions:
Set your instant pot on sauté mode, add oil, heat it up, add onion, stir and cook for 3 minutes. Add squash and stock, stir a bit, cover and cook on High for 7 minutes. Add sour cream, toss, divide into bowls and serve for breakfast. Enjoy!

Nutrition: calories 200, fat 5, fiber 5, carbs 10, protein 2

Italian Eggplant Breakfast Mix

Preparation time: 10 minutes
Cooking time: 11 minutes
Servings: 4

Ingredients:
- 3 eggplants, cubed
- 3 garlic cloves, chopped
- 1 bunch oregano, chopped
- 2 tablespoons olive oil
- ½ cup chicken stock

Directions:
Set your instant pot on sauté mode, add oil, heat it up, add garlic, stir and cook for 1 minute. Add eggplants and stock, stir, cover and cook on High for 10 minutes. Stir eggplant mix again, add oregano, toss, divide between plates and serve for breakfast. Enjoy!

Nutrition: calories 142, fat 6, fiber 2, carbs 10, protein 4

Easy Breakfast Butter

Preparation time: 10 minutes
Cooking time: 35 minutes
Servings: 2

Ingredients:
- ½ pound apples, cored and roughly chopped
- 1/3 cup apple juice
- A pinch of cinnamon powder
- A pinch of nutmeg, ground
- A pinch of cloves, ground

Directions:
In your instant pot, mix apples with apple juice, stir, cover and cook on High for 20 minutes. Blend using an immersion blender, add cinnamon, nutmeg and cloves, stir, set the pot on sauté mode and cook apple butter for 15 minutes. Serve cold for breakfast. Enjoy!

Nutrition: calories 172, fat 2, fiber 2, carbs 5, protein 3

Breakfast Apple Dumplings

Preparation time: 10 minutes
Cooking time: 10 minutes
Servings: 2

Ingredients:
- 2 ounces crescent rolls
- 1 apple, cored, peeled and cut into 4 wedges
- ¼ cup brown sugar
- 1 tablespoon butter
- A pinch of cinnamon powder
- ½ teaspoon vanilla extract
- A pinch of nutmeg, ground
- 2 tablespoons apple cider

Directions:
Roll crescents rolls on a working surface. Wrap each apple piece in crescent rolls dough. Put the butter in your instant pot, set it on sauté mode and melt it. Add vanilla, sugar, nutmeg and cinnamon and stir. Add dumplings and apple cider, cover the pot and cook on High for 10 minutes. Divide between 2 plates and serve for breakfast. Enjoy!

Nutrition: calories 213, fat 2, fiber 2, carbs 3, protein 3

Carrot Breakfast Salad

Preparation time: 5 minutes
Cooking time: 4 minutes
Servings: 5

Ingredients:
- 2 pounds carrots, shredded
- 1 tablespoon maple syrup
- 1 tablespoon olive oil
- 1 cup water
- ¼ cup raisins

Directions:
In your instant pot mix carrots with maple syrup, water and raisins, stir, cover and cook on High for 4 minutes. Stir again, divide into bowls, drizzle oil on top and serve for breakfast. Enjoy!

Nutrition: calories 80, fat 1, fiber 2, carbs 8, protein 2

Tapioca Pudding

Preparation time: 10 minutes
Cooking time: 8 minutes
Servings: 6

Ingredients:
- 1/3 cup tapioca pearls, washed and drained
- ½ cup water
- ½ cup sugar
- Zest of ½ lemon, grated
- 1 and ¼ cups milk

Directions:
In your instant pot, mix tapioca with water, sugar, milk and lemon zest, stir, cover and cook on High for 8 minutes. Transfer to bowls and serve for breakfast. Enjoy!

Nutrition: calories 140, fat 2, fiber 1, carbs 20, protein 4

Breakfast Chestnut Butter

Preparation time: 10 minutes
Cooking time: 20 minutes
Servings: 2

Ingredients:
- ½ pound chestnuts
- A splash of rum liquor
- 1 ounce sugar
- 2 ounces water

Directions:
In your instant pot, mix chestnuts with sugar and water, stir, cover and cook on High for 20 minutes. Blend well using an immersion blender, add rum, blend again and serve for breakfast. Enjoy!

Nutrition: calories 200, fat 3, fiber 1, carbs 3, protein 8

Breakfast Couscous Salad

Preparation time: 10 minutes
Cooking time: 5 minutes
Servings: 2

Ingredients:
- ½ tablespoon butter
- 1 cup chicken stock
- 3 ounces couscous
- 1 red bell pepper, chopped
- A pinch of salt and black pepper

Directions:
Set your instant pot on sauté mode, add butter and melt it. Add stock, bell pepper, couscous, salt and pepper, stir, cover and cook on High for 5 minutes. Fluff couscous with a fork, divide into 2 bowls and serve as a breakfast. Enjoy!

Nutrition: calories 163, fat 3, fiber 2, carbs 3, protein 7

Couscous and Mint

Preparation time: 10 minutes
Cooking time: 7 minutes
Servings: 4

Ingredients:
- 1 cup pearl couscous
- 2 tablespoons extra virgin olive oil
- 1 small yellow onion, thinly sliced
- 1 and ½ cups veggie stock
- 2 tablespoons mint leaves, finely chopped

Directions:
Set your instant pot on sauté mode, add oil, heat it up, add onion, stir and cook for 2 minutes. Add couscous and stock, stir, cover and cook on High for 5 minutes. Fluff with a fork, divide into bowls, sprinkle mint on top and serve for breakfast. Enjoy!

Nutrition: calories 170, fat 7, fiber 3, carbs 20, protein 6

Simple Quince Jam

Preparation time: 10 minutes
Cooking time: 10 minutes
Servings: 6

Ingredients:
- 2 pounds quince, grated
- Juice of 1 lemon
- ¼ cup water
- 10 cloves
- 2 pounds sugar

Directions:
In your instant pot, mix quince with sugar, lemon juice, water and cloves, stir, cover and cook on High for 10 minutes. Serve on toasted bread for breakfast. Enjoy!

Nutrition: calories 90, fat 3, fiber 1, carbs 14, protein 4

Veggie and Couscous Breakfast

Preparation time: 10 minutes
Cooking time: 20 minutes
Servings: 2

Ingredients:
- 2 bay leaves
- 1 tablespoon olive oil
- 1 small onion, chopped
- 1 cup carrot, grated
- 1 and ¾ cup water
- 1 and ¾ cup couscous
- ½ teaspoon garam masala
- A pinch of salt and black pepper
- 1 tablespoon cilantro, chopped
- 1 tablespoon lemon juice

Directions:
Set your instant pot on sauté mode, add oil, heat it up, add onion and bay leaves, stir and cook for 2 minutes. Add carrot and bell pepper, stir and cook for 1 minute. Add garam masala, water, salt, pepper and couscous, stir, cover and cook on Manual for 10 minutes. Fluff couscous mix with a fork, add cilantro and lemon juice, stir, divide into 2 bowls and serve for breakfast. Enjoy!

Nutrition: calories 164, fat 3, fiber 1, carbs 2, protein 3

Potato and Salmon Breakfast

Preparation time: 10 minutes
Cooking time: 25 minutes
Servings: 2

Ingredients:
- 2 salmon fillets
- ½ pound small potatoes, diced
- A pinch of salt and black pepper
- 1 teaspoon canola oil
- 1 small yellow onion, chopped
- ½ small red bell pepper, chopped
- ½ cup spinach
- 2 garlic cloves, minced
- ½ tablespoon dill, chopped
- 2 cups water+ 2 tablespoons

Directions:
Put 2 cups water in your instant pot, add the steamer basket, add potatoes, cover and cook on High for 15 minutes. Drain potatoes, transfer them to a bowl and clean the pot. Add the oil, set on Sauté mode, add salmon fillets, season with a pinch of salt, cook for 2 minutes on each side, transfer to a plate, cool them down and flake with a fork. Heat the instant pot again on sauté mode, add bell pepper, garlic and onion, stir and cook for 3 minutes more. Return potatoes, salmon, dill, spinach, salt, pepper and 2 tablespoons water, stir gently, cover and cook on High for 5 minutes. Divide between plates and serve for breakfast. Enjoy!

Nutrition: calories 193, fat 3, fiber 1, carbs 3, protein 7

Rhubarb Breakfast Spread

Preparation time: 10 minutes
Cooking time: 10 minutes
Servings: 6

Ingredients:
- 8 ounces rhubarb, chopped
- 1 tablespoon cider vinegar
- 1/3 cup honey
- ¼ cup raisins
- ¼ cup water

Directions:
In your instant pot, mix rhubarb with vinegar, honey, water and raisins, stir, cover and cook on High for 10 minutes. Pulse using an immersion blender, transfer to bowls and serve for breakfast. Enjoy!

Nutrition: calories 100, fat 2, fiber 3, carbs 17, protein 2

Strawberry and Rhubarb Breakfast Compote

Preparation time: 10 minutes
Cooking time: 30 minutes
Servings: 6

Ingredients:
- 1/3 cup water
- 3 tablespoons honey
- 2 pounds rhubarb, chopped
- 6 mint leaves, chopped
- 1 pound strawberries, chopped

Directions:
Put rhubarb and water in your instant pot, cover, cook on High for 10 minutes, add strawberries and honey and stir. Set pot in sauté mode, cook compote for 20 minutes, mix with mint, divide into bowls and serve for breakfast. Enjoy!

Nutrition: calories 100, fat 1, fiber 4, carbs 15, protein 2

Instant Pot Main Dish Recipes

Chicken Curry

Preparation time: 10 minutes
Cooking time: 45 minutes
Servings: 2

Ingredients:
- 1 bay leaf
- 1 tablespoon butter
- A small cinnamon piece
- 1 cup onion, chopped
- A pinch of cumin seeds
- ½ tablespoon garlic, minced
- 1 tablespoon tomato paste
- ½ tablespoon ginger, grated
- A pinch of turmeric powder
- 1 tablespoon coriander powder
- A pinch of salt and black pepper
- A pinch of cayenne pepper
- 1 pound chicken thighs
- 1 cup potato, cubed
- ¼ cup water
- 1 teaspoon garam masala
- 1 tablespoon cashew paste
- 2 tablespoons cilantro, chopped

Directions:
Set your instant pot on sauté mode, add butter, melt it, add cumin, bay leaf and cinnamon and stir. Also add ginger, onion and garlic, stir and sauté for 6 minutes more. Add tomato paste, stir and cook for 3 minutes more. Add turmeric, coriander, cayenne, salt, pepper, chicken and the water, stir, cover and cook on High for 15 minutes. Add garam masala and potatoes, cover and cook on Manual for 6 minutes more. Add cashew paste and cilantro, stir, divide into bowls and serve. Enjoy!

Nutrition: calories 312, fat 2, fiber 2, carbs 10, protein 17

Beef Stew

Preparation time: 10 minutes
Cooking time: 25 minutes
Servings: 2

Ingredients:
- 1 pound beef meat, cubed
- 1 tablespoon olive oil
- 1 tablespoon flour
- A pinch of salt and black pepper
- 1 small yellow onion, chopped
- 1 garlic clove, minced
- 3 tablespoons red wine
- 1 celery stalk, chopped
- 2 small carrots, chopped
- ½ pound red potatoes, chopped
- ½ tablespoon tomato paste
- 1 cup beef stock
- 2 tablespoons parsley, chopped

Directions:
In a bowl, mix beef meat with salt, pepper and flour and toss. Set your instant pot on sauté mode, add the oil and heat it up. Add beef, brown on all sides, transfer to a bowl and leave aside. Add wine to your instant pot and cook on Sauté mode for a couple more minutes. Return beef to the pot, add carrots, garlic, onions, potatoes, celery, stock and tomato paste, stir, cover and cook on High for 20 minutes. Add parsley, stir your stew, divide into 2 bowls and serve. Enjoy!

Nutrition: calories 312, fat 2, fiber 2, carbs 4, protein 6

Juicy Roast

Preparation time: 10 minutes
Cooking time: 1 hour
Servings: 4

Ingredients:
- 1 pound chuck roast
- 4 garlic cloves, minced
- 1 cup chicken stock
- 1 tablespoon soy sauce
- 1 tablespoon olive oil

Directions:
Set your instant pot on sauté mode, add oil, heat it up, add chuck roast and brown for 10 minutes on each side. Add garlic to the pot, stir and cook for a couple more minutes. Add stock and soy sauce, stir, cover and cook on High for 45 minutes. Leave roast to cool down a bit, slice, divide between plates and serve with cooking juices on top. Enjoy!

Nutrition: calories 343, fat 6, fiber 6, carbs 25, protein 18

Easy Mac and Cheese

Preparation time: 10 minutes
Cooking time: 15 minutes
Servings: 4

Ingredients:
- 16 ounces macaroni
- 4 tablespoons butter
- 4 cups water
- 14 ounces cheddar cheese, grated
- 12 ounces evaporated milk

Directions:
In your instant pot, mix macaroni with water, stir, cover and cook on High for 4 minutes. Drain macaroni and clean the pot. Add the butter to your instant pot, set it on sauté mode, melt it, add macaroni and stir well. Add cheese and milk and cook for 10 minutes stirring often. Divide into bowls and serve. Enjoy!

Nutrition: calories 321, fat 6, fiber 8, carbs 16, protein 4

Vegetarian Lentils Soup

Preparation time: 10 minutes
Cooking time: 30 minutes
Servings: two

Ingredients:
- 1 teaspoon olive oil
- ½ cup yellow onion, chopped
- ½ cup carrot, chopped
- 1/3 cup celery, chopped
- 1 tablespoon garlic, minced
- ½ teaspoon turmeric, ground
- 1 teaspoon cumin, ground
- ½ teaspoon thyme, dried
- A pinch of salt and black pepper
- 2 cups veggie stock
- ½ cup lentils
- 3 cups baby spinach

Directions:
Set your instant pot on sauté mode, add the oil, heat it up, add onion, celery and carrot, stir and cook for 5 minutes. Add turmeric, garlic, cumin, thyme, salt and pepper, stir and cook for 1 minute more. Add lentils and stock, stir, cover and cook on Manual for 12 minutes. Add spinach, stir, ladle into bowls and serve. Enjoy!

Nutrition: calories 235, fat 1, fiber 2, carbs 4, protein 7

Crispy Chicken

Preparation time: 10 minutes
Cooking time: 25 minutes
Servings: 2

Ingredients:
- 1 pound chicken breasts, skinless and boneless
- ½ teaspoon oregano, dried
- ½ teaspoon chili powder
- ½ tablespoon cumin, ground
- A pinch of salt and black pepper
- Zest and juice from ½ orange
- 2 tablespoon chicken stock
- 2 garlic cloves, minced
- 1 small yellow onion, chopped
- 1 tablespoon adobo sauce
- 2 tablespoons cilantro, chopped
- 1 tablespoon olive oil

For the sauce:
- ½ tablespoon milk
- 3 tablespoon mayonnaise
- 1 chipotle pepper
- A pinch of salt and garlic powder
- 2 tortillas for serving

Directions:
In a bowl, mix chili powder with oregano, cumin, salt, pepper and chicken breasts and toss. Set your instant pot on sauté mode, add oil, heat it up, add chicken breasts, brown for 1 minute on each side and transfer to a plate. Add garlic and onion to your instant pot, stir and cook for 2 minutes. Return chicken to your instant pot, add orange juice and zest, stock, adobo sauce, bay leaf and cilantro, stir, cover and cook on High for 10 minutes. Transfer chicken breasts to a cutting board, cool down, shred using a fork, transfer to a bowl, drizzle some of the cooking liquid from the pot and toss. Spread chicken on a lined baking sheet, introduce in preheated broiler and cook broil for 10 minutes. Meanwhile, in your blender, mix milk with mayo, chipotle pepper, salt and garlic powder and pulse well. Divide chicken on tortillas, add the sauce you've just made, roll and serve them.
Nutrition: calories 242, fat 2, fiber 2, carbs 6, protein 8

Delicious Ribs

Preparation time: 10 minutes
Cooking time: 25 minutes
Servings: 3

Ingredients:
- 1 cup water, for the instant pot
- 1 rack baby back ribs
- 4 tablespoons BBQ sauce
- Salt to the taste
- Black pepper to the taste
- A pinch of chili powder

Directions:
In a bowl, mix ribs with bbq sauce, salt, pepper and chili powder and toss well. Add the water to your instant pot, add steamer basket, add ribs inside, cover and cook on High for 25 minutes. Divide them between plates and serve. Enjoy!

Nutrition: calories 362, fat 7, fiber 7, carbs 18, protein 12

Simple Chili

Preparation time: 10 minutes
Cooking time: 35 minutes
Servings: 4

Ingredients:
- 1 pound beef, ground
- 1 green bell pepper, chopped
- 26 ounces tomatoes, chopped
- 4 teaspoons chili powder
- 1 yellow onion, chopped

Directions:
Set your instant pot on sauté mode, add beef, stir and brown for 3 minutes. Add onion, stir and cook for 2 minutes more. Add bell pepper, tomatoes and chili powder, stir, cover and cook on High for 30 minutes. Divide chili into bowls and serve. Enjoy!

Nutrition: calories 300, fat 9, fiber 7, carbs 28, protein 3

Rice and Beans

Preparation time: 10 minutes
Cooking time: 50 minutes
Servings: 2

Ingredients:
- ½ yellow onion, chopped
- 1 small red bell pepper, chopped
- 1 celery stalk, chopped
- 1 garlic clove, minced
- 1/3 pound red kidney beans
- A pinch of salt and black pepper
- A pinch of white pepper
- ½ teaspoon thyme, chopped
- 1/3 teaspoon hot sauce
- 1 bay leaf
- 3 cups water
- ½ pound chicken sausage, sliced
- 3 cups rice, already cooked

Directions:
In your instant pot, mix onion with bell pepper, celery, garlic, beans, salt, black pepper, white pepper, thyme, hot sauce, bay leaf and water, stir, cover and cook on High for 28 minutes. Add sausage, stir, cover pot again and cook on Manual for 15 minutes more. Divide rice on 2 plates, add beans mix on top and serve. Enjoy!

Nutrition: calories 194, fat 2, fiber 2, carbs 7, protein 10

Tasty Turkey Meatballs

Preparation time: 10 minutes
Cooking time: 10 minutes
Servings: 2

Ingredients:
- ½ pound turkey meat, ground
- 2 tablespoons green onion, chopped
- 2 saltine crackers, crushed
- 1 and ½ tablespoons buttermilk
- A pinch of salt and black pepper
- ½ tablespoon canola oil
- ½ tablespoon sesame seeds
- 4 tablespoons soy sauce
- 2 tablespoon rice vinegar
- 1 teaspoon ginger, grated
- 1 tablespoon canola oil
- 1 and ½ tablespoon brown sugar
- A pinch of black pepper
- ½ tablespoon cornstarch

For the sauce:
- 1 garlic clove, minced

Directions:
In a bowl, mix turkey with crackers, green onions, salt, pepper and buttermilk, stir, shape 8 meatballs and leave them aside. In another bowl, mix soy sauce with vinegar, garlic, ginger, 1 tablespoon canola, brown sugar, black pepper and cornstarch and stir well. Set your instant pot on sauté mode, add ½ tablespoon canola oil, heat it up, add meatballs and brown them for 2 minutes on each side. Add the sauce, cover and cook on High for 10 minutes. Divide between 2 plates and serve with sesame seeds sprinkled on top. Enjoy!

Nutrition: calories 293, fat 4, fiber 1, carbs 2, protein 9

Simple Shredded Chicken

Preparation time: 10 minutes
Cooking time: 15 minutes
Servings: 4

Ingredients:
- 2 pounds chicken drumsticks
- 1 tablespoon peanut oil
- 10 red chilies, dried and chopped
- ¼ cup dark soy sauce
- 2 tablespoons balsamic vinegar

Directions:
Set your instant pot on sauté mode, add peanut oil, heat it up, add chilies, stir and cook them for 3 minutes. Add chicken pieces, soy sauce and vinegar, stir, cover and cook on High for 12 minutes. Transfer meat to a cutting board, cool down a bit, shred, return to pot and toss with cooking sauce. Divide between plates and serve with a side salad. Enjoy!

Nutrition: calories 261, fat 7, fiber 3, carbs 20, protein 4

Beef Stew

Preparation time: 10 minutes
Cooking time: 36 minutes
Servings: 4

Ingredients:
- 2 pounds beef stew meat
- 1 cup baby carrots
- 4 cups beef stock
- 1 jar corn salsa
- 6 ounces canned garbanzo beans, drained

Directions:
Set your instant pot on sauté mode, add beef, stir and brown for 8 minutes on each side. Add salsa, stock, beans and baby carrots, stir, cover and cook on High for 20 minutes. Divide into bowls and serve. Enjoy!

Nutrition: calories 281, fat 6, fiber 12, carbs 26, protein 6

Tasty Pho

Preparation time: 10 minutes
Cooking time: 40 minutes
Servings: 2

Ingredients:
- 1 pound chicken pieces, bone in and skin on
- A small ginger piece, grated
- 1 small onion, cut into quarters
- ½ tablespoon coriander seeds, toasted
- ½ teaspoon cardamom pods
- ½ cardamom pods
- 2 cloves
- ½ lemongrass stalk, chopped
- ½ cinnamon stick
- 2 tablespoons fish sauce
- ½ bok choy, chopped
- ½ daikon root, cut with a spiralizer
- 1 tablespoon green onions, chopped

Directions:
In your instant pot, mix chicken with ginger, onion, coriander seeds, cardamom, cloves, lemongrass, fish sauce, daikon, bok choy and water to cover them all, stir, cover and cook on High for 30 minutes. Strain soup into another pot, shred chicken and divide into 2 bowls. Add strained soup and green onions and serve. Enjoy!

Nutrition: calories 182, fat 2, fiber 3, carbs 6, protein 7

Black Bean Soup

Preparation time: 10 minutes
Cooking time: 40 minutes
Servings: 2

Ingredients:
- 1 small yellow onion, chopped
- 1 green bell pepper, chopped
- 1 red bell pepper, chopped
- 3 ounces tomatoes, chopped
- 1 celery stalk, chopped
- ½ pound black beans
- A pinch of salt and black pepper
- 1/3 teaspoon hot sauce
- ½ tablespoon chili powder
- 1 teaspoon paprika
- ½ tablespoon cumin
- 1 bay leaf
- 2 cups veggie stock

Directions:
In your instant pot, mix onion with red bell pepper, green bell pepper, tomatoes, celery, black beans, salt, pepper, hot sauce, chili powder, cumin, paprika, bay leaf and stock, stir, cover and cook on High for 40 minutes. Ladle into 2 soup bowls and serve. Enjoy!

Nutrition: calories 300, fat 2, fiber 1, carbs 2, protein 3

Pork Chops and Tomato Sauce

Preparation time: 10 minutes
Cooking time: 20 minutes
Servings: 4

Ingredients:
- 4 pork chops, boneless
- 1 tablespoon soy sauce
- ¼ teaspoon sesame oil
- 1 and ½ cups tomato paste
- 1 yellow onion
- 8 mushrooms, sliced

Directions:
In a bowl, mix pork chops with soy sauce and sesame oil, toss and leave aside for 10 minutes. Set your instant pot on sauté mode, add pork chops and brown them for 5 minutes on each side. Add onion, stir and cook for 1-2 minutes more. Add tomato paste and mushrooms, toss, cover and cook on High for 8-9 minutes. Divide everything between plates and serve. Enjoy!

Nutrition: calories 300, fat 7, fiber 7, carbs 18, protein 4

Comforting Chicken Dish

Preparation time: 10 minutes
Cooking time: 30 minutes
Servings: 8

Ingredients:
- 7 cups water
- 1 cup jasmine rice
- 6 chicken drumsticks
- 1 tablespoon ginger, grated
- 2 tablespoons green onions, chopped

Directions:
In your instant pot, mix rice with water, chicken and ginger, stir, cover and cook on High for 30 minutes. Add onions, stir, divide into bowls and serve. Enjoy!

Nutrition: calories 251, fat 7, fiber 4, carbs 12, protein 4

Chickpea Curry

Preparation time: 10 minutes
Cooking time: 25 minutes
Servings: 2

Ingredients:
- 1 cup chickpeas, soaked for 8 hours and drained
- 1 cup water
- ½ cup tomatoes, chopped
- 1 tablespoon olive oil
- 4 tablespoons red onion, chopped
- 1 garlic clove, minced
- A pinch of chili powder
- A pinch of garam masala
- A pinch of turmeric powder
- 1 bay leaf
- ½ tablespoon curry powder
- ½ tablespoon lemon juice
- A pinch of salt and black pepper
- 1 tablespoon cilantro, chopped

Directions:
Put the oil in your instant pot, set on sauté mode, heat it up, add garlic and onion, stir and cook for 2 minutes. Add tomatoes, stir and cook for 4 minutes more. Add chili powder, garam masala, turmeric, bay leaf and curry powder, stir and cook for 1 minute more. Add chickpeas and water, stir, cover and cook on High for 10 minutes. Discard bay leaf, add lemon juice and cilantro, some salt and pepper, stir, divide into bowls and serve. Enjoy!

Nutrition: calories 310, fat 1, fiber 2, carbs 4, protein 10

Simple Beef Dish

Preparation time: 10 minutes
Cooking time: 1 hour
Servings: 2

Ingredients:
- 1 pound beef roast, cubed
- 2 garlic cloves, minced
- 1 small yellow onion, chopped
- 2 ounces green chilies, chopped
- 1 teaspoon oregano, dried
- A pinch of salt and black pepper
- 1 chipotle pepper, chopped
- Juice from 1 lime
- 1 tablespoon coconut vinegar
- 2 teaspoons cumin, ground
- ½ cup water

Directions:
In your instant pot, mix beef with garlic, onion, green chilies, oregano, salt, pepper, chipotle pepper, lime juice, vinegar, cumin and water, stir, cover and cook on Manual for 1 hour. Divide into bowls and serve. Enjoy!

Nutrition: calories 254, fat 1, fiber 2, carbs 3, protein 9

Tasty Beef and Broccoli

Preparation time: 10 minutes
Cooking time: 15 minutes
Servings: 4

Ingredients:
- 1 and ½ pounds flank steak, cut into thin strips
- 1 tablespoon olive oil
- 1 tablespoon tamari sauce
- 1 cup beef stock
- 1 pound broccoli, florets separated

Directions:
In a bowl, mix steak strips with oil and tamari, toss and leave aside for 10 minutes. Set your instant pot on sauté mode, add beef strips and brown them for 4 minutes on each side. Add stock, stir, cover and cook on High for 8 minutes. Add broccoli, stir, cover pot again and cook on High for 4 minutes more. Divide everything between plates and serve. Enjoy!

Nutrition: calories 312, fat 5, fiber 12, carbs 20, protein 4

Fast Salmon

Preparation time: 10 minutes
Cooking time: 5 minutes
Servings: 4

Ingredients:
- 4 salmon fillets, boneless
- 1 bunch dill, chopped
- 1 tablespoon butter
- ¼ cup lemon juice
- A pinch of salt
- 1 cup water, for the instant pot

Directions:
Put the water in your instant pot, add lemon juice, add steamer basket, add salmon inside, season with some salt, sprinkle dill and drizzle melted butter, cover pot and cook on Manual for 5 minutes. Divide salmon between plates and serve with a side dish. Enjoy!

Nutrition: calories 412, fat 12, fiber 8, carbs 27, protein 12

Coconut Quinoa

Preparation time: 10 minutes
Cooking time: 1 minute
Servings: 2

Ingredients:
- ½ cup quinoa
- 6 ounces coconut milk
- 2 tablespoons water
- Zest and juice from ½ lime
- A pinch of salt
- 1 tablespoon cilantro, chopped

Directions:
In your instant pot, mix quinoa with coconut milk, water, lime zest and lime juice and salt, stir, cover and cook on High for 1 minute. Leave quinoa aside for 10 minutes, fluff with a fork, divide into 2 bowls, add cilantro and serve. Enjoy!

Nutrition: calories 200, fat 1, fiber 2, carbs 3, protein 4

Chicken Wrap

Preparation time: 10 minutes
Cooking time: 10 minutes
Servings: 2

Ingredients:
- ½ pound chicken, ground
- 1 small yellow onion, chopped
- 2 teaspoons garlic, minced
- A pinch of ginger, grated
- A pinch of allspice, ground
- 4 tablespoons water chestnuts
- 2 tablespoons soy sauce
- 2 tablespoons chicken stock
- 2 tablespoons balsamic vinegar
- 2 tortillas for serving

Directions:
In your instant pot, mix chicken meat with onion, garlic, ginger, allspice, chestnuts, soy sauce, stock and vinegar, stir a bit, cover and cook on Manual for 10 minutes. Divide chicken mix on 2 tortillas, wrap and serve. Enjoy!

Nutrition: calories 231, fat 4, fiber 3, carbs 6, protein 10

Steamed Tilapia

Preparation time: 10 minutes
Cooking time: 10 minutes
Servings: 4

Ingredients:
- 1 pound tilapia fillets
- 1 tablespoon Chinese black bean paste
- 3 tablespoons soy sauce
- ¼ cup scallions, chopped
- 1 tablespoon peanut oil
- 2 cups water, for the instant pot

Directions:
In a bowl, mix soy sauce with black bean paste and whisk well. Add fish, toss and leave aside for 10 minutes. Set your instant pot on sauté mode, add oil, heat it up, add scallions, stir, cook for a couple of minutes and transfer to a bowl. Clean the pot, add the water, add steamer basket, add fish fillets inside, sprinkle scallions on top, cover pot and cook on High for 3 minutes. Divide everything between plates and serve with a side salad. Enjoy!

Nutrition: calories 152, fat 2, fiber 7, carbs 12, protein 5

Lemon Pepper Salmon

Preparation time: 10 minutes
Cooking time: 10 minutes
Servings: 4

Ingredients:
- 1 cup water, for the instant pot
- 1 lemon, sliced
- 1 pound salmon fillets, boneless and skin on
- Black pepper to the taste
- 3 teaspoons butter, melted
- 1 red bell pepper, julienned

Directions:
Put the water in your instant pot, add steamer basket, add salmon fillets, season them with black pepper, drizzle melted butter all over, divide bell pepper and lemon slices on top, cover and cook on High for 7 minutes. Divide salmon and bell pepper on plates, top with lemon slices and serve. Enjoy!

Nutrition: calories 281, fat 8, fiber 4, carbs 16, protein 6

Tasty Tikka Masala

Preparation time: 10 minutes
Cooking time: 22 minutes
Servings: 2

Ingredients:
- ½ pound chicken breasts, skinless and boneless
- ½ tablespoon butter
- ½ tablespoon olive oil
- 1 small yellow onion, chopped
- A pinch of salt and black pepper
- ½ tablespoon garam masala
- ½ teaspoon coriander, ground
- ½ teaspoon turmeric
- ½ teaspoon chili powder
- 3 garlic cloves, minced
- 1 inch ginger piece, grated
- 7 ounces canned tomatoes, crushed
- 1 and ½ tablespoon yogurt
- 1 tablespoon almond butter

Directions:
Add the butter and the oil to your instant pot, set it on sauté mode, heat it up, add onion, stir and cook for 5 minutes. Add chili powder, salt, pepper, garam masala, coriander, turmeric, ginger, garlic and tomatoes, stir and cook for 1 minute more. Add chicken breasts, cover and cook on Manual for 16 minutes. Transfer meat to a cutting board, shred using 2 forks and leave aside for now. Blend the mix from the pot using an immersion blender, add yogurt and almond butter and stir gently. Return chicken to the pot, stir a bit, divide into 2 bowls and serve. Enjoy!

Nutrition: calories 300, fat 4, fiber 4, carbs 7, protein 8

Lemon and Olive Chicken

Preparation time: 10 minutes
Cooking time: 16 minutes
Servings: 2

Ingredients:
- 2 chicken breasts, skinless and boneless
- A pinch of salt and black pepper
- A pinch of cumin, ground
- 3 tablespoons butter
- Juice from ½ lemon
- 2 lemon slices
- ½ cup chicken stock
- ½ cup green olives, pitted
- 3 tablespoons red onion, chopped

Directions:
Set your instant pot on sauté mode, add chicken breasts, season with salt, pepper and cumin and brown for 3 minutes on each side. Add butter, lemon juice, lemon slices, stock, olives and onion, stir, cover and cook on High for 10 minutes. Divide chicken mixture between 2 plates and serve. Enjoy!

Nutrition: calories 265, fat 3, fiber 4, carbs 6, protein 9

Fish Soup

Preparation time: 10 minutes
Cooking time: 8 minutes
Servings: 4

Ingredients:
- 1 pound white fish fillets, boneless, skinless and cubed
- 1 carrot, chopped
- 1 cup bacon, chopped
- 4 cups chicken stock
- 2 cups heavy cream

Directions:
In your instant pot, mix fish with carrot, bacon and stock, stir, cover and cook on High for 5 minutes. Add heavy cream, stir, set the pot on sauté mode, cook for 3 minutes more, ladle into bowls and serve. Enjoy!

Nutrition: calories 271, fat 7, fiber 16, carbs 30, protein 5

Chili Mahi Mahi

Preparation time: 10 minutes
Cooking time: 5 minutes
Servings: 2

Ingredients:
- 2 tablespoons butter
- 2 mahi mahi fillets, boneless
- ¼ cup enchilada sauce
- Salt to the taste
- Black pepper to the taste
- 1 cup water, for the instant pot

Directions:
Put the water in your instant pot, add steamer basket, add mahi mahi fillets inside, drizzle melted butter, season with salt and pepper and spread enchilada sauce all over them. Cover pot, cook on High for 5 minutes. Divide fish and sauce between plates and serve. Enjoy!

Nutrition: calories 200, fat 5, fiber 12, carbs 27, protein 7

Chicken and Tomatillo Salsa

Preparation time: 10 minutes
Cooking time: 28 minutes
Servings: 2

Ingredients:
- 4 chicken drumsticks, skin removed
- A pinch of salt and black pepper
- ½ tablespoon cider vinegar
- ½ teaspoon oregano, dried
- ½ teaspoon olive oil
- 1 cup tomatillo sauce
- 2 tablespoons cilantro, chopped
- 1 small jalapeno, chopped

Directions:
Add the oil to your instant pot, set on sauté mode, add chicken drumsticks, season with salt, pepper and oregano and brown for 4 minutes on each side. Add tomatillo sauce, jalapeno and half of the cilantro, stir, cover and cook on High for 20 minutes. Add the rest of the cilantro, stir again, divide between 2 plates and serve. Enjoy!

Nutrition: calories 264, fat 5, fiber 2, carbs 5, protein 9

Chicken with Dates

Preparation time: 10 minutes
Cooking time: 30 minutes
Servings: 2

Ingredients:
- 4 chicken thighs, skinless and boneless
- A pinch of salt and black pepper
- ½ tablespoon olive oil
- 1 teaspoon cumin, ground
- 1 teaspoon smoked paprika
- 1 teaspoon coriander, ground
- 1 garlic clove, minced
- ½ yellow onion, chopped
- 1 carrot, chopped
- 14 ounces tomatoes, chopped
- 4 tablespoons chicken stock
- 4 medjol dates, chopped
- ½ lemon, cut into wedges
- 4 tablespoons green olives, pitted
- 2 tablespoons pine nuts
- Chopped mint for serving

Directions:
In a bowl, mix chicken thighs with salt, pepper, oil, cumin, paprika and coriander and toss. Set your instant pot on sauté mode, add chicken and brown for 5 minutes on each side. Add garlic, onion, carrot, tomatoes, stock, dates and olives, stir, cover and cook on High for 20 minutes. Divide into bowls, sprinkle pine nuts and mint on top and serve. Enjoy!

Nutrition: calories 283, fat 5, fiber 4, carbs 7, protein 8

Cod and Orange Sauce

Preparation time: 10 minutes
Cooking time: 7 minutes
Servings: 4

Ingredients:
- 4 cod fillets, boneless
- A small ginger piece, grated
- Juice from 1 orange
- 4 spring onions
- 1 cup white wine

Directions:
In your instant pot, mix wine with ginger, spring onions and orange juice, stir, add steamer basket, add cod fillets inside, cover and cook on High for 7 minutes. Divide fish on plates, drizzle orange juice all over and serve. Enjoy!

Nutrition: calories 172, fat 5, fiber 3, carbs 7, protein 7

Simple Shrimp

Preparation time: 10 minutes
Cooking time: 3 minutes
Servings: 3

Ingredients:
- 2 pounds shrimp, deveined and peeled
- 2 tablespoons olive oil
- ½ cup chicken stock
- ½ cup white wine
- 1 tablespoon garlic, minced

Directions:
Set your instant pot on sauté mode, add oil, heat it up, add garlic, stir and cook for 30 seconds. Add shrimp, wine and stock, stir, cover and cook on High for 3 minutes. Divide into bowls and serve. Enjoy!

Nutrition: calories 190, fat 2, fiber 4, carbs 7, protein 2

Beef Curry

Preparation time: 1 hour
Cooking time: 55 minutes
Servings: 2

Ingredients:
For the marinade:
- 1 tablespoon coconut oil
- ½ teaspoon garlic powder
- ½ teaspoon turmeric powder
- ½ teaspoon ginger powder
- A pinch of salt and black pepper

For the curry:
- 1 pound beef roast, cubed
- 1 and ½ teaspoon coconut oil
- 1 small onion, chopped
- ½ cup coconut milk
- 2 kaffir lime leaves
- ½ cinnamon stick
- 1 small plantain, peeled and cut into medium chunks
- ½ tablespoon coriander, chopped

Directions:
In a bowl, mix beef with 1 tablespoon oil, garlic powder, turmeric powder, ginger powder, salt and pepper, toss and leave aside for 1 hour. Set your instant pot on sauté mode, add 1 and ½ teaspoons oil, heat it up, add beef, stir and brown for 5 minutes on each side. Add coconut milk, onion, lime leaves and cinnamon, stir, cover and cook on Manual for 35 minutes. Set the pot on Sauté mode again, add plantain, stir and simmer curry for a few more minutes. Divide into bowls, sprinkle coriander on top and serve. Enjoy!

Nutrition: calories 213, fat 4, fiber 2, carbs 6, protein 9

Beef and Artichokes

Preparation time: 10 minutes
Cooking time: 15 minutes
Servings: 2

Ingredients:
- ½ tablespoon olive oil
- 1 pound beef, ground
- 1 small yellow onion, chopped
- ½ teaspoon garlic powder
- ½ teaspoon oregano, dried
- ½ teaspoon dill, dried
- ½ teaspoon onion powder
- A pinch of salt and black pepper
- 10 ounces frozen artichoke hearts
- 1/3 cup water
- ½ teaspoon apple cider vinegar
- 3 tablespoons avocado mayonnaise

Directions:
Add the oil to your instant pot, set on sauté mode, heat it up, add onion, stir and cook for 5 minutes. Add beef, salt, pepper, oregano, dill, garlic and onion powder, stir and cook for 3 minutes. Add water and artichokes, stir, cover and cook on Manual for 7 minutes more. Drain excess water, add vinegar and mayo, stir, divide into bowls and serve. Enjoy!

Nutrition: calories 300, fat 4, fiber 4, carbs 6, protein 12

Shrimp Boil

Preparation time: 10 minutes
Cooking time: 35 minutes
Servings: 4

Ingredients:
- 1 cup chicken stock
- 1 tablespoon old bay seasoning
- 1 teaspoon red pepper, crushed
- 1 sweet onion, chopped
- 2 pounds shrimp, peeled and deveined

Directions:
In your instant pot, mix stock with old bay seasoning, red pepper, onion and shrimp, stir, cover and cook on Low for 30 minutes. Divide into bowls and serve. Enjoy!

Nutrition: calories 162, fat 2, fiber 4, carbs 6, protein 4

Fast Shrimp Scampi

Preparation time: 10 minutes
Cooking time: 4 minutes
Servings: 4

Ingredients:
- 1 pound shrimp, peeled and deveined
- 2 shallots, chopped
- 2 tablespoons butter
- 1 cup chicken stock
- Juice of 1 lemon

Directions:
Set your instant pot on sauté mode, add butter, heat it up, add shallots, stir and cook for 1-2 minutes. Add shrimp, lemon juice and stock, stir, cover and cook on High for 2 minutes more. Divide into bowls and serve. Enjoy!

Nutrition: calories 182, fat 5, fiber 7, carbs 12, protein 5

Pork Roast

Preparation time: 10 minutes
Cooking time: 35 minutes
Servings: 2

Ingredients:
- 1 pound pork roast
- A pinch of chili powder
- A pinch of onion powder
- A pinch of garlic powder
- A pinch of salt and black pepper
- ½ tablespoon olive oil
- 1 cup water
- 3 tablespoons apple juice

Directions:
In a bowl, mix roast with chili powder, onion powder, garlic powder, salt and pepper and rub well. Add the oil to your instant pot, set on sauté mode, add roast and brown for 5 minutes on each side. Add apple juice and water, stir a bit, cover and cook on High for 25 minutes. Slice roast, divide between 2 plates and drizzle cooking juices all over.
Enjoy!

Nutrition: calories 321, fat 4, fiber 2, carbs 4, protein 6

Pork and Pineapple Delight

Preparation time: 1 hour
Cooking time: 50 minutes
Servings: 2

Ingredients:
- 1 tablespoon olive oil
- 1 pound pork, cubed
- A pinch of salt and black pepper
- ½ tablespoon soy sauce
- 2 tablespoon cassava flour
- A pinch of cloves, ground
- A pinch of turmeric powder
- A pinch of ginger powder
- 1 small yellow onion, cut into medium chunks
- 1 garlic clove, minced
- ½ teaspoon cinnamon, ground
- ½ cup pineapple, peeled and cut into medium chunks
- 1 tablespoon dates, pitted and chopped
- 1 bay leaf
- ½ cup beef stock
- ½ bunch Swiss chard, chopped

Directions:
In a bowl, mix pork with soy sauce, salt, pepper, flour, cloves, ginger powder and turmeric powder, toss and leave aside for 1 hour. Set your instant pot on sauté mode, add the oil, heat it up, add onion and garlic, stir, cook for 2 minutes and transfer to a bowl. Add pork cubes to your instant pot and brown them for 5 minutes on each side. Return garlic and onion, also add cinnamon, pineapple, stock, dates and bay leaf, stir, cover and cook on High for 35 minutes. Set the pot on Simmer mode, add Swiss chard, cook for 1-2 minutes more, discard bay leaf, divide pork and pineapple mixture into bowls and serve. Enjoy!

Nutrition: calories 310, fat 4, fiber 1, carbs 6, protein 12

Delicious and Simple Octopus

Preparation time: 10 minutes
Cooking time: 15 minutes
Servings: 4

Ingredients:
- 2 pounds octopus, rinsed
- Water, for the instant pot
- Salt to the taste
- Black pepper to the taste
- A pinch of chili powder
- ¼ teaspoon sweet paprika

Directions:
Season octopus with salt and pepper, add to the pot, add water to cover, also add chili powder and paprika, stir a bit, cover and cook on High for 15 minutes. Cut octopus and serve with a simple side salad. Enjoy!

Nutrition: calories 112, fat 6, fiber 3, carbs 7, protein 3

Teriyaki Scallops

Preparation time: 10 minutes
Cooking time: 4 minutes
Servings: 3

Ingredients:
- 1 tablespoon avocado oil
- 1 pound sea scallops
- 3 tablespoons maple syrup
- ½ cup coconut aminos
- 1 tablespoon chives, chopped

Directions:
Set your instant pot on sauté mode, add oil, heat it up, add scallops and sear them for 1 minute on each side. Add maple syrup, aminos and chives, toss, cover pot and cook on High for 2 minutes. Divide between plates and serve scallops right away. Enjoy!

Nutrition: calories 300, fat 5, fiber 7, carbs 8, protein 12

Squash and Apple Soup

Preparation time: 10 minutes
Cooking time: 15 minutes
Servings: 2

Ingredients:
- ½ butternut squash, peeled and cubed
- A drizzle of olive oil
- A pinch of ginger powder
- 1 small apple, peeled, cored and chopped
- 2 cups veggie stock
- A pinch of salt and white pepper

Directions:
Add the oil to your instant pot, set on sauté mode, heat it up, add squash cubes and brown them for 5 minutes. Add ginger powder, apple, stock, salt and pepper, stir, cover and cook on High for 15 minutes, Puree everything using an immersion blender, divide soup into 2 bowls and serve. Enjoy!

Nutrition: calories 183, fat 1, fiber 2, carbs 3, protein 6

Chicken and Veggie Soup

Preparation time: 10 minutes
Cooking time: 30 minutes
Servings: 2

Ingredients:
- ½ pound chicken breast, skinless and boneless
- ½ yellow onion, chopped
- ½ tablespoon olive oil
- 1 garlic clove, minced
- 2 and ½ cups chicken stock
- 1 small bay leaf
- A pinch of thyme, dried
- 1 teaspoon Worcestershire sauce
- A pinch of salt and black pepper
- ½ carrot, chopped
- 1 celery stalk, chopped
- ½ zucchini, cubed
- ½ cup broccoli florets, roughly chopped
- 1 tablespoon parsley, chopped

Directions:
Add the oil to your instant pot, set on sauté mode, add garlic and onion, stir and cook for 3 minutes. Add chicken breasts, brown for 3 minutes on each side and mix with bay leaf, stock, thyme, salt, pepper and Worcestershire sauce. Stir, cover pot and cook on High for 15 minutes. Transfer meat to a cutting board, cool it down, cut into medium cubes and return to the pot. Add celery, zucchini and carrots, cover pot and cook on High for 5 minutes more. Add broccoli, set the pot on simmer mode, stir for a couple of minutes more, ladle into bowls, sprinkle parsley on top and serve. Enjoy!

Nutrition: calories 241, fat 2, fiber 1, carbs 4, protein 10

Mussels and White Wine Sauce

Preparation time: 10 minutes
Cooking time: 6 minutes
Servings: 4

Ingredients:
- 3 pounds mussels, debearded and cleaned
- 6 tablespoons butter
- 4 shallots, chopped
- 1 and ½ cups chicken stock
- 1 cup white wine

Directions:
Set the pot on sauté mode, add butter and melt it. Add shallots, stir and cook them for 2 minutes. Add wine, stir and cook for 1 minute more. Add mussels and stock, stir, cover and cook on High for 3 minutes more. Discard unopened mussels, divide the rest and the wine into bowls and serve. Enjoy!

Nutrition: calories 200, fat 2, fiber 4, carbs 6, protein 5

Beet Soup

Preparation time: 10 minutes
Cooking time: 52 minutes
Servings: 6

Ingredients:
- 8 cups beets, peeled and chopped
- 3 cups cabbage, chopped
- 6 cups chicken stock
- 1 yellow onion, chopped
- A pinch of salt
- 1 cup water, for the instant pot

Directions:
Add the water to your instant pot, add steamer basket, add beets, cover and cook on High for 7 minutes. Discard water, return beets to the pot, also add cabbage, onion, salt and stock, stir, cover and cook on Manual for 45 minutes. Ladle soup into bowls and serve. Enjoy!

Nutrition: calories 152, fat 6, fiber 4, carbs 6, protein 8

Chicken and Kale Soup

Preparation time: 10 minutes
Cooking time: 15 minutes
Servings: 2

Ingredients:
- ½ tablespoon olive oil
- 3 ounces pork chorizo, chopped
- 2 chicken thighs, boneless, skinless and chopped
- ½ yellow onion, chopped
- 1 garlic clove, minced
- 1 cup chicken stock
- 3 ounces tomatoes, chopped
- 1 small bay leaf
- 1 gold potato, peeled and cubed
- 1 ounce baby kale
- 3 ounces canned chickpeas, drained
- A pinch of salt and black pepper

Directions:
Set your instant pot on sauté mode, add the oil, heat it up, add chicken, chorizo and onion, stir and cook for 5 minutes. Add garlic, stock, bay leaf, tomatoes, potato and kale, stir, cover and cook on high for 5 minutes. Discard bay leaf, add chickpeas, salt and pepper, set the pot on simmer mode and cook soup until potatoes are done. Ladle into bowls and serve. Enjoy!

Nutrition: calories 200, fat 4, fiber 1, carbs 3, protein 7

Chicken and Fennel Soup

Preparation time: 10 minutes
Cooking time: 30 minutes
Servings: 2

Ingredients:
- ½ pound chicken breast, skinless, boneless and cubed
- 1 small yellow onion, chopped
- ½ fennel bulb, chopped
- 2 green onions, chopped
- ½ cup spinach
- 1 cup chicken stock
- 1 garlic clove, minced
- A pinch of salt and black pepper
- 2 cup water
- 1 small bay leaf
- ½ tablespoon oregano, dried

Directions:
In your instant pot, mix chicken with onion, fennel, green onions, spinach, stock, garlic, water, bay leaf, oregano, salt and pepper, stir, cover and cook on Soup mode for 30 minutes. Stir soup one more time, ladle into 2 bowls and serve. Enjoy!

Nutrition: calories 212, fat 4, fiber 2, carbs 6, protein 6

Onion Cream

Preparation time: 10 minutes
Cooking time: 40 minutes
Servings: 4

Ingredients:
- 3 pounds mixed onions, chopped
- 2 quarts chicken stock
- 6 tablespoons butter
- ½ cup dry sherry
- 1 teaspoon cider vinegar

Directions:
Set the pot on sauté mode, add butter, melt it, add onions, stir and cook for 3 minutes. Cover pot and cook onions on High for 20 minutes more. Add sherry, vinegar and stock, stir, cover and cook on High for 13 minutes. Blend soup a bit using an immersion blender, ladle into bowls and serve. Enjoy!

Nutrition: calories 300, fat 12, fiber 5, carbs 20, protein 6

Black Bean Soup

Preparation time: 10 minutes
Cooking time: 20 minutes
Servings: 4

Ingredients:
- 45 ounces canned black beans and juice
- ½ cup cilantro, chopped
- 2 and ½ cups salsa
- 1 garlic clove
- 2 teaspoons cumin, ground

Directions:
In your instant pot, mix salsa with black beans, cilantro, garlic, and cumin, stir, cover and cook on High for 15 minutes. Stir soup one more time, ladle into bowls and serve. Enjoy!

Nutrition: calories 184, fat 8, fiber 9, carbs 20, protein 7

Delicious Onion Soup

Preparation time: 10 minutes
Cooking time: 25 minutes
Servings: 2

Ingredients:
- 1 tablespoon avocado oil
- ½ tablespoon balsamic vinegar
- 4 cups yellow onion, chopped
- A pinch of salt and black pepper
- 3 cups pork stock
- 1 bay leaf
- 1 thyme sprigs, chopped

Directions:
Set your instant pot on sauté mode, add the oil and heat it up. Add onion, some salt and pepper, stir and sauté for 15 minutes. Add vinegar, thyme, bay leaf and stock, cover and cook on High for 10 minutes. Discard bay leaf, blend soup using an immersion blender, ladle into 2 bowls and serve. Enjoy!

Nutrition: calories 210, fat 2, fiber 3, carbs 4, protein 6

Chicken and Red Cabbage Soup

Preparation time: 10 minutes
Cooking time: 35 minutes
Servings: 2

Ingredients:
- ½ pound chicken pieces
- 1 garlic clove, minced
- 1 small red onion, chopped
- ½ small red cabbage, chopped
- A pinch of salt and black pepper
- 1 carrot, chopped
- ½ teaspoon ginger powder
- ½ teaspoon cinnamon powder
- ½ teaspoon turmeric powder
- ½ teaspoon white peppercorns
- ½ tablespoon tamarind paste
- Juice from 1/3 lime
- Lime wedges for serving
- 1/3 pineapple, peeled and cubed
- 1 sprigs onion, chopped

Directions:
In your instant pot, mix chicken with carrot, red onion, salt, pepper, cabbage, garlic, peppercorns and water to cover everything. Cover your instant pot and cook on Soup mode for 30 minutes. Transfer chicken to a cutting board, cool it down, shred using 2 forks and return to the pot. In a small bowl, mix 1 tablespoon soup with tamarind paste, stir and pour into the pot. Add, cinnamon, ginger, turmeric, pineapple and lime juice, stir soup, set your instant pot on sauté mode and cook for 10 minutes more. Ladle into 2 bowls, sprinkle sprigs onion on top and serve with lime wedges on the side. Enjoy!

Nutrition: calories 212, fat 1, fiber 3, carbs 4, protein 6

Minestrone Soup

Preparation time: 10 minutes
Cooking time: 6 minutes
Servings: 4

Ingredients:
- 27 ounces tomato paste
- 15 ounces canned cannellini beans, drained
- 2 cups veggie stock
- 1 cup orzo pasta, already cooker
- Grated parmesan for serving

Directions:
In your instant pot, mix tomato paste with beans and stock, stir, cover and cook on High for 6 minutes. Add pasta, stir, ladle into bowls and serve with parmesan sprinkled on top. Enjoy!

Nutrition: calories 254, fat 2, fiber 7, carbs 12, protein 4

Swiss Chard Soup

Preparation time: 10 minutes
Cooking time: 6 minutes
Servings: 4

Ingredients:
- 8 cups Swiss chard, chopped
- 3 leeks, chopped
- Salt to the taste
- 1 cup coconut milk
- 1 and ½ cups chicken stock

Directions:
In your instant pot, mix chard with leeks, salt, stock and coconut milk, stir, cover and cook on High for 6 minutes. Blend using an immersion blender, ladle into bowls and serve. Enjoy!

Nutrition: calories 142, fat 4, fiber 4, carbs 6, protein 7

Turkey Soup

Preparation time: 10 minutes
Cooking time: 12 minutes
Servings: 2

Ingredients:
- ½ pound turkey, ground
- ½ tablespoon olive oil
- ½ cup cauliflower florets
- 1 garlic clove, minced
- ½ cup yellow onion, chopped
- 10-ounce marinara sauce
- 2 cups chicken stock
- 1 cup water
- ½ cabbage head, chopped

Directions:
Add the oil to your instant pot, set on sauté mode, heat it up, add turkey, garlic and onion, stir and sauté for 5 minutes. Add cauliflower, stock, water, marinara sauce and cabbage, stir, cover and cook on High for 6 minutes. Ladle into bowls and serve. Enjoy!

Nutrition: calories 212, fat 1, fiber 3, carbs 3, protein 4

Red Pepper Soup

Preparation time: 10 minutes
Cooking time: 40 minutes
Servings: 2

Ingredients:
- ½ cauliflower head, florets separated
- 2 green onions, chopped
- 2 garlic cloves, minced
- 2 roasted red peppers, chopped
- 4 ounces canned tomatoes, chopped
- 1 carrot, chopped
- 1 red bell pepper, chopped
- 2 tablespoons Swiss chard, chopped
- 1 teaspoon onion powder
- 1 teaspoon garlic powder
- ½ tablespoon smoked paprika
- A pinch of cumin, dried
- 1 tablespoon apple cider vinegar
- 2 cups chicken stock
- A pinch of salt and black pepper

Directions:
Add the oil to your instant pot, set on sauté mode, heat it up, add red bell pepper, onion, carrot and garlic, stir and cook for 3 minutes. Add onion powder, garlic powder, paprika, cumin, vinegar, salt and pepper, stir and cook for 1 minute more. Add roasted peppers, tomatoes, cauliflower, Swiss chard and stock, stir, cover and cook on Soup mode for 30 minutes. Stir soup one more time, ladle into 2 bowls and serve. Enjoy!

Nutrition: calorie 212, fat 4, fiber 1, carbs 3, protein 4

Broccoli and Cheese Soup

Preparation time: 10 minutes
Cooking time: 10 minutes
Servings: 8

Ingredients:
- 4 cups broccoli florets
- 3 and ½ cups chicken stock
- 1 cup heavy cream
- 3 cups cheddar cheese, grated
- 4 garlic cloves, minced

Directions:
Set your instant pot on sauté mode, add garlic and cook it for 1 minute. Add broccoli, stock and cream, stir, cover and cook on High for 8-9 minutes. Add cheese, stir until it melts, ladle into bowls and serve. Enjoy!

Nutrition: calories 291, fat 20, fiber 1, carbs 8, protein 13

Potato Soup

Preparation time: 10 minutes
Cooking time: 15 minutes
Servings: 8

Ingredients:
- 3 pounds potatoes, peeled and cubed
- 1 pint milk
- A pinch of salt
- 12 green onions, chopped
- 1 cup cheddar cheese, shredded

Directions:
In your instant pot, mix potatoes with milk and salt, stir, cover and cook on High for 12 minutes. Add cheddar cheese and green onions, stir, set the pot on sauté mode, cook until cheese melts, ladle everything into bowls and serve. Enjoy!

Nutrition: calories 314, fat 12, fiber 4, carbs 17, protein 5

Potato Soup

Preparation time: 10 minutes
Cooking time: 30 minutes
Servings: 2

Ingredients:
- 4 potatoes, peeled and cubed
- 1 carrot, chopped
- 4 ounces roasted garlic paste
- 3 tablespoons celery, chopped
- 2 tablespoons baby spinach leaves, chopped
- 1 yellow onion, chopped
- ½ cup chicken stock
- A pinch of salt and black pepper
- A pinch of smoked paprika
- ½ tablespoon chia seeds
- A pinch of red pepper, crushed

Directions:
In your instant pot, mix potatoes with carrot, garlic paste, celery, spinach, onion, stock, salt, pepper, paprika, chia seeds and red pepper, stir, cover and cook on Soup mode for 30 minutes. Blend soup a bit using an immersion blender, ladle into 2 bowls and serve. Enjoy!

Nutrition: calories 213, fat 4, fiber 1, carbs 4, protein 4

Delicious Meatloaf

Preparation time: 10 minutes
Cooking time: 45 minutes
Servings: 2

Ingredients:
- ½ pound beef, ground
- 1 egg white
- 3 tablespoons breadcrumbs
- ½ yellow onion, chopped
- 3 black olives, pitted and sliced
- 2 basil leaves, chopped
- 1 tablespoon ketchup
- A pinch of salt and black pepper
- ½ teaspoon garlic, minced
- ½ tablespoon flaxseed, ground
- Cooking spray
- 1 cup water

For the glaze:
- ½ tablespoon brown mustard
- ½ tablespoon brown sugar
- 2 tablespoons ketchup

Directions:
In a bowl, mix beef with egg white, breadcrumbs, onion, olives, basil, 1 tablespoon ketchup, salt, pepper, garlic and flaxseed and stir really well. Grease a meatloaf pan with cooking spray, add beef mixture and spread well. In another bowl, mix mustard with sugar and 2 tablespoons ketchup, whisk well and brush your meatloaf with this. Add the water to your instant pot, add the trivet, add the meatloaf pan, cover and cook on Manual for 45 minutes. Leave meatloaf aside to cool down, slice, divide between 2 plates and serve. Enjoy!

Nutrition: calories 321, fat 5, fiber 2, carbs 4, protein 7

Cream of Spinach

Preparation time: 10 minutes
Cooking time: 10 minutes
Servings: 8

Ingredients:
- ½ pound mushrooms, sliced
- 1 yellow onion, chopped
- 1 and ¾ cup chicken stock
- 20 ounces cream of mushroom soup
- 20 ounces spinach, chopped

Directions:
In your instant pot, mix mushrooms with onion, cream of mushroom and stock, stir, cover and cook on High for 5 minutes. Add spinach, stir, cover and cook on High for 5 minutes more. Pulse using an immersion blender, divide into bowls and serve. Enjoy!

Nutrition: calories 172, fat 4, fiber 8, carbs 20, protein 4

Cantaloupe Soup

Preparation time: 10 minutes
Cooking time: 5 minutes
Servings: 4

Ingredients:
- 1 ounce prosciutto, chopped
- 1 cup apple juice
- 4 cups cantaloupe, chopped
- ¼ teaspoon salt
- 1 tablespoon chives, chopped

Directions:
Set your instant pot on sauté mode, add prosciutto, stir, cook for 3 minutes and transfer to a bowl Add apple juice, cantaloupe, salt and chives to the pot, stir, cover and cook on High for 2 minutes. Blend using an immersion blender, ladle into bowls, sprinkle prosciutto on top and serve. Enjoy!

Nutrition: calories 100, fat 1, fiber 1, carbs 8, protein 2

Bean Casserole

Preparation time: 10 minutes
Cooking time: 15 minutes
Servings: 2

Ingredients:
- ½ pound lima beans, soaked for 10 hours and drained
- 3 tablespoons brown sugar
- 3 tablespoons butter
- ½ tablespoon dry mustard
- 4 cups water
- ½ tablespoon dark karo syrup
- A pinch of salt
- ½ cup sour cream

Directions:
In your instant pot, mix soaked beans with the water and some salt, cover and cook on Manual for 4 minutes. Drain beans and return them to your instant pot. Add sugar, butter, mustard, karo syrup, salt and sour cream, stir, cover and cook on Manual for 10 minutes more. Divide between 2 plates and serve. Enjoy!

Nutrition: calories 212, fat 2, fiber 1, carbs 4, protein 10

Flavored Pasta

Preparation time: 10 minutes
Cooking time: 20 minutes
Servings: 2

Ingredients:
- 1 pound penne pasta
- 1 small shallot, chopped
- 1 small yellow onion, chopped
- 2 garlic cloves, minced
- 7 white mushrooms, sliced
- 1 small zucchini squash, sliced
- A pinch of basil, dried
- A pinch of oregano, dried
- A drizzle of olive oil
- A pinch of salt and black pepper

For the sauce:
- 3 ounces tomato paste
- ½ cup chicken stock
- 1 cup water
- 1 tablespoon soy sauce
- ½ tablespoon Worcestershire sauce
- ½ tablespoon fish sauce

Directions:
Set your instant pot on sauté mode, add a drizzle of oil, heat it up, add shallot, onion and garlic, stir and cook for 3 minutes. Add salt, pepper, mushroom, zucchini, oregano and basil, stir, cook for 1 more minute and transfer to a bowl. Add stock and water to your instant pot and stir really well. Add soy sauce, Worcestershire sauce and fish sauce and stir really well. Add pasta and tomato paste, cover and cook on High for 4 minutes. Divide pasta on 2 plates, add veggie mix, drizzle the sauce from the pot all over and serve. Enjoy!

Nutrition: calories 310, fat 4, fiber 1, carbs 3, protein 6

Mussels Bowls

Preparation time: 5 minutes
Cooking time: 6 minutes
Servings: 4

Ingredients:
- 2 pounds mussels, scrubbed and debearded
- 12 ounces dark beer
- 1 tablespoon olive oil
- 8 ounces spicy sausage
- 1 tablespoon paprika

Directions:
Set your instant pot on Sauté mode, add oil, heat it up, add sausages and cook for 4 minutes. Add paprika, beer and mussels, stir, cover and cook on Low for 2 minutes. Discard unopened mussels, divide everything into bowls and serve. Enjoy!

Nutrition: calories 162, fat 4, fiber 6, carbs 9, protein 6

Artichokes and Citrus Sauce

Preparation time: 10 minutes
Cooking time: 20 minutes
Servings: 4

Ingredients:
- 4 artichokes, trimmed and stems removed
- 1 tablespoon tarragon, chopped
- 2 cups chicken stock
- Lemon zest from 2 lemons, grated+ lemon pulp
- ½ cup olive oil

Directions:
Set your instant pot on sauté mode, add stock, oil, tarragon, lemon zest and lemon pulp, stir and heat up for 2-3 minutes. Add artichokes, toss them a bit, cover and cook on High for 18 minutes. Divide artichokes on plates, drizzle citrus sauce on top and serve. Enjoy!

Nutrition: calories 172, fat 3, fiber 4, carbs 12, protein 4

Beans Chili

Preparation time: 10 minutes
Cooking time: 50 minutes
Servings: 2

Ingredients:
- ½ cup mixed red, yellow and orange bell peppers, chopped
- ½ pound beef, ground
- 1 yellow onion, chopped
- 3 garlic cloves, minced
- 6 ounces canned tomatoes, chopped
- 2 cups kidney beans
- ½ tablespoon honey
- 2 teaspoons cocoa powder
- A pinch of salt and black pepper
- 1 teaspoon sweet paprika
- 1 teaspoon coriander
- 1 and ½ tablespoons chili powder
- ½ tablespoon cumin

Directions:
Set your instant pot on sauté mode, add beef, stir and brown for a few minutes. Add onion and bell pepper, stir and cook for 2 minutes more. Add garlic, tomatoes, beans, honey, cocoa powder, salt, pepper, paprika, coriander, chili powder and cumin, stir, cover and cook on Manual for 40 minutes. Ladle into 2 bowls and serve hot. Enjoy!

Nutrition: calories 242, fat 3, fiber 1, carbs 3, protein 4

Pasta and Spinach

Preparation time: 10 minutes
Cooking time: 10 minutes
Servings: 2

Ingredients:
- 1/3 pound fusilli pasta
- 2 garlic cloves, minced
- 1 and ½ cups spinach, roughly chopped
- A pinch of salt and black pepper
- 1 and ½ tablespoons butter
- 1 and ½ cups water
- 2 tablespoon parmesan, grated

Directions:
In your instant pot, mix pasta with water. Add spinach and garlic, cover and cook on High for 6 minutes. Add parmesan, salt, pepper and butter, stir, cover and leave aside for 5 minutes. Divide between 2 plates and serve. Enjoy!

Nutrition: calories 293, fat 1, fiber 2, carbs 7, protein 8

Chicken and Potatoes Mix

Preparation time: 10 minutes
Cooking time: 40 minutes
Servings: 4

Ingredients:
- 6 chicken thighs
- 1 teaspoon vegetable oil
- ½ cup white wine
- 15 ounces canned tomatoes, chopped
- 1 and ½ pounds potatoes, chopped

Directions
Set your instant pot on Sauté mode, add oil, heat it up, add chicken, stir and brown them for 4 minutes on each side. Add wine, tomatoes and potatoes, stir, cover and cook on High for 30 minutes. Divide into bowls and serve. Enjoy!

Nutrition: calories 251, fat 10, fiber 2, carbs 8, protein 27

Cajun Sausage Mix

Preparation time: 15 minutes
Cooking time: 30 minutes
Servings: 8

Ingredients:
- 1 pound smoked sausage, sliced
- 1 pound red beans, dried, soaked overnight and drained
- 2 tablespoons Cajun seasoning
- ½ green bell pepper, chopped
- 5 cups water

Directions
In your instant pot, mix beans with sausage, Cajun seasoning, bell pepper and water, stir, cover and cook on High for 30 minutes. Divide mix into bowls and serve right away. Enjoy!

Nutrition: calories 210, fat 5, fiber 10, carbs 26, protein 12

Pea and Ham Soup

Preparation time: 10 minutes
Cooking time: 17 minutes
Servings: 2

Ingredients:
- 2 and ½ cups water
- 1 cup peas
- A pinch of salt and black pepper
- 4 tablespoons ham, chopped
- 1 small yellow onion, chopped

Directions:
In your instant pot, mix peas with water, salt, pepper, ham and onion, stir, cover and cook on High for 17 minutes. Stir soup one more time, ladle into bowls and serve. Enjoy!

Nutrition: calories 193, fat 2, fiber 5, carbs 6, protein 9

Lamb Casserole

Preparation time: 10 minutes
Cooking time: 35 minutes
Servings: 2

Ingredients:
- ½ pound rack of lamb
- ½ pound baby potatoes
- 1 carrot, chopped
- ½ onion, chopped
- 1 celery stalk, chopped
- 1 tomato, chopped
- 1 cup chicken stock
- 2 garlic cloves, minced
- A pinch of salt and black pepper
- 1 teaspoon sweet paprika
- 1 teaspoon cumin, ground
- A pinch of oregano, dried
- A pinch of rosemary, dried
- 1 tablespoon ketchup
- 1 tablespoon red wine

Directions:
In your instant pot, mix lamb with baby potatoes, carrot, onion, celery, tomato, stock, garlic, salt, pepper, paprika, cumin, oregano, rosemary, ketchup and wine, cover and cook on Manual for 35 minutes. Divide everything between 2 plates and serve. Enjoy!

Nutrition: calories 278, fat 5, fiber 4, carbs 6, protein 10

Easy Turkey Mix

Preparation time: 10 minutes
Cooking time: 20 minutes
Servings: 4

Ingredients:
- 4 turkey wings
- 2 tablespoons olive oil
- 1 and ½ cups cranberries
- 1 cup orange juice
- 1 bunch thyme, roughly chopped

Directions:
Set your instant pot on Sauté mode, add oil, heat up, add turkey wings, brown them on all sides and transfer them to a bowl. Add cranberries and thyme to your instant pot, stir and cook for 2 minutes. Add orange juice, return turkey wings to pot, stir, cover, cook on High for 20 minutes and transfer turkey pieces to plates. Set the pot on sauté mode again, heat up the sauce for a couple of minutes more, drizzle over turkey winds and serve right away. Enjoy!

Nutrition: calories 293, fat 10, fiber 4, carbs 12, protein 20

Simple Chicken Fall Stew

Preparation time: 10 minutes
Cooking time: 15 minutes
Servings: 4

Ingredients:
- 4 chicken thighs
- 2 cups mushrooms, sliced
- ½ teaspoon onion powder
- ½ cup water
- 1 teaspoon Dijon mustard

Directions
Set your instant pot on sauté mode, add chicken and onion powder, stir, cook for 2 minutes on each side and transfer to a bowl. Add mushrooms to your instant pot, stir and sauté them for 2 minutes more. Return chicken to the pot, also add water and mustard, stir well, cover and cook on High for 10 minutes. Divide between plates and serve right away. Enjoy!

Nutrition: calories 243, fat 8, fiber 4, carbs 10, protein 18

Simple BBQ Ribs

Preparation time: 10 minutes
Cooking time: 40 minutes
Servings: 2

Ingredients:
- 1 rack baby back ribs
- 4 tablespoons BBQ sauce
- Salt and black pepper to the taste
- 1 cup water

Directions:
Season ribs with salt and pepper. Add the water to your instant pot, add the trivet, add ribs inside, cover and cook on High for 25 minutes. Transfer ribs to a baking sheet, brush with BBQ sauce, introduce in the oven at 450 degrees F and bake for 15 minutes. Divide between 2 plates and serve. Enjoy!

Nutrition: calories 264, fat 3, fiber 1, carbs 8, protein 7

Jambalaya

Preparation time: 10 minutes
Cooking time: 25 minutes
Servings: 2

Ingredients:
- ½ tablespoon olive oil
- 1/3 pound chicken breasts, chopped
- 1/3 pound shrimp
- ½ cup mixed bell peppers, chopped
- ½ cup yellow onion, chopped
- ½ tablespoon garlic, minced
- 2 cups chicken stock
- ½ cup rice
- ½ cup tomatoes, crushed
- 2 teaspoons Creole seasoning
- 2 teaspoons Worcestershire sauce
- 1/3 pound sausage, cooked and sliced

Directions:
Add the oil to your instant pot, set it on sauté mode, heat it up, add chicken and half of the Creole seasoning, toss, brown for a few minutes on each side and transfer to a bowl. Add bell pepper, onion and garlic to your instant pot and sauté them for 2 minutes. Add rice, stir and cook for 2 minutes more. Add the rest of the Creole seasoning, tomato, Worcestershire sauce and chicken, cover and cook on Rice mode. Add sausage and shrimp, cover and cook on Manual for 2 minutes. Divide between 2 plates and serve hot. Enjoy!

Nutrition: calories 312, fat 1, fiber 4, carbs 5, protein 12

Pork and Lemon Sauce

Preparation time: 10 minutes
Cooking time: 1 hour
Servings: 4

Ingredients:
- 1 and ½ pounds pork shoulder, chopped
- 3 garlic cloves, minced
- Juice of 1 lemon
- ½ cup water
- 2 tablespoons coconut aminos

Directions:
Set your instant pot on Sauté mode, heat it up, add pork, salt and pepper, stir and brown for 5 minutes on each side. Add garlic, aminos, water and lemon juice, stir, cover and cook on High for 50 minutes. Divide pork and sauce between plates and serve. Enjoy!

Nutrition: calories 330, fat 4, fiber 2, carbs 16, protein 24

Fennel Cream

Preparation time: 10 minutes
Cooking time: 15 minutes
Servings: 4

Ingredients:
- 2 fennel bulbs, chopped
- 3 cups water
- 2 bay leaves
- 2 tablespoon olive oil
- 4 teaspoons parmesan cheese, grated

Directions:
In your instant pot, mix fennel with bay leaves, oil and water, stir, cover and cook on High for 15 minutes. Add cheese, blend a bit using an immersion blender, ladle into bowls and serve. Enjoy!

Nutrition: calories 226, fat 3, fiber 3, carbs 9, protein 5

Cod and Beer

Preparation time: 10 minutes
Cooking time: 30 minutes
Servings: 2

Ingredients:
- ½ pound cod fillet, boneless and skinless
- ½ cup beer
- 2 potatoes, peeled and roughly chopped
- ½ red bell pepper, chopped
- ½ tablespoon olive oil
- ½ tablespoon oyster sauce
- A pinch of salt
- ½ tablespoon rock candy

Directions:
Put fish in your instant pot. Add beer, potatoes, bell pepper, oil, oyster sauce, salt and rock candy, cover and cook on Manual for 30 minutes. Divide between 2 plates and serve. Enjoy!

Nutrition: calories 221, fat 2, fiber 1, carbs 4, protein 7

Salmon with Lemon

Preparation time: 10 minutes
Cooking time: 10 minutes
Servings: 2

Ingredients:
- ¾ cup water
- 2 parsley sprigs, chopped
- 2 dill sprigs, chopped
- 2 basil leaves, chopped
- 2 teaspoons olive oil
- A pinch of salt and black pepper
- ½ lemon, sliced
- 1 zucchini, chopped
- 1 red bell pepper, chopped
- 1 carrot, chopped
- 2 salmon fillets, skin on and boneless

Directions:
Put the water in your instant pot, add dill, basil and parsley and place the trivet inside. Add salmon fillets, season with salt and pepper, drizzle the oil all over and top with lemon slices. Cover the pot and Steam fish for 3 minutes. Divide salmon between 2 plates and keep warm for now. Set your instant pot on sauté mode, add zucchini, bell pepper and carrot, stir and sauté for 4 minutes. Divide next to salmon and serve. Enjoy!

Nutrition: calories 243, fat 4, fiber 1, carbs 3, protein 7

Cauliflower Salad

Preparation time: 10 minutes
Cooking time: 5 minutes
Servings: 10

Ingredients:
- 21 ounces cauliflower, florets separated
- 1 cup red onion, chopped
- 2 tablespoons balsamic vinegar
- 1 teaspoon stevia
- 1 cup mayonnaise
- ½ cup water, for the instant pot

Directions:
Put the water in your instant pot, add steamer basket, add cauliflower, cover pot and cook on High for 5 minutes. Transfer cauliflower to a bowl, add onion, stevia and vinegar and toss. Add mayo, toss well, divide between plates and serve. Enjoy!

Nutrition: calories 171, fat 6, fiber 2, carbs 6, protein 3

Collard Greens Stew

Preparation time: 10 minutes
Cooking time: 30 minutes
Servings: 4

Ingredients:
- 2 cups bacon, chopped
- 1 pound collard greens, trimmed
- A pinch of salt and black pepper
- ½ cup chicken stock
- 3 tablespoons tomato paste

Directions:
Set your instant pot on sauté mode, add bacon, stir and brown for 5 minutes. Add collard greens, salt, pepper, tomato paste and water, cover the pot and cook on High for 20 minutes. Divide into bowls and serve. Enjoy!

Nutrition: calories 325, fat 2, fiber 5, carbs 9, protein 4

Chinese Fish

Preparation time: 20 minutes
Cooking time: 10 minutes
Servings: 2

Ingredients:
For the marinade:
- 1 tablespoon rice wine
- 1 and ½ tablespoons soy sauce
- ½ tablespoon Chinese black bean paste
- ½ teaspoon garlic, minced
- ½ teaspoon ginger, minced
- 2 tilapia fillets, skinless and boneless

For the veggies:
- 2 cups water
- 2 tablespoons ginger, grated
- ½ tablespoon peanut oil
- 2 tablespoons cilantro, chopped
- 2 tablespoons green onions, chopped

Directions:
In a bowl, mix wine with soy sauce, black bean paste, garlic, ½ teaspoon ginger and the fish, toss well and leave aside for 20 minutes. Add the water to your instant pot, add the steamer basket, place fish inside, cover and cook on Low for 2 minutes. Meanwhile, heat up a pan with the oil over medium high heat, add 2 tablespoons ginger, cilantro and green onions, stir and cook for 2 minutes. Add reserved marinade from the fish, stir well and cook for a couple more minutes. Divide fish on 2 plates, add veggie mix on the side and serve. Enjoy!

Nutrition: calories 158, fat 1, fiber 2, carbs 3, protein 3

Salmon and Risotto

Preparation time: 10 minutes
Cooking time: 15 minutes
Servings: 2

Ingredients:
- 2 salmon fillets, boneless
- 1 and ½ cups water
- Juice from 1/3 lemon

For the rice:
- 1 small yellow onion, chopped
- 12 ounces mushrooms, sliced
- 1 cup artichokes, chopped
- ½ tablespoon garlic, minced
- 1 cup Arborio rice
- 2 tablespoons white wine
- 2 cups chicken stock
- ½ cup parmesan, grated
- 1 teaspoon olive oil

Directions:
Put the water in your instant pot, add the steamer basket, add the fish inside, drizzle lemon juice, cover, Steam for 3 minutes, divide between 2 plates and leave aside for now. Clean your instant pot, add the oil and set it on Sauté mode. Heat up the oil, add onion, garlic and mushrooms, stir and cook for 3 minutes. Add artichokes, wine, ice and stock, stir, cover and cook on Manual for 7 minutes. Add parmesan, stir a bit, divide next to salmon and serve right away. Enjoy!

Nutrition: calories 212, fat 3, fiber 2, carbs 4, protein 7

Spicy Chicken Wings

Preparation time: 10 minutes
Cooking time: 14 minutes
Servings: 4

Ingredients:
- 3 pounds chicken wings pieces
- 1 tablespoon Worcestershire sauce
- 4 tablespoons butter
- 4 tablespoons cayenne pepper sauce
- A pinch of salt
- 3 ounces water, for the instant pot

Directions:
Put the water in your instant pot, add steamer basket, add chicken wings, cover and cook on High for 8 minutes. In a bowl, mix butter with Worcestershire sauce, pepper sauce and salt and whisk really well. Brush chicken pieces with this mix, return them to steamer basket, cover pot again and cook on High for 5 minutes more. Divide between plates and serve with a side salad. Enjoy!

Nutrition: calories 201, fat 6, fiber 3, carbs 12, protein 4

Rich Chicken Salad

Preparation time: 10 minutes
Cooking time: 5 minutes
Servings: 2

Ingredients:
- 1 chicken breast, skinless and boneless
- 1 cup water for the instant pot,
- 2 garlic cloves, minced
- 2 tablespoons olive oil
- 1 tablespoon balsamic vinegar
- Mixed salad greens

Directions:
Add the water to your instant pot, add steamer basket, add chicken inside, cover, cook at High for 5 minutes, transfer to a cutting board, cool down, cut in thin strips, add to a bowl and mix with salad greens. In a bowl, mix garlic with vinegar and olive oil, whisk very well, drizzle over chicken, toss, divide between plates and serve. Enjoy!

Nutrition: calories 173, fat 2, fiber 4, carbs 10, protein 6

Salmon Casserole

Preparation time: 10 minutes
Cooking time: 13 minutes
Servings: 2

Ingredients:
- 2 cups milk
- 2 salmon fillets, boneless
- 2 cups chicken stock
- ¼ cup olive oil
- A pinch of salt and black pepper
- 1 teaspoon garlic, minced
- 2 cups mixed peas and corn
- 4 ounces cream of celery soup
- ¼ teaspoon dill, chopped
- ¼ teaspoon cilantro, chopped
- 1 tablespoon parmesan, grated

Directions:
Add the oil to your instant pot, set on sauté mode, heat it up, add salmon and cook for a couple of minutes. Flake salmon a bit, add garlic and chicken stock and stir. Add milk, cream of celery, peas and corn, dill, cilantro, salt and pepper, stir gently, cover and cook on Manual for 8 minutes. Add parmesan, divide between 2 plates and serve. Enjoy!

Nutrition: calories 312, fat 2, fiber 3, carbs 6, protein 7

Salmon and Chili Sauce

Preparation time: 10 minutes
Cooking time: 5 minutes
Servings: 2

Ingredients:
- 2 salmon fillets
- 1 cup water
- A pinch of salt and black pepper
- 1 jalapeno, chopped
- 2 garlic cloves, minced
- Juice from 1 lime
- 1 tablespoon olive oil
- 1 tablespoon honey
- 1 tablespoon hot water
- 1 tablespoon parsley, chopped
- ½ teaspoon cumin, ground
- ½ teaspoon sweet paprika

Directions:
IN a bowl, mix jalapeno with lime juice, garlic, honey, oil, 1 tablespoon water, parsley, paprika and cumin, whisk really well and leave aside for now. Put 1 cup water in your instant pot, add the steamer basket, add salmon fillets inside, season with a pinch of salt and pepper, cover pot and cook on Steam mode for 5 minutes. Divide salmon on 2 plates, drizzle the sauce all over and serve. Enjoy!

Nutrition: calories 212, fat 2, fiber 3, carbs 4, protein 9

Calamari Stew

Preparation time: 10 minutes
Cooking time: 32 minutes
Servings: 3

Ingredients:
- 1 pound calamari, tentacles separated and cut into strips
- 7 ounces canned tomatoes, chopped
- ½ bunch parsley, chopped
- ¼ cup white wine
- 1 tablespoon olive oil

Directions:
Set your instant pot on Sauté mode, add oil and calamari, stir and cook for 9 minutes. Add wine, tomatoes and half of the parsley, stir, cover and cook on High for 25 minutes. Add the rest of the parsley, stir, divide into bowls and serve. Enjoy!

Nutrition: calories 160, fat 4, fiber 2, carbs 7, protein 7

Simple Lamb Ribs and Sauce

Preparation time: 10 minutes
Cooking time: 30 minutes
Servings: 2

Ingredients:
- 4 lamb ribs
- 1 carrot, chopped
- 6 ounces veggie stock
- 1 tablespoon olive oil
- 1 tablespoon white flour

Directions:
Set your instant pot on Sauté mode, add the oil, heat it up, add lamb and brown it for a few minutes on all sides. Add flour, carrot and stock stir, cover the pot, cook on High for 20 minutes. Serve lamb with carrots on the side and cooking juices drizzled all over. Enjoy!

Nutrition: calories 200, fat 4, fiber 6, carbs 14, protein 25

Salmon and Veggies

Preparation time: 10 minutes
Cooking time: 5 minutes
Servings: 2

Ingredients:
- 2 medium salmon fillets, boneless
- ½ teaspoon cumin, ground
- ½ teaspoon sweet paprika
- 1 carrot, chopped
- 1 celery stalk, chopped
- 1 yellow onion, roughly chopped
- 1 cup broccoli florets, roughly chopped
- 2 tablespoon dry sherry
- A pinch of salt and black pepper
- 1 cup water

Directions:
In a heatproof pan, mix carrot with celery, onion, broccoli, salt and pepper and toss a bit. Add salmon fillets on top, season them with salt, pepper, cumin and paprika and add dry sherry at the end. Add the water to your instant pot, add the trivet, place the pan with the fish inside, cover and cook on High for 5 minutes. Divide fish and veggies between 2 plates and serve. Enjoy!

Nutrition: calories 214, fat 2, fiber 5, carbs 7, protein 10

Pasta with Salmon and Pesto

Preparation time: 10 minutes
Cooking time: 9 minutes
Servings: 2

Ingredients:
- 8 ounces pasta
- 2 cups water
- 6 ounces smoked salmon, flaked
- A pinch of salt and black pepper
- ½ teaspoon lemon zest, grated
- ½ teaspoon lemon juice
- 2 tablespoons butter
- 2 tablespoons walnuts
- 1 garlic clove
- 5 cups spinach leaves
- 2 tablespoons olive oil
- ½ cup parmesan, grated
- 1 tablespoon lemon zest, grated
- ½ cup heavy cream

For the pesto:

Directions:
In your food processor, mix walnuts with garlic, spinach, olive oil, 1 tablespoon lemon zest, parmesan and ½ cup heavy cream, pulse well and leave aside for now. Put the pasta in your instant pot, add the water and butter, cover and cook on High for 4 minutes. Drain pasta into a bowl and clean your instant pot. Set your instant pot on sauté mode, add salmon, a pinch of salt and pepper, ½ teaspoon lemon zest, lemon juice and pasta, stir and cook for 2 minutes. Add pesto, toss well divide between plates and serve. Enjoy!

Nutrition: calories 216, fat 1, fiber 4, carbs 7, protein 8

Chicken and Salsa

Preparation time: 10 minutes
Cooking time: 15 minutes
Servings: 4

Ingredients:
- 4 chicken breasts, skinless and boneless
- ½ cup water
- 16 ounces salsa
- 1 and ½ tablespoons parsley, chopped
- 1 teaspoon chili powder

Directions:
In your instant pot, mix chicken with water, salsa, parsley and chili powder, stir, cover and cook on High for 15 minutes. Divide everything between plates and serve. Enjoy!

Nutrition: calories 187, fat 4, fiber 2, carbs 16, protein 10

Green Beans Stew

Preparation time: 10 minutes
Cooking time: 10 minutes
Servings: 4

Ingredients:
- 1 tablespoon olive oil
- 2 garlic cloves, minced
- 1 pound green beans
- 14 ounces canned tomatoes, chopped
- 1 tablespoon basil, chopped

Directions:
Set the instant pot on Sauté mode, add oil, heat it up, add garlic, stir and cook for 2 minutes. Add tomatoes and green beans cover pot and cook on High for 5 minutes. Sprinkle basil, toss, divide between plates and serve. Enjoy!

Nutrition: calories 100, fat 3, fiber 5, carbs 10, protein 2

Spicy Salmon

Preparation time: 10 minutes
Cooking time: 5 minutes
Servings: 2

Ingredients:
- 2 salmon fillets, boneless
- Juice from ½ lemon
- ½ lemon, sliced
- 1 tablespoon chili pepper, minced
- A pinch of salt and black pepper
- 1 cup water

Directions:
In a bowl, mix salmon with lemon juice, chili pepper, salt and pepper and toss. Add the water to your instant pot, add the steamer basket, place fish inside, cover with lemon slices, cover the pot and cook on High for 5 minutes. Divide between 2 plates and serve with a side salad. Enjoy!

Nutrition: calories 153, fat 1, fiber 2, carbs 3, protein 7

Mediterranean Cod

Preparation time: 10 minutes
Cooking time: 15 minutes
Servings: 2

Ingredients:
- 2 cod fillets, boneless
- 1 and ½ tablespoon butter
- Juice from 1/3 lemon
- 1 small yellow onion, chopped
- A pinch of salt and black pepper
- ½ teaspoon oregano, dried
- 12 ounces canned tomatoes, chopped

Directions:
Set your instant pot on sauté mode, add the butter and melt it. Add onion, tomatoes, salt, pepper, oregano and lemon juice, stir and cook for 10 minutes. Add fish, cover the pot and cook on High for 5 minutes. Divide everything between 2 plates and serve. Enjoy!

Nutrition: calories 211, fat 1, fiber 2, carbs 2, protein 6

Spinach Pasta

Preparation time: 5 minutes
Cooking time: 15 minutes
Servings: 4

Ingredients:
- 1 pound spinach
- 1 pound fusilli pasta
- 2 garlic cloves, minced
- A drizzle of olive oil
- ½ cup veggie stock

Directions:
Set instant pot on Sautee, add olive oil, heat it up, add spinach and garlic, stir and cook for 6-8 minutes. Add pasta and stock, stir, cover and cook on Low for 6 minutes. Stir again, divide between plates and serve. Enjoy!

Nutrition: calories 214, fat 1, fiber 4, carbs 15, protein 6

Chickpeas Cakes

Preparation time: 10 minutes
Cooking time: 25 minutes
Servings: 6

Ingredients:
- 1 cup dried chickpeas, soaked for 8 hours and drained
- 1 teaspoon cumin
- 1 teaspoon garlic powder
- 3 tablespoons tomato paste
- ½ cup whole wheat flour
- 1 cup water, for the instant pot + water for boiling the chickpeas

Directions:
Put chickpeas in your instant pot, add water to cover, cumin and garlic powder, stir, cover and cook on High for 15 minutes. Transfer chickpeas to your food processor, pulse very well, add tomato paste and flour, blend again and shape 6 cakes out of this mix. Add 1 cup water to your instant pot, add steamer basket, add chickpeas inside, cover and cook on High for 10 minutes. Serve chickpeas cakes right away with a side salad. Enjoy!

Nutrition: calories 110, fat 1, fiber 4, carbs 20, protein 3

Fish and Orange Sauce

Preparation time: 10 minutes
Cooking time: 7 minutes
Servings: 2

Ingredients:
- 2 cod fillets, boneless
- Zest and juice from ½ orange
- 1 inch ginger, grated
- A drizzle of olive oil
- 2 sprigs onions, chopped
- ½ cup fish stock
- A pinch of salt and black pepper

Directions:
Season with salt and pepper, drizzle oil and rub well. In your instant pot, mix stock with orange zest, juice, ginger and sprigs onions and stir. Add the steamer basket, place fish inside, cover pot and cook on High for 7 minutes. Divide between 2 plates and serve with the orange sauce drizzled all over. Enjoy!

Nutrition: calories 212, fat 2, fiber 1, carbs 3, protein 4

Tasty and Easy Shrimp

Preparation time: 10 minutes
Cooking time: 2 minutes
Servings: 2

Ingredients:
- 1 pound shrimp
- 1 tablespoon olive oil
- 1 tablespoon butter
- ½ tablespoon garlic, minced
- ¼ cup white wine
- ¼ cup chicken stock
- ½ tablespoon lemon juice
- 1 tablespoon parsley, chopped
- A pinch of salt and black pepper
- Your favorite pasta, already cooked for serving

Directions:
Set your instant pot on sauté mode, add butter and oil, heat them up, add garlic, stir and cook for 1 minute. Add stock and wine and stir. Add shrimp and parsley, cover and cook on High for 2 minutes. Divide shrimp on plates and serve with pasta on the side. Enjoy!

Nutrition: calories 198, fat 1, fiber 2, carbs 3, protein 5

Pork Tenderloin and Pomegranate Sauce

Preparation time: 10 minutes
Cooking time: 40 minutes
Servings: 4

Ingredients:
- 2 pounds pork tenderloin, trimmed
- ¼ cup sugar
- 3 cups pomegranate juice
- A pinch of salt
- A pinch of black pepper

Directions:
Set your instant pot on sauté mode, add pomegranate juice, heat it up, add sugar, stir and cook until sugar starts to melt. Add pork, salt and pepper, toss a bit, cover and cook on High for 40 minutes. Leave pork to cool down, slice, divide between plates and serve with pomegranate sauce on top. Enjoy!

Nutrition: calories 215, fat 4, fiber 1, carbs 20, protein 24

Lemon Lamb Chops

Preparation time: 10 minutes
Cooking time: 15 minutes
Servings: 4

Ingredients:
- ½ teaspoon oregano, dried
- 2 tablespoons lemon juice
- 1 teaspoon olive oil
- 8 lamb chops, trimmed
- 1 cup chicken stock

Directions:
In your instant pot, mix lamb chops with oregano, lemon juice, oil and stock, toss well, cover and cook on High for 15 minutes. Divide lamb chops between plates and serve right away. Enjoy!

Nutrition: calories 220, fat 10, fiber 1, carbs 2, protein 28

Instant Pot Side Dish Recipes

Baked Sweet Potatoes

Preparation time: 10 minutes
Cooking time: 10 minutes
Servings: 2

Ingredients:
- 2 big sweet potatoes, scrubbed
- 1 cup water
- A pinch of salt and black pepper
- ½ teaspoon smoked paprika
- ½ teaspoon cumin, ground

Directions:
Put the water in your instant pot, add the steamer basket, add sweet potatoes inside, cover and cook on High for 10 minutes. Split potatoes, add salt, pepper, paprika and cumin, divide them between plates and serve as a side dish. Enjoy!

Nutrition: calories 152, fat 2, fiber 3, carbs 4, protein 4

Broccoli Pasta

Preparation time: 10 minutes
Cooking time: 4 minutes
Servings: 2

Ingredients:
- 2 cups water
- ½ pound pasta
- 8 ounces cheddar cheese, grated
- ½ cup broccoli
- ½ cup half and half

Directions:
Put the water and the pasta in your instant pot. Add the steamer basket, add the broccoli, cover the pot and cook on High for 4 minutes. Drain pasta, transfer it as well as the broccoli, and clean the pot. Set it on sauté mode, add pasta and broccoli, cheese and half and half, stir well, cook for 2 minutes, divide between plates and serve as a side dish for chicken. Enjoy!

Nutrition: calories 211, fat 4, fiber 2, carbs 6, protein 7

Tasty Carrots Mix

Preparation time: 10 minutes
Cooking time: 10 minutes
Servings: 6

Ingredients:
- 2 and ½ pounds baby carrots
- 2 tablespoons olive oil
- 3 shallots, chopped
- 1 teaspoon thyme
- ¼ cup Greek yogurt
- 1 cup water, for the instant pot

Directions:
In a bowl, mix baby carrots with thyme and oil and toss. Add the water to your instant pot, add steamer basket, add carrots inside, cover, cook on High for 5 minutes and transfer them to a bowl. Clean the pot, set on sauté mode, add shallots and brown them for a couple of minutes. Add carrots, toss and heat them up. Add yogurt, toss, divide between plates and serve as a side dish. Enjoy!

Nutrition: calories 162, fat 4, fiber 5, carbs 12, protein 5

Minty Carrots

Preparation time: 10 minutes
Cooking time: 5 minutes
Servings: 4

Ingredients:
- 16 ounces baby carrots
- 1 tablespoon butter
- 1 tablespoon mint, chopped
- 1 teaspoon sweet paprika
- Salt to the taste
- 1 cup water, for the instant pot

Directions:
In your instant pot, mix carrots with water, cover, cook on High for 3 minutes, drain and transfer to a bowl. Clean the pot, set on sauté mode, add butter and heat it up. Add mint, stir and cook for 1 minute. Add carrots, salt and paprika, toss, divide between plates and serve as a side dish. Enjoy!

Nutrition: calories 172, fat 3, fiber 7, carbs 8, protein 4

Simple Cauliflower Rice

Preparation time: 10 minutes
Cooking time: 12 minutes
Servings: 2

Ingredients:
- 1 tablespoon olive oil
- ½ cauliflower head, florets separated
- A pinch of salt and black pepper
- A pinch of parsley flakes
- ¼ teaspoon cumin, ground
- ¼ teaspoon turmeric powder
- ¼ teaspoon paprika
- 1 cup water
- ½ tablespoon cilantro, chopped
- Juice from 1/3 lime

Directions:
Put the water in your instant pot, add the steamer basket, add cauliflower florets, cover and cook on High for 2 minutes. Discard water, transfer cauliflower to a plate and leave aside. Clean your instant pot, add the oil, set on sauté mode and heat it up. Add cauliflower, mash using a potato masher, add salt, pepper, parsley, cumin, turmeric, paprika, cilantro and lime juice, stir well, cook for 10 minutes more, divide between 2 plates and serve as a side dish. Enjoy!

Nutrition: calories 191, fat 1, fiber 2, carbs 4, protein 5

Refried Beans

Preparation time: 10 minutes
Cooking time: 35 minutes
Servings: 2

Ingredients:
- 1 pound pinto beans, soaked for 20 minutes and drained
- 1 cup onion, chopped
- 2 garlic cloves, minced
- 1 teaspoon oregano, dried
- ½ jalapeno, chopped
- 1 teaspoon cumin, ground
- A pinch of salt and black pepper
- 1 and ½ tablespoon olive oil
- 2 cups chicken stock

Directions:
In your instant pot, mix oil with onion, jalapeno, garlic, oregano, cumin, salt, pepper, stock and beans, stir, cover and cook on Manual for 30 minutes. Stir beans one more time, divide them between 2 plates and serve as a side dish. Enjoy!

Nutrition: calories 200, fat 1, fiber 3, carbs 7, protein 7

Tasty Carrots and Walnuts Salad

Preparation time: 10 minutes
Cooking time: 5 minutes
Servings: 4

Ingredients:
- 2 pounds baby carrots
- 1 cup water, for the instant pot
- 2 tablespoons butter
- 3 ounces canned walnuts in syrup
- Salt to the taste
- A splash of vinegar

Directions:
Put the water in your instant pot, add carrots, stir, cover, cook on High for 3 minutes, drain and transfer to a bowl. Clean the pot, set it on sauté mode, add butter, heat it up, add carrots, stir and cook for 1 minute. Add walnuts and syrup, salt and vinegar, toss, cook for 1 minute more, divide between plates and serve as a side dish. Enjoy!

Nutrition: calories 172, fat 3, fiber 6, carbs 10, protein 4

Sweet and Sour Side Salad

Preparation time: 10 minutes
Cooking time: 7 minutes
Servings: 8

Ingredients:
- 1 cup water, for the instant pot
- 3 pounds rainbow carrots, chopped
- 1 onion, chopped
- 3 tablespoons butter
- 3 tablespoons vinegar
- 3 tablespoons honey

Directions:
Add the water to your instant pot, add carrots, cover, cook on High for 3 minutes, drain and transfer to a bowl. Clean the pot, set on sauté mode, add butter, melt it, add onion, stir and cook for 2 minutes. Add vinegar, honey and return carrots, stir, cover and cook on High for 2 minutes more. Divide between plates and serve as a side dish. Enjoy!

Nutrition: calories 192, fat 3, fiber 4, carbs 10, protein 3

Sweet Brussels Sprouts

Preparation time: 10 minutes
Cooking time: 4 minutes
Servings: 2

Ingredients:
- ½ pounds Brussels sprouts
- 2 teaspoon buttery spread
- ½ teaspoon orange zest, grated
- 1 tablespoon orange juice
- ½ tablespoon maple syrup
- A pinch of salt and black pepper

Directions:
In your instant pot, mix Brussels sprouts with buttery spread, orange zest, orange juice, maple syrup, salt and pepper, stir, cover and cook on High for 4 minutes. Divide between 2 plates and serve as a side dish. Enjoy!

Nutrition: calories 65, fat 2, fiber 3, carbs 10, protein 3

Simple Roasted Potatoes

Preparation time: 10 minutes
Cooking time: 15 minutes
Servings: 2

Ingredients:
- ½ pound potatoes, cut into wedges
- ¼ teaspoon onion powder
- ½ teaspoon garlic powder
- 2 tablespoons avocado oil
- A pinch of salt and black pepper
- ½ cup chicken stock

Directions:
Set your instant pot on sauté mode, add the oil and heat it up. Add potatoes, onion powder, garlic powder, salt and pepper, stir and sauté for 8 minutes. Add stock, cover and cook on High for 7 minutes more. Divide between 2 plates and serve as a side dish. Enjoy!

Nutrition: calories 192, fat 1, fiber 4, carbs 8, protein 8

Pearl Onions Side Dish

Preparation time: 10 minutes
Cooking time: 10 minutes
Servings: 6

Ingredients:
- 1 pound rainbow carrots, cut into quarters
- 2 cups pearl onions
- ½ cup water, for the instant pot
- 3 tablespoons butter
- 2 tablespoons balsamic vinegar
- 2 tablespoons parsley, chopped

Directions:
In your instant pot, mix carrots with onions and water, cover, cook on High for 4 minutes, drain and transfer to a bowl. Clean the pot, set on sauté mode, add butter, melt it, add onions and carrots, vinegar and parsley, stir and sauté for 5 minutes. Toss again, divide between plates and serve as a side dish. Enjoy!

Nutrition: calories 162, fat 4, fiber 8, carbs 12, protein 4

Haricots Verts Side Salad

Preparation time: 10 minutes
Cooking time: 8 minutes
Servings: 4

Ingredients:
- 4 ounces pancetta, chopped
- 2 pounds haricots verts
- ½ cup dates, sliced
- ½ cup chicken stock
- Black pepper to the taste

Directions
Set your instant pot on sauté mode, add pancetta, stir and cook for 3 minutes. Add haricot verts, dates and black pepper, stir and cook for 2 minutes more. Add stock, stir a bit more, cover and cook on High for 3 minutes. Divide everything between plates and serve as a side dish. Enjoy!

Nutrition: calories 128, fat 3, fiber 6, carbs 16, protein 4

Squash Risotto

Preparation time: 10 minutes
Cooking time: 13 minutes
Servings: 2

Ingredients:
- 1 small yellow onion, chopped
- A drizzle of olive oil
- 1 garlic clove, minced
- ½ red bell pepper, chopped
- 1 cup butternut squash, chopped
- 1 cup Arborio rice
- 1 and ½ cups veggie stock
- 3 tablespoons dry white wine
- 4 ounces mushrooms, chopped
- A pinch of salt and black pepper
- A pinch of oregano, dried
- ¼ teaspoon coriander, ground
- 1 and ½ cups mixed kale and spinach
- 1 tablespoon nutritional yeast

Directions:
Set your instant pot on sauté mode, add the oil and heat it up. Add onion, bell pepper, squash and garlic, stir and cook for 5 minutes. Add rice, stock, wine, salt, pepper, mushrooms, oregano and coriander, stir, cover and cook on High for 5 minutes. Add mixed kale and spinach, parsley and yeast, stir and leave aside for 5 minutes. Divide between 2 plates and serve as a side dish. Enjoy!

Nutrition: calories 163, fat 1, fiber 2, carbs 3, protein 6

Cabbage Side Dish

Preparation time: 10 minutes
Cooking time: 10 minutes
Servings: 2

Ingredients:
- ½ pound turkey sausage, sliced
- ½ cabbage head, shredded
- 2 garlic cloves, minced
- ½ yellow onion, chopped
- 1 teaspoon sugar
- 1 teaspoon balsamic vinegar
- 1 teaspoon mustard
- A drizzle of olive oil
- A pinch of salt and black pepper

Directions:
Set your instant pot on sauté mode, add the oil and heat it up. Add onion, sausage and garlic, stir and sauté for 5 minutes. Add cabbage, sugar, vinegar, mustard, salt and pepper, stir, cover and cook on High for 5 minutes more. Divide between 2 plates and serve. Enjoy!

Nutrition: calories 200, fat 3, fiber 1, carbs 8, protein 3

Green Beans and Cranberries Side Dish

Preparation time: 10 minutes
Cooking time: 6 minutes
Servings: 6

Ingredients:
- ½ cup water, for the instant pot
- 2 pounds green beans
- 3 tablespoons oil
- ¼ cup cranberries, dried
- ¼ cup almonds, chopped
- A pinch of salt

Directions:
Put the water in your instant pot, add steamer basket, add green beans and cranberries, cover, cook on High for 2 minutes and transfer to a bowl. Clean the pot, set on sauté mode, add oil, heat it up, add green beans and cranberries, almonds and a pinch of salt, toss and cook for 4 minutes more. Divide everything between plates and serve as a side dish. Enjoy!

Nutrition: calories 130, fat 3, fiber 3, carbs 7, protein 4

Delicious Green Beans and Blue Cheese

Preparation time: 10 minutes
Cooking time: 7 minutes
Servings: 4

Ingredients:
- ½ cup water, for the instant pot
- 1 and ½ pounds green beans
- ½ cup almonds, chopped
- ¼ cup olive oil
- 2 tablespoons blue cheese, crumbled
- 2 tablespoons lemon juice

Directions:
Put the water in your instant pot, add steamer basket, add green beans inside, cover, cook on High for 2 minutes, drain and transfer them to a bowl. Clean the pot, set on sauté mode, add oil, heat it up, add green beans, stir and cook for 3 minutes. Add lemon juice and almonds, stir and cook for 2 minutes more. Divide on plates, sprinkle blue cheese all over and serve as a side dish. Enjoy!

Nutrition: calories 200, fat 4, fiber 4, carbs 7, protein 4

Beans and Chorizo

Preparation time: 10 minutes
Cooking time: 42 minutes
Servings: 2

Ingredients:
- ½ tablespoon vegetable oil
- 3 ounces chorizo, chopped
- ½ pound black beans
- ½ yellow onion, chopped
- 3 garlic cloves, minced
- ½ orange
- 1 bay leaf
- 1 quart chicken stock
- A pinch of salt and black pepper
- 1 tablespoon cilantro, chopped

Directions:
Set your instant pot on sauté mode, add the oil and heat it up. Add chorizo, stir and cook for 2 minutes. Add garlic, onion, beans, orange, bay leaf, salt, pepper and stock, stir, cover and cook on High for 40 minutes. Discard bay leaf and orange, add cilantro, stir, divide between plates and serve as a side dish. Enjoy!

Nutrition: calories 224, fat 1, fiber 2, carbs 7, protein 10

Spanish Rice

Preparation time: 10 minutes
Cooking time: 12 minutes
Servings: 2

Ingredients:
- ½ tablespoon olive oil
- ½ tablespoon butter
- ½ cup rice
- ½ cup chicken stock
- ½ cup tomato sauce
- 1 teaspoon chili powder
- ½ teaspoon cumin, ground
- ¼ teaspoon oregano, dried
- A pinch of salt and black pepper
- 2 tablespoons tomatoes, chopped

Directions:
Put the oil in your instant pot, set on sauté mode and heat it up. Add rice, stir and cook for 4 minutes. Add stock, tomato sauce, chili powder, cumin, oregano, tomatoes, salt and pepper, stir, cover and cook on High for 8 minutes. Stir rice one more time, divide between 2 plates and serve as a side dish. Enjoy!

Nutrition: calories 174, fat 1, fiber 2, carbs 6, protein 8

Tasty Spinach and Salami

Preparation time: 10 minutes
Cooking time: 6 minutes
Servings: 4

Ingredients:
- 3 salami slices, chopped
- 3 garlic cloves, minced
- 3 tablespoons olive oil
- 10 ounces baby spinach
- ½ cup chicken stock

Directions:
Set your instant pot on sauté mode, add oil, heat it up, add garlic, stir and cook for 1 minute. Add salami, stir and cook for 2 minutes more. Add spinach and stock, stir a bit, cover and cook on high for 3 minutes. Divide between plates and serve as a side dish. Enjoy!

Nutrition: calories 172, fat 3, fiber 6, carbs 12, protein 3

Creamy Spinach

Preparation time: 10 minutes
Cooking time: 6 minutes
Servings: 4

Ingredients:
- 10 ounces spinach, roughly chopped
- 2 tablespoons butter
- 2 shallots, chopped
- 2 cups heavy cream
- A pinch of nutmeg, ground

Directions:
Set your instant pot on sauté mode, add butter, melt it, add shallots, stir and cook for 2 minutes. Add spinach, stir and cook for 30 seconds more. Add cream and nutmeg, stir, cover and cook on High for 3 minutes. Divide everything between plates and serve as a side dish. Enjoy!

Nutrition: calories 200, fat 3, fiber 5, carbs 15, protein 3

Garlic Green Beans

Preparation time: 10 minutes
Cooking time: 7 minutes
Servings: 4

Ingredients:
- 1 cup water, for the instant pot
- 4 garlic cloves, minced
- ½ teaspoon red pepper flakes
- 1 and ½ pounds green beans
- 3 tablespoons olive oil
- 1 tablespoon parmesan, shaved

Directions:
Put the water in your instant pot, add steamer basket, add green beans inside, cover, cook on High for 2 minutes, drain and transfer to a bowl. Clean the pot, set it on sauté mode, add oil, heat it up, add garlic, stir and cook for 30 seconds. Return green beans, also add pepper flakes, stir and sauté everything or 4 minutes more. Divide green beans on plates, sprinkle shaved parmesan on top and serve as a side dish. Enjoy!

Nutrition: calories 172, fat 3, fiber 3, carbs 6, protein 4

Kale Sauté

Preparation time: 10 minutes
Cooking time: 7 minutes
Servings: 4

Ingredients:
- 1 pound kale, trimmed
- 1 tablespoon olive oil
- 3 garlic cloves
- ½ cup veggie stock
- Juice of ½ lemon

Directions:
Set your instant pot on sauté mode, add oil, heat it up, add garlic, stir and cook for 2 minutes. Add kale, stock and lemon juice, stir a bit, cover and cook on High for 5 minutes. Stir kale mix one more time, divide between plates and serve as a side dish. Enjoy!

Nutrition: calories 132, fat 3, fiber 6, carbs 8, protein 2

Spaghetti Squash Delight

Preparation time: 10 minutes
Cooking time: 33 minutes
Servings: 2

Ingredients:
- 1 cup water
- 1 small spaghetti squash
- ½ cup apple juice
- 1 tablespoon duck fat
- A pinch of salt and black pepper

Directions:
Put the water in your instant pot, add the steamer basket, add the squash inside, cover and cook on High for 30 minutes. Cut squash in half, scoop seeds and take out squash spaghetti. Clean the instant pot, set it on sauté mode, add duck fat and heat it up. Add apple juice, salt and pepper, stir and simmer for 3 minutes. Divide squash spaghetti between 2 plates, drizzle the sauce all over, toss a bit and serve as a side dish. Enjoy!

Nutrition: calories 183, fat 3, fiber 3, carbs 7, protein 8

Artichokes Side Dish

Preparation time: 10 minutes
Cooking time: 20 minutes
Servings: 2

Ingredients:
- 2 artichokes, trimmed and tops cut off
- 1 cup water
- 1 lemon wedges

Directions:
Rub artichokes with the lemon wedge. Add the water to your instant pot, add the steamer basket, place artichokes inside, cover and cook on High for 20 minutes. Divide between 2 plates and serve as a side dish. Enjoy!

Nutrition: calories 100, fat 1, fiber 1, carbs 1, protein 3

Cabbage and Cream

Preparation time: 10 minutes
Cooking time: 10 minutes
Servings: 2

Ingredients:
- ½ cup bacon, chopped
- ½ yellow onion, chopped
- 1 cup beef stock
- 1 pound Savoy cabbage, chopped
- A pinch of nutmeg, ground
- ½ cup coconut milk
- 1 small bay leaf
- 1 tablespoon parsley flakes
- A pinch of salt

Directions:
Set your instant pot on sauté mode, add bacon and onion, stir and cook for 3 minutes. Add stock, bay leaf and cabbage, cover the pot and cook on Manual for 4 minutes. Set the pot on sauté mode again, add coconut milk, nutmeg and a pinch of salt, discard bay leaf, stir cabbage and simmer for 4 minutes. Sprinkle parsley flakes at the end, divide between 2 plates and serve. Enjoy!

Nutrition: calories 229, fat 2, fiber 4, carbs 9, protein 6

Carrots and Kale

Preparation time: 10 minutes
Cooking time: 11 minutes
Servings: 2

Ingredients:
- 10 ounces kale, roughly chopped
- 1 tablespoon butter
- 3 carrots, sliced
- 1 yellow onion, chopped
- 4 garlic cloves, minced
- ½ cup chicken stock
- A pinch of salt and black pepper
- A splash of balsamic vinegar
- ¼ teaspoon red pepper flakes

Directions:
Set your instant pot on sauté mode, add butter and melt it. Add onion and carrots, stir and cook for 3 minutes. Add garlic, stir and cook for 1 minute more. Add kale and stock, cover and cook on High for 7 minutes. Add vinegar and pepper flakes, stir, divide between 2 plates and serve. Enjoy!

Nutrition: calories 183, fat 2, fiber 3, carbs 6, protein 8

Braised Collard Greens

Preparation time: 10 minutes
Cooking time: 20 minutes
Servings: 4

Ingredients:
- 1 bunch collard greens, trimmed
- 2 tablespoons olive oil
- ½ cup chicken stock
- 2 tablespoons tomatoes, chopped
- 1 tablespoon balsamic vinegar

Directions:
In your instant pot, mix collard greens with stock, oil, tomatoes and vinegar, stir, cover and cook on Manual for 20 minutes. Divide kale mix on plates and serve as a side dish. Enjoy!

Nutrition: calories 122, fat 7, fiber 4, carbs 10, protein 4

Collard Greens and Peas

Preparation time: 10 minutes
Cooking time: 40 minutes
Servings: 5

Ingredients:
- 1 pound collard greens, trimmed and roughly chopped
- 1 pound black-eyed peas, dried
- 1-quart chicken stock
- 1 onion, chopped
- 1 smoked ham hock

Directions:
In your instant pot, mix peas with stock, onion and ham hock, stir, cover and cook on manual for 38 minutes. Add collard greens, stir, cover the pot again and cook on High for 2 minutes more. Divide collard greens and peas between plates and serve as a side dish. Enjoy!

Nutrition: calories 271, fat 4, fiber 7, carbs 12, protein 4

Beets Side Dish

Preparation time: 10 minutes
Cooking time: 25 minutes
Servings: 2

Ingredients:
- 2 beets
- 1 tablespoon balsamic vinegar
- ½ bunch parsley, chopped
- A pinch of salt and black pepper
- 1 small garlic clove, minced
- ½ tablespoon olive oil
- 1 tablespoon capers
- 1 cup water

Directions:
Put the water in your instant pot, add the steamer basket, add beets inside, cover and cook on High for 25 minutes. Transfer beets to a cutting board, leave aside to cool down, peel, slice and transfer to a bowl. In another bowl, mix parsley with salt, pepper, garlic, oil and capers and whisk really well. Divide beets on plates, drizzle vinegar all over, add parsley dressing and serve as a side dish. Enjoy!

Nutrition: calories 76, fat 2, fiber 1, carbs 4, protein 1

Sweet Potato Puree

Preparation time: 10 minutes
Cooking time: 20 minutes
Servings: 2

Ingredients:
- 2 tablespoons butter
- A pinch of sea salt and black pepper
- 1 pounds sweet potatoes, roughly chopped
- A pinch of baking soda
- ½ teaspoon chipotle powder, dried
- 2 tablespoons brown sugar
- 3 tablespoons water

Directions:
Set your instant pot on sauté mode, add the butter and melt it. Add sweet potatoes, baking soda, sugar, chipotle powder, water, salt and pepper, stir, cover and cook on High for 16 minutes. Mash using a potato masher, divide between 2 plates and serve as a side dish. Enjoy!

Nutrition: calories 121, fat 1, fiber 2, carbs 3, protein 7

Chinese Mustard Greens

Preparation time: 10 minutes
Cooking time: 7 minutes
Servings: 4

Ingredients:
- 2 Chinese sausages, chopped
- 2 teaspoons ginger, grated
- 2 tablespoons vegetable oil
- 2 pounds mustard greens, chopped
- ½ cup veggie stock

Directions:
Set your instant pot on sauté mode, add oil, heat it up, add ginger, stir and cook for 30 seconds. Add Chinese sausages, stir and cook for 1 minute more. Add mustard greens and stock, stir, cover and cook on High for 4 minutes. Divide everything between plates and serve as a side dish. Enjoy!

Nutrition: calories 178, fat 5, fiber 3, carbs 8, protein 9

Acorn Squash Side Dish

Preparation time: 10 minutes
Cooking time: 15 minutes
Servings: 4

Ingredients:
- 2 acorn squash, halved and cut into medium wedges
- 1 cup water, for the instant pot
- 4 tablespoons butter
- 1 tablespoon brown sugar
- 1 teaspoon smoked paprika
- 3 tablespoons pepitas, roasted

Directions:
Put the water in your instant pot, add steamer basket, add acorn wedges inside, cover, cook on High for 5 minutes and transfer to a bowl. Clean the pot, set it on sauté mode, add butter, melt it, add acorn wedges, sugar, paprika and pepitas, stir and cook for 10 minutes. Divide between plates and serve as a side dish. Enjoy!

Nutrition: calories 128, fat 4, fiber 3, carbs 6, protein 8

Beet and Cabbage Mix

Preparation time: 10 minutes
Cooking time: 20 minutes
Servings: 2

Ingredients:
- 1 small apple, cored and chopped
- 2 cups chicken stock
- ½ small green cabbage head, chopped
- ½ yellow onion, chopped
- 1 beet, chopped
- 1 carrot, chopped
- ½ tablespoons ginger, grated
- ½ teaspoon gelatin
- 1 tablespoon parsley
- A pinch of salt

Directions:
In your instant pot, mix apple with beet, cabbage, onion, carrot, ginger, gelatin, stock, salt and parsley, stir, cover and cook on High for 20 minutes. Divide between 2 plates and serve as a side dish. Enjoy!

Nutrition: calories 100, fat 1, fiber 2, carbs 2, protein 4

Broccoli and Garlic

Preparation time: 10 minutes
Cooking time: 15 minutes
Servings: 2

Ingredients:
- 1 broccoli head, florets separated
- 5 garlic cloves, minced
- ½ cup water
- 1 tablespoon olive oil
- 1 tablespoon rice wine
- A pinch of salt and black pepper

Directions:
Put the water in your instant pot, add the steamer basket, add broccoli, cover pot and cook on High for 10 minutes. Transfer broccoli to a bowl filled with ice water, cool it down, drain and transfer to a bowl. Clean your instant pot, set on sauté mode, add the oil and heat it up. Add garlic, stir and cook for 1-2 minutes. Add salt, pepper and wine, stir and cook for 1 minute more. Add broccoli, stir, cook everything for 1-2 minutes more, divide between plates and serve as a side dish. Enjoy!

Nutrition: calories 121, fat 2, fiber 1, carbs 2, protein 4

Tasty Maple Acorn Squash Dish

Preparation time: 10 minutes
Cooking time: 10 minutes
Servings: 4

Ingredients:
- 2 acorn squash, halved and cut into medium wedges
- 3 tablespoons butter
- ¼ cup maple syrup
- 2 teaspoons sriracha sauce
- 4 thyme sprigs, chopped

Directions:
Set your instant pot on sauté mode add butter, melt it, add acorn squash wedges, stir and cook for 1-2 minutes. Add maple syrup, sriracha sauce and thyme, stir, cover and cook on Manual for 8 minutes. Toss squash wedges gently, divide between plates and serve as a side dish. Enjoy!

Nutrition: calories 200, fat 2, fiber 4, carbs 5, protein 4

Red Onions and Apples Mix

Preparation time: 10 minutes
Cooking time: 6 minutes
Servings: 4

Ingredients:
- 2 red onions, cut into wedges
- ½ cup chicken stock
- 3 apples, cored and cut into medium wedges
- 3 tablespoons vegetable oil
- 3 tablespoons maple syrup

Directions:
Set your instant pot on sauté mode, add oil, heat it up, add onion and apple wedges, stir and cook for 2-3 minutes. Add maple syrup and stock, stir a bit, cover and cook on High for 4 minutes. Toss well, divide between plates and serve as a side dish. Enjoy!

Nutrition: calories 110, fat 3, fiber 6, carbs 4, protein 2

Creamy Corn

Preparation time: 10 minutes
Cooking time: 10 minutes
Servings: 2

Ingredients:
- 4 ounces cream cheese
- ½ cup milk
- 30 ounces canned corn, drained
- ½ stick butter
- ½ tablespoon sugar
- A pinch of salt and black pepper

Directions:
In your instant pot, mix corn with cream cheese, milk, butter, sugar, salt and pepper, stir, cover and cook on Low for 10 minutes. Divide between plates and serve as a side dish. Enjoy!

Nutrition: calories 211, fat 2, fiber 4, carbs 6, protein 4

Tasty Rice and Quinoa

Preparation time: 10 minutes
Cooking time: 13 minutes
Servings: 2

Ingredients:
- 1 cup sprouted rice and quinoa
- 1 and ½ cups water
- A pinch of salt and white pepper
- ½ teaspoon cumin, ground
- A pinch of smoked paprika

Directions:
In your instant pot, mix rice and quinoa with water, salt, pepper, cumin and paprika, stir, cover and cook on High for 13 minutes. Fluff with a fork, divide between 2 plates and serve as a side dish. Enjoy!

Nutrition: calories 100, fat 1, fiber 2, carbs 2, protein 6

Tasty Mushrooms and Rosemary

Preparation time: 10 minutes
Cooking time: 10 minutes
Servings: 6

Ingredients:
- 3 pounds mixed mushroom caps
- ¾ cup olive oil
- 4 garlic cloves, minced
- 3 rosemary sprigs, chopped
- ½ cup white wine

Directions:
Set your instant pot on sauté mode, add oil, heat up, add garlic and rosemary, stir and cook for 2-3 minutes. Add mushroom caps and wine, stir, cover and cook on High for 7-8 minutes. Stir mushroom mix again, divide between plates and serve as a side dish. Enjoy!

Nutrition: calories 172, fat 3, fiber 4, carbs 17, protein 3

Chestnut Mushrooms

Preparation time: 10 minutes
Cooking time: 10 minutes
Servings: 4

Ingredients:
- 1 cup jarred chestnuts, halved
- 6 bacon slices, chopped
- 2 pounds mushrooms, halved
- 1 teaspoon Worcestershire sauce
- ½ cup veggie stock

Directions:
Set your instant pot on sauté mode, add bacon, stir and cook for a couple of minutes. Add chestnuts, stir and cook for 1 minute more. Add mushrooms, Worcestershire sauce and stock, stir, cover and cook on High for 8 minutes. Divide everything between plates and serve as a side dish. Enjoy!

Nutrition: calories 180, fat 2, fiber 4, carbs 10, protein 2

Delicious Mushrooms Side Dish

Preparation time: 10 minutes
Cooking time: 6 minutes
Servings: 2

Ingredients:
- 1 and ½ tablespoons olive oil
- 2 small garlic cloves, minced
- ½ pound mushrooms, sliced
- 1 and ½ tablespoons balsamic vinegar
- 1 and ½ tablespoons white wine
- A pinch of salt and black pepper

Directions:
Set your instant pot on sauté mode, add the oil and heat it up. Add garlic and mushrooms, stir and cook for 3 minutes. Add wine and vinegar, stir, cover and cook on High for 2 minutes. Add salt and pepper, stir, divide between 2 plates and serve as a side dish. Enjoy!

Nutrition: calories 121, fat 2, fiber 3, carbs 4, protein 5

Mashed Potatoes

Preparation time: 10 minutes
Cooking time: 8 minutes
Servings: 2

Ingredients:
- 2 big potatoes, peeled and cubed
- ½ cup chicken stock
- 1 garlic clove, minced
- 2 tablespoons milk
- 1 and ½ tablespoon butter
- 1 rosemary sprigs, chopped
- 1 tablespoon sour cream
- A pinch of salt and black pepper

Directions:
In your instant pot, mix potatoes with stock, garlic and rosemary, cover and cook on High for 8 minutes. Transfer potatoes to a bowl, mash using a potato masher, add milk, butter, salt and pepper and whisk really well. Add sour cream, stir mashed potatoes again, divide between 2 plates and serve as a side dish. Enjoy!

Nutrition: calories 165, fat 3, fiber 2, carbs 4, protein 5

Delicious Shiitake Mushrooms Mix

Preparation time: 10 minutes
Cooking time: 10 minutes
Servings: 4

Ingredients:
- 1 pound shiitake mushroom caps, quartered
- 3 tablespoons butter
- 2 cups edamame
- 2 teaspoons ginger
- 1 cup veggie stock

Directions:
Set your instant pot on sauté mode, add butter, melt it, add ginger, stir and cook for 30 seconds. Add mushrooms, stir and cook for 1-2 minutes. Add edamame and stock, stir, cover and cook on High for 8 minutes. Divide between plates and serve as a side dish. Enjoy!

Nutrition: calories 164, fat 3, fiber 6, carbs 8, protein 3

Brussels Sprouts Side Salad

Preparation time: 10 minutes
Cooking time: 5 minutes
Servings: 4

Ingredients:
- 1 pound Brussels sprouts, halved
- ½ cup pecans, chopped
- 1/3 cup olive oil
- 3 tablespoons balsamic vinegar
- 2 teaspoons Dijon mustard

Directions
Set your instant pot on sauté mode, add oil, heat it up, add sprouts, stir and cook for 2 minutes. Add pecans, vinegar and mustard, toss, cover and cook on High for 3 minutes. Divide Brussels sprouts mix on plates and serve as a side dish. Enjoy!

Nutrition: calories 167, fat 4, fiber 4, carbs 6, protein 4

Mushrooms and Asparagus

Preparation time: 10 minutes
Cooking time: 4 minutes
Servings: 2

Ingredients:
- ½ pound asparagus crowns
- 4 tablespoons mushrooms, sliced
- 3 tablespoons chicken stock
- Salt and black pepper to the taste

Directions:
In your instant pot, mix asparagus with mushrooms, stock, salt and pepper, stir, cover and cook on Low for 2 minutes. Divide between 2 plates and serve as a side dish. Enjoy!

Nutrition: calories 110, fat 1, fiber 1, carbs 2, protein 4

Onion, Celery and Bread Side Dish

Preparation time: 10 minutes
Cooking time: 20 minutes
Servings: 2

Ingredients:
- ½ yellow onion, chopped
- ½ cup celery, chopped
- 3 tablespoons butter
- 1 cup chicken stock
- A pinch of salt and black pepper
- 1 small sourdough bread, cubed and toasted
- ½ teaspoon poultry seasoning
- 1 and ½ cups water

Directions:
Put the stock in a small pot and bring to a simmer over medium heat. Add butter, onion and celery, stir and simmer for 5 minutes. Add salt, pepper and poultry seasoning, stir and take off heat. In a bowl, mix bread cubes with stock mix, stir well, pour everything into a Bundt pan and cover with tin foil. Add the water to your instant pot, add the trivet, place pan inside, cover pot and cook on high for 15 minutes. Divide between 2 plates and serve as a side dish. Enjoy!

Nutrition: calories 192, fat 2, fiber 2, carbs 6, protein 6

Cauliflower and Grapes

Preparation time: 10 minutes
Cooking time: 10 minutes
Servings: 4

Ingredients:
- 1 cup water, for the instant pot
- 1 cauliflower head, florets separated
- 1 and ½ cups grapes
- 2 tablespoons capers
- 3 tablespoons olive oil
- 1 teaspoon lemon zest, grated

Directions:
Put the water in your instant pot, add steamer basket, add cauliflower florets inside, cover, cook on High for 6 minutes, drain and transfer to a bowl. Clean your instant pot, set on sauté mode, add oil, heat it up, return cauliflower, stir and cook for 2 minutes. Add grapes, capers and lemon zest, stir, cook for 2 minutes more, divide between plates and serve as a side dish. Enjoy!

Nutrition: calories 114, fat 3, fiber 3, carbs 5, protein 2

Brussels Sprouts and Chestnuts

Preparation time: 10 minutes
Cooking time: 5 minutes
Servings: 5

Ingredients:
- 2 pounds Brussels sprouts, halved
- 3 tablespoons olive oil
- 1 cup jarred chestnuts, halved
- 1 splash of red vinegar
- ¼ cup veggie stock

Directions:
Set your instant pot on sauté mode, add oil, heat it up, add Brussels sprouts, stir and cook for 2 minutes. Add chestnuts, stock and vinegar, stir, cover and cook on High for 3 minutes. Divide everything between plates and serve as a side dish. Enjoy!

Nutrition: calories 182, fat 3, fiber 4, carbs 6, protein 4

Cranberry Side Dish

Preparation time: 10 minutes
Cooking time: 7 minutes
Servings: 2

Ingredients:
- ½ pound cranberries, fresh
- ½ cup sugar
- 2 tablespoons lime zest, grated
- Juice from ½ orange

Directions:
In your instant pot, mix cranberries with sugar, lime zest and orange juice, stir, cover and cook on High for 7 minutes. Serve as a side dish for a tasty steak. Enjoy!

Nutrition: calories 100, fat 0, fiber 0, carbs 0, protein 2

Green Beans and Bacon

Preparation time: 10 minutes
Cooking time: 3 minutes
Servings: 2

Ingredients:
- 1 cup water
- ½ pound green beans, trimmed
- 2 tablespoon bacon, chopped
- 2 teaspoons butter
- A pinch of salt and black pepper

Directions:
Put the water in your instant pot, add the steamer basket, add green beans, cover and cook on High for 3 minutes. Transfer beans to a bowl, add butter and stir until it melts. Add bacon, salt and pepper, toss, divide between 2 plates and serve as a side dish. Enjoy!

Nutrition: calories 142, fat 2, fiber 4, carbs 6, protein 6

Tasty Vidalia Onions Mix

Preparation time: 10 minutes
Cooking time: 15 minutes
Servings: 4

Ingredients:
- 4 Vidalia onions, sliced
- 1 tablespoon sage, chopped
- ½ cup cornbread stuffing cubes
- 2 tablespoons butter
- ¼ cup chicken stock

Directions:
Set your instant pot on sauté mode, add butter, melt it, add onions and sage, toss a bit and cook for 3 minutes, Add stock, stir, cover and cook on High for 7 minutes. Add cornbread stuffing cubes, set the pot in sauté mode again, toss and cook everything for 3-4 minutes more. Divide everything between plates and serve as a side dish. Enjoy!

Nutrition: calories 146, fat 4, fiber 6, carbs 8, protein 5

Parmesan Zucchini Fries

Preparation time: 10 minutes
Cooking time: 8 minutes
Servings: 4

Ingredients:
- 4 zucchinis, cut into quarters lengthwise
- ½ teaspoon oregano, dried
- ½ cup parmesan, grated
- 2 tablespoons olive oil
- 2 tablespoons parsley, chopped
- 1 cup water, for the instant pot

Directions:
In a bowl, mix parmesan with parsley and oregano and toss. In another bowl, mix zucchini fries with the oil and toss well. Combine zucchini fries with parmesan mix and toss well. Put the water in your instant pot, add steamer basket, add zucchini fries inside, cover and cook on High for 8 minutes. Arrange on plates and serve as a side dish. Enjoy!

Nutrition: calories 162, fat 3, fiber 5, carbs 5, protein 4

Beans and Avocado Salsa

Preparation time: 10 minutes
Cooking time: 45 minutes
Servings: 2

Ingredients:
- ½ pound pinto beans, soaked and drained
- 1 tablespoon olive oil
- ½ yellow onion, chopped
- ½ poblano pepper, chopped
- ½ red bell pepper, chopped
- ½ green bell pepper, chopped
- ½ tablespoon garlic, minced
- ½ tablespoon cumin, ground
- 1 teaspoon oregano, dried
- 1 and ½ cups veggie stock
- A pinch of salt and black pepper

For the salsa:
- 2 tablespoons lime juice
- 1 avocado, peeled, pitted and chopped
- ½ red onion, chopped
- ½ poblano pepper, chopped
- 1 tablespoon olive oil

Directions:
Put beans, stock and ½ tablespoon oil in your instant pot, cover and cook on High for 30 minutes. Meanwhile, heat up a pan with ½ tablespoon oil over medium high heat, add ½ poblano pepper, yellow onion, green and red bell pepper, stir and cook for 5 minutes. Add oregano, garlic, salt, pepper and cumin, stir and cook for 2 minutes more. Drain beans, clean your instant pot, add beans and set the pot on sauté mode. Add bell peppers, mix, stir, cover and cook on High for 6 minutes. In a bowl, mix avocado with ½ red onion, ½ poblano pepper, 1 tablespoon oil, lime juice, and whisk really well. Add this to beans, toss and serve as a side dish. Enjoy!

Nutrition: calories 182, fat 2, fiber 2, carbs 6, protein 6

Spicy Zucchini

Preparation time: 10 minutes
Cooking time: 1 minute
Servings: 2

Ingredients:
- 2 zucchinis, sliced
- 1/3 cup water
- ½ tablespoon butter
- 1 tablespoon Cajun seasoning
- ½ teaspoon smoked paprika
- ½ teaspoon garlic powder

Directions:
In your instant pot, mix zucchini slices with butter, water, Cajun seasoning, paprika and garlic powder, stir, cover and cook on High for 1 minute. Divide between 2 plates and serve as a side dish. Enjoy!

Nutrition: calories 113, fat 1, fiber 1, carbs 1, protein 2

Flavored Parmesan Mushrooms

Preparation time: 10 minutes
Cooking time: 10 minutes
Servings: 4

Ingredients:
- 1 and ½ pounds cremini mushrooms, sliced
- 3 tablespoons olive oil
- ¼ cup parmesan, grated
- ¼ cup lemon juice
- Salt to the taste
- 1 cup water, for the instant pot

Directions:
In a bowl, mix mushrooms with oil, lemon juice, parmesan and salt and toss well. Add the water to your instant pot, add steamer basket, add mushrooms inside, cover and cook on High for 10 minutes. Divide between plates and serve as a side dish. Enjoy!

Nutrition: calories 128, fat 4, fiber 4, carbs 9, protein 4

Simple Buttery Potatoes

Preparation time: 10 minutes
Cooking time: 15 minutes
Servings: 4

Ingredients:
- 3 pounds red potatoes, halved
- 2 tablespoons butter
- ½ teaspoon basil
- ¼ cup parmesan, grated
- Salt to the taste
- 1 cup water, for the instant pot

Directions:
Put the water in your instant pot, add potatoes, cover, cook on High for 10 minutes, drain and transfer to a bowl. Clean the pot, set it on sauté mode, add butter, melt it, add potatoes, basil, salt and parmesan, toss, cook for 5 minutes, divide between plates and serve as a side dish. Enjoy!

Nutrition: calories 137, fat 3, fiber 6, carbs 10, protein 3

Mexican Zucchini Side Dish

Preparation time: 10 minutes
Cooking time: 15 minutes
Servings: 2

Ingredients:
- ½ tablespoon olive oil
- 1 poblano pepper, cut into thin strips
- 1 small yellow onion, chopped
- 1 teaspoon butter
- ½ tablespoon garlic, minced
- ½ zucchini, roughly chopped
- ½ yellow squash, peeled and roughly chopped
- A pinch of salt and black pepper
- 3 tablespoons chicken stock
- ¼ teaspoon cumin, ground
- ½ tablespoon sour cream

Directions:
Set your instant pot on sauté mode, add the oil and heat it up. Add poblano strips, stir and cook for 10 minutes Add butter, garlic and onion, stir and cook for 2 minutes more. Add zucchini, squash, salt, pepper, cumin and stock, stir, cover and cook on Low for 2 minutes more Add sour cream, toss to coat, divide between 2 plates and serve as a side dish. Enjoy!

Nutrition: calories 104, fat 1, fiber 2, carbs 3, protein 1

Zucchini and Mushrooms

Preparation time: 10 minutes
Cooking time: 6 minutes
Servings: 2

Ingredients:
- ½ tablespoon olive oil
- 1 cup yellow onion, chopped
- 1 garlic clove, minced
- 4 ounces mushrooms, sliced
- 1 teaspoon basil, dried
- A pinch of salt and black pepper
- 2 zucchinis, sliced
- 5 ounces tomatoes and juice, crushed

Directions:
Add the oil to your instant pot, set on sauté mode and heat it up. Add mushroom, garlic and onion, stir and cook for 4 minutes. Add salt, pepper and basil and stir. Add zucchinis and toss a bit, Add tomatoes, cover and cook on Low for 1 minute. Divide between 2 plates and serve as a side dish. Enjoy!

Nutrition: calories 142, fat 2, fiber 2, carbs 5, protein 5

Green Beans Fries

Preparation time: 10 minutes
Cooking time: 9 minutes
Servings: 4

Ingredients:
- 1 cup water, for the instant pot
- 1 and ½ pounds green beans, trimmed
- 1 cup panko
- ½ cup parmesan, grated
- Salt to the taste
- 2 eggs, whisked

Directions:
Put the water in your instant pot, add steamer basket, add green beans, cover, cook on High for 5 minutes and transfer to a bowl. In a bowl, mix panko with parmesan and salt and stir. Put the eggs in a separate bowl. Dredge green beans in panko and then in eggs mix. Set the pot on sauté mode, heat it up, add green beans fries, cook them for 2-3 minutes on each side, arrange them on plates and serve as a side dish. Enjoy!

Nutrition: calories 174, fat 3, fiber 6, carbs 7, protein 7

Mixed Veggies

Preparation time: 10 minutes
Cooking time: 10 minutes
Servings: 4

Ingredients:
- 2 cups butternut squash, roughly chopped
- 1 red onion, cut into wedges
- 2 tablespoons olive oil
- 1 red bell pepper, chopped
- 2 tablespoons balsamic vinegar
- 1 cup water, for the instant pot

Directions:
In a bowl, mix squash with red onion, oil, bell pepper and vinegar and toss well. Add the water to your instant pot, add steamer basket, add mixed veggies inside, cover and cook on High for 10 minutes. Divide mixed veggies between plates and serve as a side dish. Enjoy!

Nutrition: calories 128, fat 3, fiber 7, carbs 9, protein 8

Yellow Squash and Zucchini

Preparation time: 10 minutes
Cooking time: 6 minutes
Servings: 2

Ingredients:
- 1 cup zucchini, sliced
- 1 cup yellow squash, peeled, sliced and then roughly chopped
- ½ teaspoon Italian seasoning
- A pinch of salt and black pepper
- ½ teaspoon garlic powder
- 2 tablespoons butter
- ½ cup veggie stock
- 2 tablespoons parmesan, grated
- 2 tablespoons pork rinds, crushed

Directions:
Set your instant pot on sauté mode, add the garlic and heat it up. Add zucchini, squash, Italian seasoning, salt, pepper and garlic powder, stir and sauté for 5 minutes. Add stock, cover and cook on Low for 1 minute. Add parmesan and pork rinds, toss a bit, divide between 2 plates and serve as a side dish. Enjoy!

Nutrition: calories 121, fat 2, fiber 3, carbs 3, protein 5

Bell Peppers Stir Fry

Preparation time: 10 minutes
Cooking time: 15 minutes
Servings: 2

Ingredients:
- 2 red bell peppers, cut into medium strips
- 1 tablespoon olive oil
- 4 small potatoes, cubed
- ½ teaspoon cumin seeds
- 1 tablespoon water
- 3 garlic cloves, minced
- ½ teaspoon dry mango powder
- 1 tablespoon cilantro, chopped
- ¼ teaspoon turmeric powder
- ½ teaspoon cayenne pepper
- 2 teaspoons coriander powder

Directions:
Set your instant pot on sauté mode, add the oil and heat it up. Add garlic and cumin, stir and cook for 1 minute. Add potatoes, bell peppers, turmeric, water, cayenne and coriander, stir, cover and cook on High for 2 minutes. Add mango powder and cilantro, toss a bit, divide between 2 plates and serve as a side dish. Enjoy!

Nutrition: calories 124, fat 2, fiber 1, carbs 3, protein 4

Simple Corn Side Dish

Preparation time: 10 minutes
Cooking time: 12 minutes
Servings: 4

Ingredients:
- 6 ounces cream cheese
- 2 cups corn kernels
- ¼ cup butter
- 1/3 cup milk
- 3 garlic cloves, minced

Directions:
Set the pot on sauté mode, add butter, melt it, add garlic, stir and cook for 2 minutes. Add corn, stir and cook for 2 minutes more. Add cream cheese and milk, stir, cover and cook on Manual for 7 minutes. Toss creamy corn one more time, divide between plates and serve as a side dish. Enjoy!

Nutrition: calories 200, fat 3, fiber 7, carbs 10, protein 3

Tomatoes Side Salad

Preparation time: 10 minutes
Cooking time: 6 minutes
Servings: 4

Ingredients:
- 15 ounces canned garbanzo beans, drained
- 2 pints mixed cherry tomatoes, halved
- ¼ teaspoon parsley, chopped
- 1 tablespoons sherry vinegar
- 2 tablespoons olive oil

Directions:
Set your instant pot on sauté mode, add oil, heat it up, add garbanzo beans and tomatoes, stir and cook for 3 minutes. Add parsley and vinegar, stir, cover and cook on High for 3 minutes more. Divide everything between plates and serve as a side dish. Enjoy!

Nutrition: calories 132, fat 3, fiber 4, carbs 7, protein 5

Bell Peppers and Sausages

Preparation time: 10 minutes
Cooking time: 25 minutes
Servings: 2

Ingredients:
- 5 sausages, sliced
- 2 green bell peppers, cut into strips
- 14 ounces canned tomatoes, chopped
- 6 ounces tomato sauce
- ½ cup water
- ½ tablespoon basil, chopped
- 1 teaspoon garlic powder
- ½ tablespoon Italian seasoning

Directions:
In your instant pot, mix sausage slices with bell pepper strips, tomatoes, tomato sauce, water, basil, garlic powder and Italian seasoning, stir a bit, cover and cook on High for 25 minutes. Divide between 2 plates and serve as a side dish. Enjoy!

Nutrition: calories 176, fat 3, fiber 2, carbs 4, protein 6

Mixed Veggies Side Dish

Preparation time: 10 minutes
Cooking time: 10 minutes
Servings: 2

Ingredients:
- 2 tablespoons olive oil
- ½ sweet onion, sliced
- 1 tablespoon garlic, crushed
- 1 tablespoon tomato paste
- 1 small eggplant, cut into small cubes
- 1 small green bell pepper, cut into small chunks
- 1 small red bell pepper, cut into small chunks
- 1 small green zucchini, chopped
- ½ yellow squash, peeled and cubed
- 6 ounces canned tomatoes, chopped
- 1 teaspoon Italian seasoning
- A pinch of salt and black pepper
- 1/3 cup veggie stock

Directions:
Set your instant pot on sauté mode, add the oil and heat it up. Add onions, stir and cook for 3 minutes. Add tomato paste and garlic, stir and cook for a few seconds more. Add eggplant, green bell pepper, red bell pepper, zucchini, squash, tomatoes, salt, pepper, Italian seasoning and stock, stir, cover and cook on High for 7 minutes. Divide between 2 plates and serve as a side dish. Enjoy!

Nutrition: calories 126, fat 2, fiber 2, carbs 4, protein 7

Tomatoes and Corn Side Salad

Preparation time: 10 minutes
Cooking time: 7 minutes
Servings: 6

Ingredients:
- 6 sweet corn ears, shucked
- 4 tomatoes, roughly chopped
- ¼ cup mint leaves
- 1 tablespoons olive oil
- 3 ounces goat cheese, crumbled
- 1 and ½ cups water, for the instant pot

Directions:
Put the water in your instant pot, add corn, cover, cook on High for 5 minutes, drain and transfer to a bowl. Clean the pot, set it on sauté mode, add oil, heat it up, add corn and tomatoes, stir and cook for 2 minutes. Add mint, stir, cook for 2 minutes more, divide between plates and serve with cheese on top. Enjoy!

Nutrition: calories 122, fat 3, fiber 3, carbs 6, protein 4

Sweet Pearl Onion Mix

Preparation time: 10 minutes
Cooking time: 5 minutes
Servings: 4

Ingredients:
- 1 pound pearl onions, peeled
- A pinch of salt
- ½ cup water
- 4 tablespoons balsamic vinegar
- 1 tablespoon sugar

Directions:
In your instant pot, mix pearl onions with salt, water, vinegar and sugar, stir, cover and cook on Low for 5 minutes. Toss onions again, divide them between plates and serve as a side dish. Enjoy!

Nutrition: calories 130, fat 2, fiber 1, carbs 7, protein 1

Braised Endives

Preparation time: 10 minutes
Cooking time: 10 minutes
Servings: 2

Ingredients:
- ½ pounds Belgian endives, halved
- A pinch of salt and black pepper
- ½ tablespoon olive oil
- 1 small garlic clove, minced
- A pinch of nutmeg, ground
- 2 teaspoons brown sugar
- 2 ounces water

Directions:
Set your instant pot on sauté mode, add the oil and heat it up. Add endives, cook for 2 minutes and mix with garlic, nutmeg and sugar. Stir gently, cook for 1 minute, add water, cover and cook on High for 7 minutes. Divide between 2 plates and serve as a side dish. Enjoy!

Nutrition: calories 172, fat 2, fiber 1, carbs 2, protein 4

Simple Bok Choy Side Dish

Preparation time: 10 minutes
Cooking time: 15 minutes
Servings: 2

Ingredients:
- ½ tablespoon peanut oil
- 1 small garlic clove, minced
- 1 small ginger piece, grated
- ½ pound baby bok choy, trimmed
- A pinch of salt and black pepper
- 1/3 cup water
- A pinch of red pepper flakes
- ½ tablespoon soy sauce
- ½ tablespoon rice vinegar
- ½ teaspoon sesame oil

Directions:
Put the peanut oil in your instant pot, set the pot on sauté mode and heat it up. Add garlic and ginger, stir and cook for 3 minutes. Add bok choy, salt, pepper and water, cover and cook on High for 5 minutes. In a bowl, mix vinegar with sesame oil and soy sauce and whisk really well. Divide bok choy between 2 plates, drizzle the sauce all over, sprinkle red pepper flakes and serve as a side dish. Enjoy!

Nutrition: calories 100, fat 1, fiber 2, carbs 3, protein 3

Tomatoes and Burrata Side Salad

Preparation time: 10 minutes
Cooking time: 3 minutes
Servings: 4

Ingredients:
- 4 tomatoes, different colors, cut into wedges
- 2 tablespoons olive oil
- 5 ounces burrata cheese, shredded
- ½ teaspoon oregano, dried
- 1 tablespoon water

Directions:
In your instant pot, mix tomatoes with oil, oregano and water, toss a bit, cover and cook on High for 3 minutes. Divide on plates, add burrata on top and serve an as a side dish. Enjoy!

Nutrition: calories 111, fat 2, fiber 3, carbs 3, protein 3

Arborio Rice Side Salad

Preparation time: 10 minutes
Cooking time: 4 minutes
Servings: 4

Ingredients:
- 2 cups Arborio rice
- 4 cups water
- A pinch of salt
- 1 cup black olives in oil, pitted and sliced
- 1 bunch basil, chopped

Directions:
In your instant pot, mix rice with water, cover, cook on High for 4 minutes, drain and transfer to a salad bowl. Add a pinch of salt, olives and basil, toss well, divide between plates and serve as a side salad. Enjoy!

Nutrition: calories 120, fat 4, fiber 2, carbs 5, protein 2

Bok Choy and Rice

Preparation time: 10 minutes
Cooking time: 5 minutes
Servings: 2

Ingredients:
- ½ tablespoon olive oil
- 2 tablespoons yellow onion, chopped
- 1 garlic clove, minced
- 1 cup Arborio rice
- 3 tablespoons white wine
- 2 cups veggie stock
- 1 and ½ cups bok choy, trimmed and roughly chopped
- A pinch of red pepper flakes
- A pinch of salt and black pepper

Directions:
Set your instant pot on sauté mode, add the oil, heat it up, add onion and garlic, stir and cook for 1 minute. Add rice and wine, stir and cook for 1 minute more. Add stock, cover pot and cook on High for 4 minutes. Add bok choy, salt, pepper and pepper flakes, stir everything, divide between 2 plates and serve as a side dish. Enjoy!

Nutrition: calories 100, fat 2, fiber 1, carbs 3, protein 4

Collard Greens and Bacon

Preparation time: 10 minutes
Cooking time: 30 minutes
Servings: 2

Ingredients:
- 1 cup bacon, chopped
- ½ pound collard greens, trimmed
- A pinch of salt and black pepper
- 4 tablespoons water

Directions:
Set your instant pot on sauté mode, add bacon, stir and brown for 5 minutes. Add collard greens, salt, pepper and water, cover the pot and cook on High for 20 minutes. Divide between 2 plates and serve as a side dish. Enjoy!

Nutrition: calories 165, fat 2, fiber 2, carbs 3, protein 5

Simple Spinach Side Dish

Preparation time: 10 minutes
Cooking time: 5 minutes
Servings: 3

Ingredients:
- 1 teaspoon olive oil
- ½ teaspoon garam masala
- ½ teaspoon turmeric powder
- ½ cup veggie stock
- 6 ounces spinach leaves

Directions:
Set your instant pot on sauté mode, add oil, heat it up, add spinach, stir and toss for 1-2 minutes. Add garam masala, turmeric and stock, stir, cover and cook on High for 3 minutes. Divide between plates and serve as a side dish. Enjoy!

Nutrition: calories 100, fat 3, fiber 1, carbs 6, protein 1

Squash and Apple Mash

Preparation time: 10 minutes
Cooking time: 8 minutes
Servings: 4

Ingredients:
- 1 cup water, for the instant pot
- 2 apples, peeled, cored and sliced
- 1 butternut squash, peeled and cut into medium chunks
- 2 tablespoons maple syrup
- A pinch of salt
- 1 yellow onion, roughly chopped

Directions:
Put the water in your instant pot, add steamer basket, add squash, onion and apple pieces, inside, cover and cook on High for 8 minutes. Transfer all of them to a bowl, mash using a potato masher, add a pinch of salt and maple syrup, whisk well, divide between plates and serve as a side dish. Enjoy!

Nutrition: calories 161, fat 2, fiber 3, carbs 5, protein 3

Simple Collard Greens Side Dish

Preparation time: 10 minutes
Cooking time: 6 minutes
Servings: 2

Ingredients:
- 1 bunch collard greens, trimmed and cut into medium strips
- ½ yellow onion, roughly chopped
- 1 tablespoon water
- 2 garlic cloves, minced
- ½ cup water
- A pinch of salt
- A pinch of red pepper flakes

Directions:
Set your instant pot on sauté mode, add 1 tablespoon water and onion, stir and cook for 2 minutes. Add pepper flakes, salt and garlic, stir and cook for 1 minute more. Add collard greens and 1 cup water, stir, cover and cook on High for 3 minutes. Divide between 2 plates and serve as a side dish. Enjoy!

Nutrition: calories 87, fat 1, fiber 2, carbs 2, protein 3

Spicy Collard Greens

Preparation time: 10 minutes
Cooking time: 30 minutes
Servings: 2

Ingredients:
- 1 bunch collard greens, cut into strips
- 2 cups chicken stock
- 2 bacon slices, chopped
- 1 garlic clove, minced
- 1 small jalapeno, chopped
- 2 teaspoons Creole seasoning
- A splash of apple cider vinegar

Directions:
Set your instant pot on sauté mode, add bacon, stir and cook for 4 minutes. Add garlic, stir and cook for 1 minute more. Add jalapeno, collard greens, Creole seasoning and stock, stir, cover and cook on High for 25 minutes. Divide between plates, add a splash of vinegar all over and serve as a side dish. Enjoy!

Nutrition: calories 103, fat 1, fiber 1, carbs 2, protein 3

Brown Rice Salad

Preparation time: 10 minutes
Cooking time: 20 minutes
Servings: 2

Ingredients:
- ½ cup brown rice
- ½ cup mung beans
- ½ teaspoon cumin seeds
- 4 cups water
- 1 teaspoon lemon juice

Directions:
In your instant pot, mix mung beans with rice, water, lemon juice and cumin, stir, cover and cook on High for 13 minutes. Divide between plates and serve as a side dish. Enjoy!

Nutrition: calories 170, fat 6, fiber 7, carbs 12, protein 4

Kidney Beans and Corn Side Dish

Preparation time: 10 minutes
Cooking time: 10 minutes
Servings: 2

Ingredients:
- 1 cup kidney beans, already cooked
- ½ cup corn
- 1 small red onion, chopped
- ½ teaspoon chili powder
- 1 and ½ cups chicken stock

Directions:
In your instant pot, mix beans with corn, onion, chili powder and stock, stir, cover and cook on High for 10 minutes. Divide between plates and serve as a side dish. Enjoy!

Nutrition: calories 203, fat 7, fiber 5, carbs 9, protein 2

Eggplant and Cashews Mix

Preparation time: 10 minutes
Cooking time: 15 minutes
Servings: 3

Ingredients:
- 2 tablespoons cashews, chopped
- 1 tablespoon coriander seeds
- 4 baby eggplants, roughly chopped
- 1 cup veggie stock
- 1 teaspoon lime juice

Directions:
In your instant pot, mix eggplants with stock and coriander, stir, cover and cook on High for 10 minutes. Add cashews and lime juice, stir, divide between plates and serve as a side dish. Enjoy!

Nutrition: calories 170, fat 4, fiber 4, carbs 7, protein 3

Green Cabbage and Tomatoes Side Dish

Preparation time: 10 minutes
Cooking time: 5 minutes
Servings: 4

Ingredients:
- 3 tablespoons olive oil
- 1 green cabbage head, chopped
- 15 ounces canned tomatoes, chopped
- ½ cup yellow onion, chopped
- 2 teaspoons turmeric powder

Directions:
Set your instant pot on Sauté mode, add oil, heat it up, add onion, stir and cook for 2 minutes. Add cabbage, tomatoes and turmeric, stir, cover, cook on High for 4 minutes, divide between plates and serve as a side dish. Enjoy!

Nutrition: calories 152, fat 5, fiber 8, carbs 9, protein 7

Rice and Edamame

Preparation time: 10 minutes
Cooking time: 12 minutes
Servings: 2

Ingredients:
- 1 small yellow onion, chopped
- ½ tablespoon olive oil
- ½ tablespoon butter
- 1 cup white rice
- 2 cups chicken stock
- A pinch of salt and black pepper
- 3 tablespoons white wine
- ½ cup edamame

Directions:
Set your instant pot on sauté mode, add the oil and the butter and heat them up. Add onion, stir and cook for 3 minutes. Add rice, stir and cook for 2 minutes more. Add wine, stock, salt, pepper and edamame, stir, cover and cook on High for 7 minutes. Stir rice one more time, divide between plates and serve. Enjoy!

Nutrition: calories 110, fat 1, fiber 1, carbs 2, protein 4

Poached Fennel

Preparation time: 10 minutes
Cooking time: 10 minutes
Servings: 2

Ingredients:
- 2 fennel bulbs, sliced
- A pinch of salt and white pepper
- 1 tablespoon butter
- 1 tablespoon white flour
- 1 and ½ cups milk
- A pinch of nutmeg, ground

Directions:
Set your instant pot on sauté mode, add the butter and heat it up. Add fennel slices, stir and brown for a few minutes more. Add salt, pepper, nutmeg, flour and milk, toss well, cover pot and cook on High for 6 minutes. Divide fennel on 2 plates and serve as a side dish. Enjoy!

Nutrition: calories 76, fat 1, fiber 2, carbs 2, protein 4

Fennel and Shallots

Preparation time: 10 minutes
Cooking time: 10 minutes
Servings: 2

Ingredients:
- 1 big fennel bulb, sliced
- A pinch of salt and black pepper
- ½ pound shallots, sliced
- 2 tablespoons olive oil
- ½ cup orange juice
- 1 teaspoon parsley, chopped
- ½ teaspoon orange zest, grated

Directions:
Set your instant pot on sauté mode, add the oil and heat it up. Add shallots, stir and cook for 4 minutes. Add fennel, salt, pepper, orange juice and zest and parsley, stir a bit, cover and cook on high for 7 minutes. Divide fennel mix on 2 plates and serve as a side dish. Enjoy!

Nutrition: calories 92, fat 1, fiber 1, carbs 2, protein 3

Pea Rice

Preparation time: 10 minutes
Cooking time: 10 minutes
Servings: 2

Ingredients:
- 2 tablespoons butter
- 1 yellow onion, chopped
- 2 celery sticks, chopped
- A pinch of salt and black pepper
- 1 cup white rice
- 1 cup baby peas
- 2 garlic cloves, minced
- Zest from ½ lemon, grated
- 2 cup veggie stock
- 2 tablespoons lemon juice
- 1 ounce parmesan, grated

Directions:
Set your instant pot on sauté mode, add the butter and melt it. Add onion, salt, pepper and celery, stir and cook for 4 minutes. Add peas, rice, garlic, lemon zest, stock, salt and pepper, stir, cover and cook on High for 5 minutes. Add lemon juice and parmesan, stir again, divide between plates and serve as a side dish. Enjoy!

Nutrition: calories 198, fat 3, fiber 5, carbs 6, protein 7

Radishes Side Salad

Preparation time: 10 minutes
Cooking time: 8 minutes
Servings: 3

Ingredients:
- 7 ounces red radishes, halved
- ½ cup veggie stock
- 2 tablespoons sour cream
- 2 bacon slices, chopped
- 1 tablespoon green onions, chopped

Directions:
Set your instant pot on sauté mode, add bacon, stir and cook for a couple of minutes. Add radishes and stock, stir, cover and cook on High for 4 minutes. Add sour cream and green onions, stir, cover pot again, cook on High for 2 minutes more, divide between plates and serve as a side dish. Enjoy!

Nutrition: calories 187, fat 6, fiber 3, carbs 10, protein 8

Turnip Mash

Preparation time: 10 minutes
Cooking time: 5 minutes
Servings: 4

Ingredients:
- 4 turnips, peeled and chopped
- ½ cup chicken stock
- Salt to the taste
- 1 yellow onion, chopped
- ¼ cup heavy cream

Directions:
In your instant pot, mix turnips with stock and onion, stir, cover, cook on High for 5 minutes and blend using an immersion blender. Add salt and cream blend again, divide between plates and serve as a side dish. Enjoy!

Nutrition: calories 140, fat 3, fiber 3, carbs 7, protein 3

Garlic Beets Salad

Preparation time: 10 minutes
Cooking time: 20 minutes
Servings: 4

Ingredients:
- 3 beets, washed
- 2 cups water, for the instant pot
- 1 tablespoon olive oil
- Salt to the taste
- 2 garlic cloves, minced
- 1 teaspoon lemon juice

Directions:
Put the water in your instant pot, add steamer basket, add beets inside, cover, cook on High for 15 minutes, drain, transfer them to a cutting board, peel and cut them in medium cubes. Clean your instant pot, set it on sauté mode, add oil, heat it up, add beets, stir and cook for 4 minutes. Add garlic, lemon juice and salt, toss, divide between plates and serve as a side dish. Enjoy!

Nutrition: calories 121, fat 1, fiber 2, carbs 6, protein 2

Mango Side Salad

Preparation time: 10 minutes
Cooking time: 8 minutes
Servings: 4

Ingredients:
- 1 shallot, chopped
- 1 tablespoon olive oil
- 4 big mangos, peeled and roughly cubed
- 2 red hot chilies, chopped
- 1 tablespoon balsamic vinegar

Directions:
Set your instant pot on Sauté mode, add oil, heat it up, add shallot, stir and cook for 3 minutes. Add hot peppers, mangos and vinegar, stir, cover and cook on High for 5 minutes. Divide between plates and serve as a side dish. Enjoy!

Nutrition: calories 120, fat 2, fiber 1, carbs 4, protein 3

Rice with Fennel

Preparation time: 10 minutes
Cooking time: 15 minutes
Servings: 2

Ingredients:
- ½ brown onion, chopped
- 1 tablespoon olive oil
- 1 small fennel bulb, chopped
- ½ small asparagus bunch, chopped
- A pinch of salt and black pepper
- 1 garlic clove, minced
- 1 cup Arborio rice
- 3 tablespoons white wine
- Zest from 1/3 lemon, grated
- 1 cup veggie stock
- 1 cup chicken stock
- 1 tablespoon butter
- 2 tablespoons parmesan, grated

Directions:
Set your instant pot on sauté mode, add the oil and heat it up. Add onion, stir and cook for 5 minutes. Add asparagus, fennel, salt and garlic and stir. Add rice, wine, lemon zest, chicken stock and chicken stock, stir, cover and cook on High for 5 minutes. Add parmesan and butter, stir rice, divide between 2 plates and serve as a side dish. Enjoy!

Nutrition: calories 183, fat 3, fiber 1, carbs 3, protein 4

Coconut Cabbage

Preparation time: 10 minutes
Cooking time: 10 minutes
Servings: 2

Ingredients:
- ½ tablespoon coconut oil
- ½ brown onion, chopped
- A pinch of salt and black pepper
- 1 garlic clove, minced
- ½ chili pepper, chopped
- ½ tablespoon mustard seeds
- ½ tablespoon curry powder
- ½ tablespoon turmeric powder
- ½ cabbage head, shredded
- ½ carrot, chopped
- 1 tablespoon lime juice
- 4 tablespoons coconut, desiccated
- ½ tablespoon olive oil
- 3 tablespoons water

Directions:
Set your instant pot on sauté mode, add the coconut oil and heat it up. Add onion, a pinch of salt and black pepper, stir and cook for 3 minutes. Add chili pepper garlic, mustard seeds, curry powder, turmeric powder, cabbage, carrot, lime juice, coconut, olive oil and water, stir, cover and cook on High for 6 minutes. Stir cabbage one more time, divide between 2 plates and serve as a side dish. Enjoy!

Nutrition: calories 200, fat 2, fiber 3, carbs 4, protein 6

Sweet Potato Side Salad

Preparation time: 10 minutes
Cooking time: 5 minutes
Servings: 6

Ingredients:
- 3 green onions, chopped
- 6 sweet potatoes
- 1 cup water
- 3 teaspoons dill, chopped
- 3 ounces mayonnaise

Directions:
Put potatoes in your instant pot, add the water, cover, cook on High for 5 minutes, transfer them to a cutting board, peel them, roughly chop and transfer to a salad bowl. Add onion, dill and mayo, toss, divide between plates and serve as a side salad. Enjoy!

Nutrition: calories 170, fat 2, fiber 1 carbs 8, protein 4

Sweet Potatoes Mash

Preparation time: 10 minutes
Cooking time: 15 minutes
Servings: 10

Ingredients:
- 3 pounds sweet potatoes, peeled and cubed
- 1 cup milk, hot
- 6 garlic cloves, minced
- 28 ounces veggie stock
- 4 tablespoons butter, melted

Directions:
Put potatoes in your instant pot, add stock and garlic, stir, cover and cook on High for 15 minutes Drain potatoes, transfer them to a bowl, mash using a potato masher, mix with hot milk and butter, whisk really well, divide between plates and serve as a side dish. Enjoy!

Nutrition: calories 155, fat 4, fiber 2, carbs 9, protein 2

Corn on the Cob

Preparation time: 10 minutes
Cooking time: 5 minutes
Servings: 2

Ingredients:
- 3 cobs of corn, halved
- ½ cup water
- 1 and ½ tablespoons butter
- 1 small garlic clove, minced
- 1 teaspoon sweet paprika
- 1 teaspoon onion powder
- A pinch of cayenne pepper
- 1 teaspoon oregano, dried
- A pinch of salt and black pepper
- ½ lime, cut into wedges
- 1 tablespoon cilantro, chopped

Directions:
Put the water in your instant pot, add the steamer basket, add corn inside, cover and cook on High for 3 minutes. Transfer corn to a plate and clean up your instant pot. Set the pot on sauté mode, add the butter and melt it. Add garlic, stir and cook for a few seconds. Add corn, paprika, onion powder, cayenne, oregano, salt and pepper, stir and sauté for 2 minutes. Sprinkle cilantro on top and serve as a side dish with lime wedges on the side. Enjoy!

Nutrition: calories 127, fat 3, fiber 1, carbs 4, protein 4

Steamed Leeks

Preparation time: 10 minutes
Cooking time: 7 minutes
Servings: 2

Ingredients:
- 2 leeks, trimmed and cut into halves lengthwise
- 1/3 cup water
- A pinch of salt and black pepper
- ½ tablespoon butter

Directions:
Put the water in your instant pot, add the steamer basket, add leeks inside, season with salt and pepper, cover and cook on High for 5 minutes. Clean your instant pot and transfer leeks to a plate. Set the pot on sauté mode, add the butter, melt it, add leeks, stir, cook for a couple of minutes, divide between 2 plates and serve as a side dish. Enjoy!

Nutrition: calories 100, fat 1, fiber 2, carbs 2, protein 4

Turnips and Chili Pepper Side Dish

Preparation time: 10 minutes
Cooking time: 14 minutes
Servings: 4

Ingredients:
- 20 ounces turnips, peeled and chopped
- 1 cup water
- 2 tablespoons olive oil
- 3 green chili peppers, chopped
- 2 tomatoes, chopped

Directions:
Set your instant pot on Sauté mode, add the oil, heat it up, add green chilies, stir and cook for 1 minute. Add tomatoes, turnips and water, stir, cover and cook on Low for 13 minutes. Divide between plates and serve as a side dish. Enjoy!

Nutrition: calories 130, fat 2, fiber 2, carbs 5, protein 4

Spinach and Squash Mix

Preparation time: 10 minutes
Cooking time: 20 minutes
Servings: 4

Ingredients:
- 1 butternut squash, cut into medium wedges
- 1 cup water, for the instant pot
- 6 cups spinach
- 2 tablespoons balsamic vinegar
- 1 teaspoon Dijon mustard
- 6 tablespoons olive oil

Directions:
In a bowl, mix squash with half of the oil and toss. Add the water to your instant pot, add the steamer basket, add squash, cover and cook on High for 10 minutes. In a bowl, mix vinegar with the rest of the oil and mustard and whisk very well. Put spinach in a salad bowl, add squash wedges, add salad dressing, toss to coat well, divide between plates and serve as a side dish. Enjoy!

Nutrition: calories 131, fat 3, fiber 2, carbs 6, protein 5

Sautéed Escarole

Preparation time: 10 minutes
Cooking time: 5 minutes
Servings: 2

Ingredients:
- 4 cups escarole, roughly chopped
- 2 garlic cloves, minced
- 2 tablespoons water
- 1 tablespoon olive oil
- ¼ teaspoon red pepper flakes
- A pinch of salt and black pepper
- 2 tablespoons parmesan, grated

Directions:
Set your instant pot on sauté mode, add the oil and heat it up. Add garlic and pepper flakes, stir and cook for 2 minutes. Add escarole, water, salt and pepper, cover and cook on High for 3 minutes. Add parmesan, toss, divide between 2 plates and serve as a side dish. Enjoy!

Nutrition: calories 93, fat 1, fiber 2, carbs 2, protein 3

Stir Fried Okra

Preparation time: 10 minutes
Cooking time: 10 minutes
Servings: 2

Ingredients:
- 1 onion, chopped
- 1 pound okra, cut into medium pieces
- 1 tablespoon olive oil
- 1 tomato, chopped
- ½ teaspoon cumin seeds
- 2 garlic cloves, minced
- ¼ teaspoon turmeric powder
- 1 teaspoon coriander powder
- A pinch of cayenne pepper
- A pinch of salt and black pepper
- 1 teaspoon lemon juice

Directions:
Set your instant pot on sauté mode, add the oil and heat it up. Add garlic and cumin seeds, stir and cook for 1 minute. Add onion, stir and cook for 2 minutes. Add okra, tomato, turmeric, coriander, cayenne, salt, pepper and lemon juice, stir, cover and cook on Low for 5 minutes. Divide between 2 plates and serve as a side dish. Enjoy!

Nutrition: calories 92, fat 1, fiber 1, carbs 2, protein 3

Instant Pot Snack and Appetizer Recipes

Fish Balls

Preparation time: 10 minutes
Cooking time: 20 minutes
Servings: 16

Ingredients:
- 1 and ½ cups fish stock
- 1 and ½ pound pike fillets, skinless, boneless and ground
- 3 egg whites
- ¼ cup potato starch
- 1 carrot, grated

Directions:
In a bowl, mix fish meat with egg whites, potato starch and carrot and whisk well. Put the stock in your instant pot, add fish balls, cover and cook on Low for 10 minutes. Drain fish balls, arrange them on a platter and serve as an appetizer. Enjoy!

Nutrition: calories 162, fat 3, fiber 4, carbs 8, protein 4

Baby Carrots Snack

Preparation time: 10 minutes
Cooking time: 2 minutes
Servings: 6

Ingredients:
- 1 pound baby carrots
- ¼ cup soy sauce
- ¼ cup Chinese wine
- ¼ cup veggie stock
- 1 tablespoon liquid smoke

Directions:
In your instant pot, mix baby carrots with soy sauce, Chinese wine, stock and liquid smoke, toss, cover and cook on High for 2 minutes. Drain carrots, arrange them on a platter and serve them as a snack with a dip on the side. Enjoy!

Nutrition: calories 176, fat 3, fiber 6, carbs 4, protein 4

Beef Dip

Preparation time: 10 minutes
Cooking time: 20 minutes
Servings: 2

Ingredients:
- ½ cup mushrooms, chopped
- ½ yellow onion, chopped
- 2 tablespoons beer
- ½ pound beef, ground
- A pinch of salt and black pepper
- ½ teaspoon garlic powder
- 2 ounces cream cheese
- ½ tablespoons white flour
- ½ cup cheddar cheese, shredded

Directions:
Set your instant pot on sauté mode, add the oil, heat it up, add mushrooms, beef and onion, stir and cook for 5 minutes. Add salt, pepper, garlic powder and beer, cover and cook on High for 10 minutes. Add cream cheese and flour, stir, turn the pot on sauté mode again and cook for 5 minutes. Add cheddar cheese, toss a bit, transfer to a bowl and serve at a casual gathering. Enjoy!

Nutrition: calories 212, fat 2, fiber 3, carbs 6, protein 7

Potato Wedges

Preparation time: 10 minutes
Cooking time: 10 minutes
Servings: 2

Ingredients:
- 1 cup water
- A pinch of salt and black pepper
- A pinch of baking soda
- 1 teaspoon onion powder
- ½ teaspoon garlic powder
- A pinch of cayenne pepper
- ½ teaspoon oregano, dried
- 2 big potatoes, cut into medium wedges
- 3 quarts sunflower oil+ 2 tablespoons
- 1 cup flour
- 3 tablespoons cornstarch
- ½ cup buttermilk

Directions:
Put the water in your instant pot, add some salt and the baking soda, stir and place the steamer basket inside. In a bowl, mix onion powder with garlic powder, salt, pepper, oregano and cayenne and stir. Add potatoes, toss them well, add them to the pot, cover and cook on High for 2 minutes. In a bowl, mix cornstarch with flour and stir. In another bowl, mix buttermilk with a pinch of baking soda and whisk. Drain potato wedges, dredge them in flour mix and then dip them in buttermilk. Heat up a large pan with 3 quarts water over medium high heat, add potato wedges, cook them for 4 minutes and transfer them to paper towels. Drain grease, transfer wedges to a bowl and serve them as a snack. Enjoy!

Nutrition: calories 284, fat 1, fiber 2, carbs 5, protein 7

Greek Meatballs

Preparation time: 10 minutes
Cooking time: 4 minutes
Servings: 20

Ingredients:
- 1 pound beef, ground
- ¼ cup white vinegar
- 3 tablespoons olive oil
- ¼ cup mint, chopped
- 1 egg, whisked

Directions:
In a bowl, mix beef with mint and egg, whisk well and shape 20 meatballs out of this mix. Set your instant pot on sauté mode, add oil, heat it up, add meatballs and brown them for a few minutes on each side. Add vinegar, toss, cover and cook on High for 4 minutes. Arrange meatballs on a platter and serve them with a yogurt dip on the side. Enjoy!

Nutrition: calories 200, fat 4, fiber 4, carbs 8, protein 10

Cocktail Boiled Peanuts

Preparation time: 10 minutes
Cooking time: 1 hour and 10 minutes
Servings: 4

Ingredients:
- 1 pound peanuts
- ½ cup sugar
- 2 tablespoons lime juice
- ½ cup sea salt
- A pinch of chili powder
- Water, for the instant pot

Directions:
In your instant pot, mix peanuts with sugar, lime juice, sea salt and chili powder and toss. Add water to cover peanuts and cook them on High for 1 hour and 10 minutes. Drain peanuts, divide them into bowls and serve as a snack. Enjoy!

Nutrition: calories 100, fat 4, fiber 4, carbs 5, protein 2

BBQ Chicken Wings

Preparation time: 10 minutes
Cooking time: 25 minutes
Servings: 2

Ingredients:
- 2 pounds chicken wings
- ½ cup BBQ sauce
- 1 cup water

Directions:
Put the water in your instant pot, add the steamer basket, add chicken wings, cover and cook on High for 5 minutes. Put BBQ sauce in a bowl, add chicken wings, toss them well and spread on a lined baking sheet. Introduce in the oven at 450 degrees F and bake for 18 minutes. Serve as an appetizer for a casual snack. Enjoy!

Nutrition: calories 263, fat 3, fiber 5, carbs 8, protein 8

Beef Meatballs

Preparation time: 10 minutes
Cooking time: 30 minutes
Servings: 2

Ingredients:
- 1 tablespoon olive oil
- ½ yellow onion, chopped
- 1 garlic clove, minced
- 7 ounces tomato sauce
- ½ cup water
- ½ tablespoon Worcestershire sauce
- ½ pound beef, ground
- 4 tablespoons rice
- A pinch of salt and black pepper

Directions:
Set your instant pot on sauté mode, add the oil and heat it up. Add half of the garlic and onion, stir and cook for 4 minutes. Add water, Worcestershire sauce and tomato sauce, stir and bring to a simmer. Meanwhile, in a bowl, mix beef with rice, salt, pepper, the rest of the garlic and onion and stir well. Shape meatballs out of this mix, add the to your instant pot, cover and cook on High for 15 minutes. Transfer meatballs on a platter and serve as an appetizer. Enjoy!

Nutrition: calories 221, fat 2, fiber 3, carbs 4, protein 7

Chinese Style Peanuts

Preparation time: 10 minutes
Cooking time: 1 hour and 20 minutes
Servings: 4

Ingredients:
- 1 pound raw peanuts
- 3 garlic cloves
- 3 cinnamon sticks
- 4 red chilies, dried and crushed
- 3-star anise
- Water, for the instant pot

Directions:
In your instant pot mix peanuts with garlic, cinnamon, chilies and star anise. Add water to cover them and cook on High for 1 hour and 20 minutes. Drain peanuts, divide them into bowls and serve as a snack. Enjoy!

Nutrition: calories 89, fat 3, fiber 3, carbs 6, protein 2

Southern Peanuts

Preparation time: 10 minutes
Cooking time: 1 hour and 15 minutes
Servings: 4

Ingredients:
- 1 pound peanuts
- 1 tablespoon Cajun seasoning
- 2 garlic cloves
- 1 jalapeno pepper, chopped
- ¼ cup sea salt
- Water, for the instant pot

Directions:
In your instant pot mix peanuts with sea salt, Cajun seasoning, garlic and jalapeno. Add water to cover, cook on High for 1 hour and 15 minutes, drain, transfer to bowls and serve as a snack. Enjoy!

Nutrition: calories 100, fat 4, fiber 3, carbs 7, protein 2

Stuffed Chicken Breasts

Preparation time: 10 minutes
Cooking time: 30 minutes
Servings: 2

Ingredients:
- 2 chicken breasts, skinless, boneless and butterflied
- 1 ounce ham, chopped
- 6 asparagus spears
- 14 bacon strips
- 4 mozzarella slices
- A pinch of salt and black pepper
- 3 cups water

Directions:
Flatten chicken breasts with a meat mallet and place them on a plate. In a bowl, mix 2 cups water with a pinch of salt and whisk well. Add chicken breasts, cover and leave aside for 30 minutes. Pat dry chicken breasts and place them on a cutting board. Add 2 slices of mozzarella on each, divide ham and asparagus as well. Season with a pinch of salt and pepper and roll chicken breasts. Line bacon slices on a cutting board, add rolled chicken breasts and wrap each in bacon. Secure with toothpicks and place all rolls on a plate. Add 1 cup water to your instant pot, add the trivet, add chicken rolls inside, cover and cook on High for 10 minutes. Arrange on a platter and serve as an appetizer. Enjoy!

Nutrition: calories 231, fat 4, fiber 5, carbs 7, protein 8

Baby Back Ribs Appetizer

Preparation time: 10 minutes
Cooking time: 40 minutes
Servings: 2

Ingredients:
- 2 carrots, chopped
- 1 rack baby back ribs
- 3 drops liquid smoke
- 2 tablespoons brown sugar
- 2 teaspoon chili powder
- A pinch of salt and black pepper
- 1 teaspoon garlic powder
- 1 teaspoon onion powder
- 1 teaspoon cinnamon powder
- ½ teaspoon fennel seeds, ground
- ½ teaspoon cumin seeds
- A pinch of cayenne pepper

For the sauce:
- 1 cup ketchup
- 3 garlic cloves, minced
- 1 yellow onion, chopped
- 1/8 cup maple syrup
- ½ cup water
- 1/8 cup honey
- 2 tablespoons apple cider vinegar
- 2 tablespoons mustard
- 1 tablespoon brown sugar

Directions:
In a bowl, mix ribs with carrots, liquid smoke and toss. Add 2 tablespoons brown sugar, chili powder, a pinch of salt, black pepper, onion powder, garlic powder, cinnamon powder, cumin seeds, fennel seeds and cayenne and toss really well. In another bowl, mix onion with garlic, ketchup, water, maple syrup, honey, vinegar, mustard and 1 tablespoon sugar and whisk really well. Add this to your instant pot, add ribs, cover and cook on High for 25 minutes. Transfer ribs to a platter and leave aside. Turn your instant pot on Sauté mode again and simmer sauce for a few minutes until it thickens. Serve your ribs with the sauce on the side.

Nutrition: calories 242, fat 5, fiber 5, carbs 8, protein 12

Simple Red Pepper Hummus

Preparation time: 10 minutes
Cooking time: 1 hour and 30 minutes
Servings: 4

Ingredients:
- 7 cups water, for the instant pot
- 1 pound chickpeas
- 3 red peppers, roasted
- 2 tablespoons sesame oil
- ½ cup lemon juice
- 1 tablespoon tahini paste

Directions:
In your instant pot, mix chickpeas with water, cover and cook on High for 1 hour and 30 minutes. Drain chickpeas, transfer to a food processor, add roasted peppers, sesame oil, lemon juice and tahini paste, pulse well, divide into bowls and serve as an appetizer. Enjoy!

Nutrition: calories 162, fat 4, fiber 4, carbs 7, protein 8

Asian Wings

Preparation time: 10 minutes
Cooking time: 7 minutes
Servings: 4

Ingredients:
- 4 pounds chicken wings
- 2 tablespoon black soy sauce
- ¼ cup honey
- ¼ cup brown sugar
- ¼ cup water

Directions:
In your instant pot, mix chicken wings with black soy sauce, honey, sugar and water, stir, cover and cook on High for 5 minutes. Transfer chicken wings to a baking sheet, broil for a few minutes, divide into bowls and serve as a snack and appetizer. Enjoy!

Nutrition: calories 221, fat 3, fiber 7, carbs 10, protein 6

Crispy Chicken

Preparation time: 10 minutes
Cooking time: 20 minutes
Servings: 2

Ingredients:
- 6 chicken thighs
- 1 yellow onion, chopped
- 4 garlic cloves, minced
- 1 cup water
- A pinch of rosemary, chopped
- A pinch of salt and black pepper
- 1 and ½ cups panko bread crumbs
- 2 tablespoons olive oil
- 2 tablespoons butter
- 1 cup flour
- 2 eggs, whisked

Directions:
In your instant pot, mix garlic with onion, rosemary and water and stir. Put the steamer basket in your instant pot, add chicken thighs, cover and cook on High for 9 minutes. Meanwhile, heat up a pan with 2 tablespoons oil, 2 tablespoons butter and panko, stir and cook for a couple of minutes. Pat dry chicken thighs and season them with salt and pepper. Coat chicken with flour, dip in eggs, coat in panko and place on a lined baking sheet. Introduce in the oven at 400 degrees F and bake for 5 minutes. Arrange on a platter and serve as an appetizer. Enjoy!

Nutrition: calories 222, fat 4, fiber 5, carbs 8, protein 7

Boiled Peanuts

Preparation time: 10 minutes
Cooking time: 1 hour
Servings: 2

Ingredients:
- ½ pound raw peanuts
- 2 tablespoons salt
- ½ tablespoon Cajun seasoning
- 2 garlic cloves, minced
- 1 small jalapeno, chopped

Directions:
Put peanuts in your instant pot, add salt and water to cover. Add the trivet over peanuts, cover pot and cook on High for 1 hour. Transfer peanuts to a bowl, add Cajun seasoning, jalapeno and garlic, toss well and serve as a snack. Enjoy!

Nutrition: calories 195, fat 4, fiber 1, carbs 4, protein 3

Mexican Corn on the Cob

Preparation time: 10 minutes
Cooking time: 15 minutes
Servings: 4

Ingredients:
- 1 cup water, for the instant pot
- 4 ears of corn, husks removed
- ¼ cup mayonnaise
- 1 tablespoon butter
- A pinch of cayenne pepper
- ¾ cup feta cheese, crumbled

Directions:
Brush corn with mayo and butter and season with cayenne pepper. Add the water to your instant pot, add steamer basket, add corn inside, cover and cook on High for 15 minutes. Arrange corn on a platter, sprinkle cheese all over and serve as a snack. Enjoy!

Nutrition: calories 172, fat 4, fiber 6, carbs 5, protein 3

BBQ Square Ribs

Preparation time: 10 minutes
Cooking time: 20 minutes
Servings: 3

Ingredients:
- 1 rack pork spare ribs
- 1 onion, chopped
- 1 cup apple juice
- 1 cup bbq sauce
- 1 teaspoon liquid smoke

Directions:
In your instant pot, mix spare ribs with onion, apple juice, bbq sauce and liquid smoke, toss, cover and cook on High for 20 minutes. Arrange ribs on a platter, drizzle bbq sauce all over and serve as an appetizer or snack. Enjoy!

Nutrition: calories 300, fat 8, fiber 5, carbs 12, protein 4

Roasted Hummus

Preparation time: 10 minutes
Cooking time: 1 hour and 30 minutes
Servings: 2

Ingredients:
- 3 cups water
- ½ pound garbanzo beans
- A pinch of salt
- 1 small yellow onion, chopped
- 2 garlic cloves, minced
- 1 tablespoon olive oil
- A pinch of cumin, ground
- 2 tablespoons lemon juice
- ½ tablespoon sesame oil
- ½ cup sesame seeds, toasted

Directions:
Put the beans in your instant pot, add the water and some salt, cover and cook on High for 1 hour and 30 minutes. Meanwhile, heat up a pan with the oil over medium high heat, add onion and garlic, stir and cook for 2 minutes. Transfer beans to your food processor, add garlic and onion, cumin, lemon juice, sesame seeds and sesame oil and pulse really well. Transfer hummus to a bowl and serve as an appetizer. Enjoy!

Nutrition: calories 253, fat 4, fiber 2, carbs 4, protein 8

Pasta Appetizer Salad

Preparation time: 10 minutes
Cooking time: 4 minutes
Servings: 2

Ingredients:
- 4 bacon slices, cooked and crumbled
- 2 cups water
- ½ pound gemelli pasta
- A pinch of salt and black pepper
- 4 tablespoons mayonnaise
- 2 tablespoons sour cream
- ½ teaspoon lemon juice
- 2 tablespoons red onion, chopped
- ½ teaspoon Worcestershire sauce
- ½ teaspoon sugar
- 1 teaspoon apple cider vinegar
- 2 ounces cheddar cheese, grated
- 5 ounces peas

Directions:
In your instant pot, mix pasta with a pinch of salt and water, cover and cook on High for 4 minutes. Drain pasta and transfer to a bowl. Add peas, salt, pepper, bacon, red onion, mayo, sour cream, lemon juice, Worcestershire sauce, sugar, vinegar and cheddar cheese, toss well and serve as an appetizer. Enjoy!

Nutrition: calories 213, fat 4, fiber 3, carbs 4, protein 8

Grated Carrot Appetizer Salad

Preparation time: 10 minutes
Cooking time: 3 minutes
Servings: 4

Ingredients:
- 1 pound carrots
- ¼ cup water, for the instant pot
- 1 tablespoon lemon juice
- 1 teaspoon red pepper flakes
- 1 tablespoon parsley, chopped
- Salt to the taste

Directions:
In your instant pot, mix carrots with water and salt, cover and cook on High for 3 minutes. Drain carrots, cool them down, grated and transfer them to a bowl. Add lemon juice, pepper flakes and parsley, toss, divide into smaller bowls and serve as an appetizer Enjoy!

Nutrition: calories 152, fat 3, fiber 3, carbs 4, protein 3

Green Beans Salad

Preparation time: 10 minutes
Cooking time: 2 minutes
Servings: 4

Ingredients:
- 1 pound green beans, trimmed
- ½ cup water, for the instant pot
- 2 red onions, sliced
- 1 tablespoon Creole mustard
- 1 tablespoon red wine vinegar
- A drizzle of olive oil

Directions:
In your instant pot, mix green beans with water, cover and cook on High for 2 minutes. Drain green beans, transfer to a bowl, add onion slices, mustard, vinegar and oil, toss, divide on appetizer plates and serve as an appetizer. Enjoy!

Nutrition: calories 121, fat 4, fiber 4, carbs 6, protein 4

Honey Chicken Appetizer

Preparation time: 10 minutes
Cooking time: 10 minutes
Servings: 2

Ingredients:
- 2 pound chicken wings pieces
- ½ cup ketchup
- ½ tablespoon liquid smoke
- 3 tablespoons brown sugar
- 1 garlic clove, minced
- 2 tablespoons onion, chopped
- 3 tablespoons water
- 2 tablespoons bourbon
- 1 teaspoon smoked paprika
- A pinch of cayenne pepper
- A pinch of salt and black pepper
- 1 and ½ tablespoons honey

Directions:
In your instant pot, mix ketchup with smoke, sugar, garlic, onion, water, bourbon, paprika, salt, pepper, cayenne and honey, whisk well, set on sauté mode and simmer for a few minutes. Add chicken wings, toss, cover and cook on High for 5 minutes. Transfer chicken wings to a lined baking sheet, introduce in the oven at 400 degrees F and roast for 5 minutes. Serve as an appetizer. Enjoy!

Nutrition: calories 243, fat 4, fiber 4, carbs 7, protein 9

Hot Wings

Preparation time: 10 minutes
Cooking time: 10 minutes
Servings: 2

Ingredients:
- 1 and ½ pounds chicken wings pieces
- ½ tablespoon Worcestershire sauce
- 2 tablespoons butter
- 2 tablespoons cayenne pepper sauce
- 1 tablespoon brown sugar
- A pinch of salt
- 3 ounces water

Directions:
Put the water in your instant pot, add the trivet, add chicken wings, cover and cook on High for 5 minutes. In a bowl, mix butter with Worcestershire sauce, pepper sauce, sugar and salt and whisk really well. Brush chicken pieces with this mix, spread them on a lined baking sheet, introduce in the oven at 400 degrees F and roast for 5 minutes. Serve as an appetizer. Enjoy!

Nutrition: calories 251, fat 5, fiber 3, carbs 6, protein 8

Watercress Appetizer Salad

Preparation time: 10 minutes
Cooking time: 2 minutes
Servings: 4

Ingredients:
- 1 big bunch watercress, roughly torn
- 2 peaches, stones removed and cut into medium wedges
- 1 watermelon, cubed
- A drizzle of olive oil
- 1 tablespoon lemon juice
- ½ cup water, for the instant pot

Directions:
In your instant pot, mix watercress with water, cover and cook on High for 2 minutes. Drain, transfer to a bowl, add peaches, watermelon, oil and lemon juice, toss, divide on appetizer plates and serve as an appetizer. Enjoy!

Nutrition: calories 111, fat 3, fiber 4, carbs 5, protein 3

Ham and Cheese Dip

Preparation time: 10 minutes
Cooking time: 12 minutes
Servings: four

Ingredients:
- 8 ounces cream cheese
- 1 cup Swiss cheese
- 1 cup cheddar cheese, grated
- 2 tablespoons parsley, chopped
- 8 ham slices, chopped

Directions:
Set your instant pot on sauté mode, add ham, stir and brown for 3-4 minutes. Add Swiss, cheddar and cream cheese, stir, cover and cook on High for 6 minutes. Add parsley, divide into bowls and serve as an appetizer. Enjoy!

Nutrition: calories 243, fat 4, fiber 7, carbs 7, protein 4

Italian Dip

Preparation time: 10 minutes
Cooking time: 55 minutes
Servings: 2

Ingredients:
- 1 pound beef roast, cut into medium chunks
- 1 tablespoon Italian seasoning
- 3 ounces beef stock
- 2 tablespoons water
- 4 ounces pepperoncini peppers

Directions:
In your instant pot, mix beef with seasoning, stock, water and pepperoncini peppers, cover and cook on High for 55 minutes. Shred meat using 2 forks, stir your dip and serve it with sandwiches. Enjoy!

Nutrition: calories 242, fat 4, fiber 4, carbs 6, protein 7

Mussels Appetizer

Preparation time: 10 minutes
Cooking time: 6 minutes
Servings: 2

Ingredients:
- 1 pound mussels, scrubbed
- ½ onion, chopped
- ½ radicchio, cut into strips
- ½ pound baby spinach
- 3 tablespoons white wine
- 4 tablespoons water
- 1 small garlic clove, minced
- 1 tablespoon olive oil

Directions:
Set your instant pot on Sauté mode, add oil, heat it up, add garlic, wine and onion, stir and cook for 5 minutes. Add the steamer basket inside, add mussels, cover and cook on Low for 1 minute. Divide spinach and radicchio on 2 plates, also divide mussels, drizzle the cooking liquid from the pot and serve as an appetizer.

Nutrition: calories 65, fat 2, fiber 2, carbs 2, protein 7

Scallion Spread

Preparation time: 10 minutes
Cooking time: 3 minutes
Servings: 6

Ingredients:
- ½ cup scallions, chopped
- 1 cup sour cream
- ¼ cup mayonnaise
- 3 tablespoons dill, chopped
- 1 tablespoon lemon zest, grated

Directions:
Set your instant pot on sauté mode, add scallions, stir and brown for 1 minute. Add sour cream, stir, cover and cook on High for 2 minutes. Leave this mix to cool down, add mayo, dill and lemon zest, stir well, divide into bowls and serve with tortilla chips on the side. Enjoy!

Nutrition: calories 222, fat 4, fiber 5, carbs 8, protein 4

Crab Spread

Preparation time: 10 minutes
Cooking time: 15 minutes
Servings: 4

Ingredients:
- 8 ounces crab meat
- ½ cup sour cream
- ¼ cup half and half
- ½ bunch scallions, chopped
- 1 teaspoon Worcestershire sauce

Directions:
In your instant pot, mix crab meat with sour cream, half-and-half, scallions and Worcestershire sauce, stir, cover and cook on High for 15 minutes. Leave spread to cool down, divide into bowls and serve as an appetizer. Enjoy!

Nutrition: calories 241, fat 4, fiber 6, carbs 8, protein 3

Italian Mussels

Preparation time: 10 minutes
Cooking time: 6 minutes
Servings: 2

Ingredients:
- 20 ounces canned tomatoes, chopped
- 3 tablespoons onion, chopped
- 1 jalapeno peppers, chopped
- 2 tablespoons white wine
- 2 tablespoons olive oil
- 2 tablespoons balsamic vinegar
- 1 and ½ pounds mussels, scrubbed
- 1 tablespoon red pepper flakes
- 1 garlic cloves, minced
- A pinch of salt
- 2 tablespoons basil, chopped

Directions:
Set your instant pot on sauté mode, add the oil, heat it up, add onion and garlic, stir and cook for 2 minutes. Add tomatoes, jalapeno, wine, vinegar, pepper flakes and salt, stir and simmer for 2 minutes more. Add mussels, stir, cover and cook on High for 2 minutes. Discard unopened mussels, divide them between 2 bowls and serve with basil sprinkled on top. Enjoy!

Nutrition: calories 94, fat 1, fiber 2, carbs 2, protein 2

Clams Appetizer

Preparation time: 10 minutes
Cooking time: 5 minutes
Servings: 4

Ingredients:
- 12 clams
- 1 garlic clove, minced
- 2 tablespoons butter
- 2 tablespoons parsley, chopped
- 2 tablespoons parmesan cheese, grated
- ½ teaspoon oregano, chopped
- ½ cup breadcrumbs
- 1 cup water

Directions:
In a bowl, mix breadcrumbs with parmesan, oregano, parsley, butter and garlic, stir, open clams and divide this into them. Add the water into your instant pot, add the steamer basket, add clams inside, cover and cook on High for 5 minutes. Divide clams on a platter and serve as an appetizer with lemon wedges on the side. Enjoy!

Nutrition: calories 100, fat 3, fiber 1, carbs 2, protein 5

Tasty Black Bean Salsa

Preparation time: 10 minutes
Cooking time: 8 minutes
Servings: 4

Ingredients:
- 1 small white onion, chopped
- 8 ounces canned black beans, drained
- 2 tablespoons lime juice
- 1 tablespoon olive oil
- 2 red jalapenos, chopped

Directions:
Set your instant pot on sauté mode, add oil, heat it up, add onion, stir and cook for 2-3 minutes. Add black beans, lime juice and jalapenos, stir, cover and cook on High for 3 minutes. Divide into bowls and serve warm. Enjoy!

Nutrition: calories 172, fat 3, fiber 4, carbs 6, protein 3

Special Ranch Spread

Preparation time: 10 minutes
Cooking time: 10 minutes
Servings: 12

Ingredients:
- 1 cup sour cream
- 1 pound bacon, chopped
- 1 cup mayonnaise
- 1 cup Monterey jack cheese, shredded
- 4 green onions, chopped

Directions:
Set your instant pot on sauté mode, add bacon, stir and cook until it is crispy. Add sour cream and green onions, stir, cover and cook on High for 6 minutes. Add cheese and mayo, stir well, leave aside for a few minutes, divide into bowls and serve as an appetizer. Enjoy!

Nutrition: calories 261, fat 4, fiber 6, carbs 7, protein 4

Beet Appetizer Salad

Preparation time: 30 minutes
Cooking time: 30 minutes
Servings: 2

Ingredients:
- 2 cups water
- 2 small beets
- 1 small red onion, sliced
- 1 ounce goat cheese
- 2 tablespoons apple cider vinegar
- Salt and black pepper to the taste
- ½ tablespoons sugar
- 1 cup mixed cherry tomatoes, halved
- 2 tablespoons pecans
- ½ tablespoon olive oil

Directions:
Add 1 cup water to your instant pot, add the steamer basket, add beets inside, cover and cook on High for 20 minutes. Transfer beets to a cutting board, cool them down, peel, roughly chop them, put them into a bowl, add tomatoes and leave aside for now. Clean your instant pot, add the rest of the water, vinegar and sugar, stir, set the pot on sauté mode and simmer for 2 minutes. Strain this into a bowl, add onion and leave aside for 20 minutes. Drain onions, add them to your salad and toss. In a bowl, mix 1 tablespoon liquid from the onions with oil and whisk. Add this to salad, also add, salt, pepper, goat cheese and pecans, toss, divide between 2 appetizer plates and serve. Enjoy!

Nutrition: calories 183, fat 2, fiber 3, carbs 8, protein 5

Onion Dip

Preparation time: 10 minutes
Cooking time: 30 minutes
Servings: 2

Ingredients:
- 2 tablespoons butter
- 1 pound yellow onion, chopped
- Salt and black pepper to the taste
- A pinch of baking soda

Directions:
Set your instant pot on Sauté mode, add butter, melt it, add onion and soda, stir, sauté for 3 minutes, cover the pot and cook on High for 20 minutes. Set the pot on sauté mode again, add salt and pepper, stir and cook the dip for a few minutes more until it thickens. Transfer to bowls and serve as a snack. Enjoy!

Nutrition: calories 142, fat 1, fiber 1, carbs 4, protein 3

Chicken Dip

Preparation time: 10 minutes
Cooking time: 15 minutes
Servings: 6

Ingredients:
- 3 cups chicken, cooked and shredded
- 4 ounces cream cheese
- 1 cup mozzarella cheese, shredded
- ½ cup hot sauce
- 1 cup Greek yogurt

Directions:
In your instant pot, mix chicken with cream cheese and hot sauce, stir, cover and cook on High for 15 minutes. Add yogurt and mozzarella, stir, leave aside for a few minutes, divide into bowls and serve as an appetizer. Enjoy!

Nutrition: calories 188, fat 4, fiber 7, carbs 8, protein 4

Blue Cheese Dip

Preparation time: 10 minutes
Cooking time: 4 minutes
Servings: 6

Ingredients:
- 4 tablespoons blue cheese, crumbled
- 1 cup sour cream
- 2 tablespoons chives, chopped
- 1 and ½ teaspoons rosemary, chopped
- Black pepper to the taste

Directions:
In your instant pot, mix blue cheese with sour cream, rosemary and black pepper, stir, cover and cook on Manual for 4 minutes. Add chives, whisk dip, divide into bowls and serve as an appetizer. Enjoy!

Nutrition: calories 200, fat 7, fiber 5, carbs 7, protein 4

Chili Dip

Preparation time: 10 minutes
Cooking time: 17 minutes
Servings: 2

Ingredients:
- 2 ounces red chilies, chopped
- 1 and ½ tablespoons sugar
- 1.5 ounces bird's eye chilies, chopped
- 5 garlic cloves, minced
- 2 ounces white vinegar
- 2 ounces water

Directions:
In your instant pot, mix water with sugar, red chilies, bird's eye chilies and garlic, stir, cover and cook on High for 7 minutes. Add vinegar, blend everything using an immersion blender, set the pot on sauté mode and simmer for 10 minutes. Divide into bowls and serve as a snack with tortilla chips. Enjoy!

Nutrition: calories 100, fat 1, fiber 0, carbs 2, protein 4

Corn Dip

Preparation time: 10 minutes
Cooking time: 6 minutes
Servings: 2

Ingredients:
- ½ yellow onion, chopped
- ½ tablespoon olive oil
- ½ teaspoon white flour
- 1 cup chicken stock
- 2 tablespoons white wine
- 1 teaspoon thyme, dried
- 2 cups corn kernels
- Salt and black pepper to the taste
- 1 teaspoons butter

Directions:
Set your instant pot on Sauté mode, add oil, heat it up, add onion, stir and cook for 3 minutes. Add flour and wine, stir and cook for 2 minutes more. Add thyme, stock and corn, stir, cover and cook at High for 2 minutes. Transfer everything to your blender, add salt, pepper and butter and pulse really well. Return corn mix to your instant pot, set it on sauté mode again and simmer for a couple of minutes until it thickens. Serve as a snack. Enjoy!

Nutrition: calories 121, fat 3, fiber 2, carbs 5, protein 5

Chunky Warm Salsa

Preparation time: 10 minutes
Cooking time: 4 minutes
Servings: 5

Ingredients:
- 1 red bell pepper, cut into medium pieces
- 2 peaches, roughly chopped
- 1 red onion, roughly chopped
- A drizzle of olive oil
- 2 tablespoons lime juice

Directions:
Set your instant pot on sauté mode, add oil, heat it up, add onion, stir and cook for 1 minute. Add red pepper, peaches and lime juice, toss, cover and cook on High for 3 minutes. Leave this appetizer to cool down, divide into small bowls and serve. Enjoy!

Nutrition: calories 152, fat 2, fiber 3, carbs 4, protein 4

Cumin Dip

Preparation time: 10 minutes
Cooking time: 2 minutes
Servings: 4

Ingredients:
- 1 cup sour cream
- 1/3 cup mayonnaise
- 1 and ¼ teaspoon cumin, ground
- 1 tablespoon hot sauce
- 1 tablespoon lime juice

Directions:
In your instant pot, mix sour cream with cumin and hot sauce, stir, cover and cook on High for 2 minutes. Leave dip to cool down, add mayo and lime juice, stir, divide into bowls and serve. Enjoy!

Nutrition: calories 209, fat 6, fiber 3, carbs 7, protein 7

Cabbage Rolls

Preparation time: 15 minutes
Cooking time: 35 minutes
Servings: 2

Ingredients:
- ½ tablespoon olive oil
- ½ cup brown rice
- 4 cups water
- 1 and ½ cups mushrooms, chopped
- ½ yellow onion, chopped
- 1 garlic clove, minced
- Salt and black pepper to the taste
- 6 green cabbage leaves
- ½ teaspoon walnuts, chopped
- ½ teaspoon caraway seeds
- A pinch of cayenne pepper

Directions:
Put 2 cups water and rice in your instant pot, cover, cook on High for 15 minutes, drain rice and transfer to a bowl. Heat up a pan with the oil over medium high heat, add onion, mushrooms, garlic, walnuts, caraway seeds, salt, pepper and cayenne, stir, cook for 5 minutes, add to rice and stir well. Meanwhile, put the rest of the water into a pot, bring to a boil over medium high heat, add cabbage leaves, blanch them for 1 minute, drain them well, arrange on a working surface, divide rice mix in the middle, roll and seal edges. Transfer cabbage rolls to your instant pot, add water to cover them, cover and cook on High for 10 minutes more. Arrange cabbage rolls on a platter and serve as an appetizer. Enjoy!

Nutrition: calories 193, fat 2, fiber 6, carbs 8, protein 5

Tofu Appetizer

Preparation time: 10 minutes
Cooking time: 8 minutes
Servings: 2

Ingredients:
- ½ yellow onion, sliced
- 3 mushrooms, sliced
- 1 and ½ teaspoons tamari
- 4 ounces tofu, cubed
- 3 tablespoons red bell pepper, chopped
- 3 tablespoons green beans
- 2 tablespoons veggie stock
- Salt and white pepper to the taste

Directions:
Set your instant pot on sauté mode, add onion and mushroom, stir and brown for 2 minutes. Add tofu and tamari, stir and cook for 2 minutes more. Add stock, stir a bit, cover and cook on High for 3 minutes. Add bell pepper and green beans, salt and pepper, cover and cook on High for 1 minute. Divide into 2 small bowls and serve as an appetizer. Enjoy!

Nutrition: calories 143, fat 3, fiber 2, carbs 9, protein 6

Pinto Bean Dip

Preparation time: 10 minutes
Cooking time: 8 minutes
Servings: 4

Ingredients:
- 8 ounces canned pinto beans, drained
- 4 rosemary sprigs, chopped
- 1 and ¼ cup parsley, chopped
- 3 tablespoons lemon juice
- 2 tablespoons tomatoes, chopped

Directions:
In your instant pot, mix pinto beans with rosemary and tomatoes, stir, cover and cook on High for 8 minutes. Blend using an immersion blender, add parsley and lemon juice, stir again, divide into bowls and serve as an appetizer. Enjoy!

Nutrition: calories 272, fat 3, fiber 8, carbs 9, protein 8

Light Lemon Dip

Preparation time: 10 minutes
Cooking time: 10 minutes
Servings: 6

Ingredients:
- 2 lemons, roasted in the oven and pulp separated
- 1 tablespoon olive oil
- 1 cup sour cream
- ½ cup chives, chopped
- 1 cup mayonnaise

Directions:
In your instant pot, mix lemon pulp with sour cream and oil, whisk well, cover and cook on High for 5 minutes. Leave aside dip to cool down, add chives and mayo, whisk well, divide into bowls and serve as an appetizer. Enjoy!

Nutrition: calories 200, fat 3, fiber 4, carbs 6, protein 8

Lentils Patties

Preparation time: 15 minutes
Cooking time: 40 minutes
Servings: 2

Ingredients:
- ½ teaspoon ginger, grated
- 2 tablespoons mushrooms, chopped
- 1 small yellow onion, chopped
- ½ cup red lentils
- 1 cup veggie stock
- 1 small sweet potato, chopped
- Cooking spray
- ½ tablespoon parsley, finely chopped
- ½ tablespoon hemp seeds
- ½ tablespoon cilantro, finely chopped
- 2 teaspoons curry powder
- 2 tablespoons quick oats
- 1 tablespoon rice flour
- Salt and pepper to the taste

Directions:
Set your instant pot on Sauté more, add onion, mushroom and ginger, stir and cook for 3 minutes. Add stock, sweet potatoes and lentils, stir, cover, cook on High for 6 minutes, transfer everything to a bowl and leave aside to cool down. Add parsley, curry powder, salt, pepper, hemp seeds and cilantro, stir well and mash everything using a potato masher. Add oats and rice flour and stir. Shape 4 patties out of this mix, arrange them on a baking sheet after you've sprayed it with cooking spray, introduce in the oven, bake at 375 degrees F for 10 minutes, flip and cook for 10 minutes more. Arrange patties on a platter and serve as an appetizer. Enjoy!

Nutrition: calories 140, fat 4, fiber 4, carbs 7, protein 11

Black Beans Patties

Preparation time: 15 minutes
Cooking time: 35 minutes
Servings: 2

Ingredients:
- ½ cup black beans, soaked for a few hours and drained
- ½ tablespoon flaxseed mixed with ½ tablespoon water
- ½ red onion, chopped
- 1 and ½ tablespoons olive oil
- 3 tablespoons quick oats
- A pinch of cumin, ground
- 1 teaspoon chipotle powder
- Salt to the taste
- 1 garlic clove, minced
- 1 teaspoon lemon zest, grated

Directions:
Put beans in your instant pot, add water to cover, cook on High for 20 minutes, drain beans, transfer them to a bowl, mash using a potato masher and leave aside for now. Heat up a pan with half of the oil, over medium high heat, add onion and garlic, stir and cook for 5 minutes. Cool this mix down, add to the bowl with the beans, also add flaxseed, oats, cumin, chipotle powder, salt to the taste and lemon zest, stir well and shape small patties out of this mix. Heat up a pan with the rest of the oil over medium high heat, add patties, cook for 3 minutes on each side, transfer them to paper towels, drain grease, arrange on a platter and serve as an appetizer. Enjoy!

Nutrition: calories 271, fat 3, fiber 4, carbs 8, protein 10

Green Olive Pate

Preparation time: 10 minutes
Cooking time: 2 minutes
Servings: 4

Ingredients:
- 2 cups green olives, pitted
- 2 anchovy fillets
- 2 garlic cloves, minced
- 1 tablespoon capers, chopped
- ½ cup olive oil

Directions:
In a food processor, mix olives with anchovy fillets, garlic, capers and olive oil, pulse well, transfer to your instant pot, cover and cook on High for 2 minutes. Divide into bowls and serve cold as an appetizer. Enjoy!

Nutrition: calories 118, fat 2, fiber 2, carbs 5, protein 4

Shrimp and Tomatoes Appetizer Mix

Preparation time: 10 minutes
Cooking time: 4 minutes
Servings: 6

Ingredients:
- 1 and ½ cups onion, chopped
- 2 tablespoons butter
- 15 ounces canned tomatoes, chopped
- 1 pound shrimp, shelled
- 1 cup feta cheese, crumbled

Directions:
Set your instant pot on sauté mode, add butter, melt it, add onion, stir and cook for 2 minutes. Add shrimp and tomatoes, toss a bit, cover and cook on Low for 2 minutes. Divide shrimp and tomatoes mix into small bowls and serve as an appetizer with feta cheese on top. Enjoy!

Nutrition: calories 201, fat 3, fiber 4, carbs 7, protein 4

Chickpeas Appetizer

Preparation time: 10 minutes
Cooking time: 20 minutes
Servings: 2

Ingredients:
- ½ cup chickpeas, soaked for a couple of hours and drained
- ½ teaspoon thyme, dried
- ½ teaspoon cumin, ground
- 1 bay leaf
- A pinch of salt and black pepper
- ½ teaspoon garlic powder
- 1 and ½ tablespoons tomato paste
- 3 tablespoons whole wheat flour

Directions:
Put chickpeas in your instant pot, add water to cover, cumin powder, bay leaf, garlic powder, thyme, onion, salt and pepper, stir, cover, cook on High for 15 minutes, discard bay leaf, drain chickpeas, transfer them to your blender and pulse really well. Add tomato paste and flour, blend again and shape small patties out of this mix. Place them on preheated grill over medium high heat, cook them for a couple of minutes on each side, arrange on a platter and serve them as an appetizer. Enjoy!

Nutrition: calories 122, fat 1, fiber 4, carbs 8, protein 4

Mushroom Cakes

Preparation time: 10 minutes
Cooking time: 15 minutes
Servings: 2

Ingredients:
- ½ tablespoon canola oil
- 1 small garlic clove, minced
- 2 green onions, chopped
- ½ yellow onion, chopped
- A pinch of cumin, ground
- 7 ounces canned pinto beans, drained
- ½ cup mushrooms, chopped
- ½ teaspoon parsley, chopped
- Salt and black pepper to the taste
- 2 tablespoons olive oil

Directions:
Set your instant pot on Sauté mode, add canola oil, heat it up, add garlic, yellow onion, green onions, mushrooms, salt, pepper and cumin, stir, sauté for 5 minutes, cover pot, cook on Low for 5 minutes, transfer to a bowl and cool down. Put the beans in your food processor, pulse them, add them and parsley to mushrooms mix, stir well and shape small cakes out of this mixture. Heat up a pan with the olive oil over medium high heat, add cakes, cook for 3 minutes on each side, arrange them on a platter and serve as an appetizer. Enjoy!

Nutrition: calories 170, fat 2, fiber 3, carbs 8, protein 10

Tomatoes Appetizer Salad

Preparation time: 10 minutes
Cooking time: 30 minutes
Servings: 6

Ingredients:
- 1 and ½ cups water, for the instant pot
- 8 beets, trimmed
- 1 pint mixed cherry tomatoes, halved
- 1 cup apple cider vinegar
- 1 red onion, chopped
- 2 teaspoons sugar

Directions:
Put the water in your instant pot, add steamer basket, add beets inside, cover and cook on High for 20 minutes. Drain beets, cool them down, peel, grate them and transfer to a bowl. Clean the pot, set on sauté mode, add mixed cherries and sugar, toss them and cook for a couple of minutes. Add onion and vinegar, stir and cook for 2 minutes more. Add beets, stir, sauté everything for another 2 minutes, divide everything on appetizer plates and serve. Enjoy!

Nutrition: calories 118, fat 3, fiber 2, carbs 5, protein 3

Kale and Carrots Salad

Preparation time: 10 minutes
Cooking time: 7 minutes
Servings: 4

Ingredients:
- 10 ounces kale, roughly chopped
- 3 carrots, sliced
- ½ cup chicken stock
- 1 tablespoon olive oil
- 1 red onion, chopped

Directions:
Set your instant pot on sauté mode, add oil, heat it up, add onion and carrots, stir and cook for 1-2 minutes. Add kale and stock, stir a bit, cover and cook on High for 5 minutes. Divide into small bowls and serve as an appetizer. Enjoy!

Nutrition: calories 128, fat 2, fiber 4, carbs 8, protein 4

Beets Cakes

Preparation time: 15 minutes
Cooking time: 20 minutes
Servings: 2

Ingredients:
- 1 beet
- 1 potato
- A pinch of turmeric powder
- ½ teaspoon fennel powder
- A pinch of red chili powder
- Salt and black pepper to the taste
- A pinch of coriander powder
- A pinch of garam masala powder
- A pinch of chaat masala
- 1 small green chili, chopped
- 1 teaspoon lemon juice
- 1 teaspoon ginger, grated
- 1 tablespoon semolina
- ½ slice of whole wheat bread, soaked and squeezed
- Vegetable oil

Directions:
Put beetroot and potato in your instant pot, add water to cover, cook on High for 10 minutes, drain, cool them down, peel, grated them and put in a bowl. Add turmeric, fennel powder, red chili powder, coriander powder, garam masala, chaat masala, green chili, lemon juice, ginger, salt, pepper and bread, stir well, shape small cakes out of this mix and coat them in semolina. Heat up a pan with vegetable oil over medium high heat, add cakes, cook for a few minutes on each side, transfer to a platter and serve as an appetizer. Enjoy!

Nutrition: calories 180, fat 3, fiber 4, carbs 7, protein 9

Mango Salsa

Preparation time: 10 minutes
Cooking time: 22 minutes
Servings: 2

Ingredients:
- ½ shallot, chopped
- 2 teaspoons olive oil
- A pinch of cinnamon powder
- 2 teaspoons ginger, grated
- A pinch of cardamom
- 1 small red hot chili pepper, minced
- 1 small apple, peeled, cored and chopped
- 1 mango, peeled and chopped
- A pinch of salt
- 1 tablespoon raisins
- 2 tablespoons white vinegar
- 2 tablespoons white wine

Directions:
Set your instant pot on Sauté mode, add the oil, heat it up, add shallot, ginger, cinnamon, chili peppers and cardamom, stir and cook for 3 minutes. Add mango, apple, salt, raisins, sugar and vinegar, stir, cover pot, cook on High for 15 minutes, transfer to a bowl and serve with crackers on the side. Enjoy!

Nutrition: calories 80, fat 1, fiber 2, carbs 7, protein 1

Kale and Wild Rice Appetizer Salad

Preparation time: 10 minutes
Cooking time: 4 minutes
Servings: 4

Ingredients:
- 1 cup wild rice, already cooked
- 1 avocado, peeled, pitted and chopped
- 1 kale bunch, roughly chopped
- 1 teaspoon olive oil
- 3 ounces goat cheese, crumbled

Directions:
Set your instant pot on sauté mode, add oil, heat it up, add rice and toast it for 2-3 minutes stirring often. Add kale, stir, cover and cook on Manual for 2 minutes. Add avocado, toss, divide on appetizer plates, sprinkle cheese on top and serve. Enjoy!

Nutrition: calories 182, fat 3, fiber 2, carbs 4, protein 3

Minty Kale Salad

Preparation time: 10 minutes
Cooking time: 3 minutes
Servings: 4

Ingredients:
- 1 bunch kale, roughly chopped
- 1 teaspoon sesame oil
- 2 tablespoons lemon juice
- 1 cup pineapple, chopped
- 2 tablespoons mint, chopped

Directions:
Set your instant pot on sauté mode, add oil, heat it up, add kale, stir and cook for 1 minute. Add pineapple, lemon juice and mint, toss, divide on appetizer plates and serve. Enjoy!

Nutrition: calories 121, fat 1, fiber 2, carbs 4, protein 2

Mushroom Dip

Preparation time: 10 minutes
Cooking time: 20 minutes
Servings: 2

Ingredients:
- 5 mushrooms, chopped
- ½ yellow onion, chopped
- 1 garlic clove, minced
- ½ teaspoon thyme, dried
- ½ cup veggie stock
- A pinch of rosemary, dried
- ¼ teaspoon sage, dried
- ½ teaspoon sherry
- ½ tablespoon water
- ½ tablespoon nutritional yeast
- ½ tablespoon soy sauce
- Salt and black pepper to the taste
- 2 tablespoons milk
- 1 tablespoon white flour

Directions:
Set your instant pot on Sauté mode, add onion, brown for 5 minutes, add mushrooms, garlic and the water, stir and cook for 4 minutes more. Add water, stock, yeast, sherry, soy sauce, salt, pepper, sage, thyme and rosemary, stir, cover and cook on High for 4 minutes. Add milk mixed with flour, stir, cover, cook on High for 6 minutes, transfer to a bowl and serve as a dip Enjoy!

Nutrition: calories 90, fat 4, fiber 3, carbs 6, protein 2

Cauliflower Dip

Preparation time: 10 minutes
Cooking time: 10 minutes
Servings: 2

Ingredients:
- ½ cup cauliflower florets
- ¼ teaspoon onion powder
- ½ cup water
- 1 garlic clove, minced
- ¼ teaspoon mustard powder
- ¼ teaspoon smoked paprika
- A pinch of turmeric
- 1 tablespoon nutritional yeast
- 2 teaspoons chickpea miso
- 2 teaspoons cornstarch
- Salt to the taste
- 2 teaspoons lemon juice

Directions:
Put the water, cauliflower, garlic, paprika, powder, turmeric and mustard in your instant pot, stir, cover and cook on High for 10 minutes. Transfer everything to your blender, add yeast, chickpea miso, cornstarch, lemon juice and salt to the taste, blend well, transfer to a bowl and serve with veggie sticks on the side. Enjoy!

Nutrition: calories 80, fat 1, fiber 2, carbs 4, protein 2

Broccoli Appetizer Salad

Preparation time: 10 minutes
Cooking time: 10 minutes
Servings: 4

Ingredients:
- 1 broccoli head, florets separated
- ½ cup almonds, chopped
- 2 tablespoons olive oil
- ¼ cup apple juice
- 2 tablespoons tamari sauce
- 1 and ½ cups water, for the instant pot

Directions:
Put the water in your instant pot, add steamer basket, add broccoli florets, cover, cook on High for 4 minutes, drain and transfer to a bowl. Clean the pot, set it on sauté mode, add oil, heat it up, add kale, stir and cook for 2 minutes. Return broccoli, also add, apple juice and tamari, stir, cover and cook on High for 2 minutes more. Add almonds, toss, divide into bowls and serve as an appetizer. Enjoy!

Nutrition: calories 192, fat 2, fiber 4, carbs 7, protein 4

Creamy Broccoli Appetizer

Preparation time: 10 minutes
Cooking time: 3 minutes
Servings: 4

Ingredients:
- 1 broccoli head, florets separated
- 1 apple, cored and cut into medium wedges
- ½ cup Greek yogurt
- 2 tablespoons mayonnaise
- 1 tablespoon honey
- 1 cup water, for the instant pot

Directions:
Put the water in your instant pot, add steamer basket, add broccoli inside, cover and cook on High for 3 minutes. Drain broccoli florets, transfer to a bowl, add apple, mayo, yogurt and honey, toss well, divide on appetizer plates and serve. Enjoy!

Nutrition: calories 200, fat 3, fiber 4, carbs 7, protein 3

Red Pepper Dip

Preparation time: 10 minutes
Cooking time: 2 hours
Servings: 2

Ingredients:
- 3 cups water
- 2 red bell peppers
- Salt to the taste
- ½ tablespoon sesame oil
- 1/3 pound garbanzo beans
- A pinch of cumin
- 2 tablespoons lemon juice
- 2 teaspoons olive oil
- 1 garlic clove, roasted
- 2 tablespoons sesame seeds, toasted

Directions:
Put beans in your instant pot, add water and salt, cover and cook on High for 1 hour and 30 minutes. Transfer beans to a bowl and reserve cooking liquid. Add some water to the pot, add the steamer basket, add bell peppers inside, cover and cook on High for 15 minutes. Peel peppers, chop them and put them in another bowl. Heat up a pan with half of the sesame oil over medium high heat, add sesame seeds and garlic , stir and cook for 6 minutes. In your blender, mix beans with toasted sesame seeds and garlic, peppers, lemon juice, olive oil, the rest of the sesame oil, some of the cooking liquid from the beans, salt and cumin, pulse well and serve as a dip with pita bread. Enjoy!

Nutritional value: calories 80, fat 6, carbs 6, fiber 2, protein 2

Artichokes Spread

Preparation time: 15 minutes
Cooking time: 15 minutes
Servings: 2

Ingredients:
- ½ cup cannellini beans, soaked overnight and drained
- ½ pound artichokes, cut lengthwise
- ½ cup water
- 2 tablespoons lemon juice
- 1 garlic clove, minced
- 2 tablespoons Greek yogurt
- Salt and pepper to the taste

Directions:
Put artichokes in a bowl, add the lemon juice, leave aside for 15 minutes, add them to instant pot, also add beans, cover and cook on High for 15 minutes. Discard excess water, transfer artichokes and beans to your blender, add garlic, salt, pepper and yogurt, pulse well and serve as a snack. Enjoy!

Nutrition: calories 100, fat 3, fiber 4, carbs 7, protein 3

Broccoli and Bacon Appetizer Salad

Preparation time: 10 minutes
Cooking time: 4 minutes
Servings: 4

Ingredients:
- 1 broccoli head, florets separated
- ¼ cup cilantro, chopped
- 4 bacon slices, chopped
- 2 tablespoons olive oil
- ½ tablespoon apple cider vinegar
- 1 and ½ cups water, for the instant pot

Directions:
Put the water in your instant pot, add steamer basket, add broccoli, cover, cook on High for 3 minutes, drain and transfer to a bowl. Clean the pot, set on sauté mode, add bacon, stir and cook until it's crispy. Roughly chop broccoli, add to instant pot, stir and cook for 1 minute more. Add oil, cilantro and vinegar, toss well, divide into bowls and serve as an appetizer. Enjoy!

Nutrition: calories 200, fat 4, fiber 5, carbs 6, protein 4

Cheesy Broccoli Appetizer Salad

Preparation time: 10 minutes
Cooking time: 4 minutes
Servings: 4

Ingredients:
- 1 broccoli head, florets separated
- 4 ounces cheddar cheese, cubed
- 1/8 cup pumpkin seeds
- 1 cup mayonnaise
- 2 tablespoons balsamic vinegar
- 1 and ½ cups water, for the instant pot

Directions:
Put the water in your instant pot, add steamer basket, add broccoli, cover, cook on High for 3 minutes, drain, chop and transfer to a bowl. Add cheese, pumpkin seeds, mayo and vinegar, toss well, divide on appetizer plates and serve. Enjoy!

Nutrition: calories 182, fat 4, fiber 5, carbs 7, protein 4

Easy Tortillas

Preparation time: 10 minutes
Cooking time: 14 minutes
Servings: 2

Ingredients:
- ½ yellow onion, finely chopped
- ½ tablespoon olive oil
- 1 garlic clove, minced
- ½ green bell pepper, sliced
- 1 and ½ cups canned pinto beans, drained
- 1 hot chili peppers, minced
- 2 tablespoon cilantro, chopped
- Salt to the taste
- ½ cup water
- ½ teaspoon cumin powder
- 4 whole wheat tortillas
- Salsa for serving
- 1 cup cheddar cheese, shredded
- Black olives, for serving

Directions:
Set your instant pot on Sauté mode, add the oil, heat it up, add onion and garlic, stir and cook for 4 minutes Add green pepper, pinto beans, chili peppers, salt, water, cumin and cilantro, stir, cover pot and cook on High for 10 minutes. Transfer mix to a bowl, mash everything, divide this on each tortilla, also divide cheese, salsa and olives, roll them up and serve as a snack. Enjoy!

Nutrition: calories 170, fat 3, fiber 8, carbs 10, protein 12

White Beans Dip

Preparation time: 10 minutes
Cooking time: 13 minutes
Servings: 2

Ingredients:
- ½ cup white beans, soaked overnight and drained
- 1 and ½ tablespoons lemon juice
- 1 garlic clove, minced
- 2 tablespoons olive oil
- 1 teaspoon cumin, ground
- 1 teaspoon chili powder
- A pinch of red pepper flakes
- Salt and black pepper to the taste
- 1 and ½ tablespoons cilantro, chopped

Directions:
Put beans in your instant pot, add water to cover and cook on High for 13 minutes. Drain beans, transfer them to your food processor, add garlic, lemon juice, oil, cumin, chili powder, pepper flakes, salt and pepper and pulse really well. Add cilantro, stir a bit, transfer to a bowl and serve as a snack. Enjoy!

Nutrition: calories 211, fat 4, fiber 5, carbs 12, protein 14

Brussels Sprouts and Broccoli Appetizer Salad

Preparation time: 10 minutes
Cooking time: 5 minutes
Servings: 6

Ingredients:
- 1 pound Brussels sprouts, halved
- 1 broccoli head, florets separated
- ½ cup walnut oil
- ¼ cup balsamic vinegar
- 2 teaspoons mustard
- 1 and ½ cups water, for the instant pot

Directions:
Put the water in your instant pot, add steamer basket, add broccoli and Brussels sprouts, cover, cook on High for 4 minutes, drain and transfer to a bowl. Clean the pot, set on sauté mode, add oil, heat it up, add broccoli and Brussels sprouts, stir and cook for 1 minute. Add vinegar, toss, cook for a couple of seconds more and transfer to a bowl. Add mustard, toss well, divide on appetizer plates and serve. Enjoy!

Nutrition: calories 200, fat 6, fiber 7, carbs 8, protein 5

Crunchy Brussels Sprouts Salad

Preparation time: 10 minutes
Cooking time: 6 minutes
Servings: 4

Ingredients:
- 1 tablespoon brown sugar
- 1 pound Brussels sprouts, halved
- ½ cup pecans, chopped
- 1 tablespoon olive oil
- 2 tablespoons apple cider vinegar
- 1 and ½ cups water, for the instant pot

Directions:
Put the water in your instant pot, add steamer basket, add Brussels sprouts, cover, cook on High for 4 minutes, drain and transfer to a bowl. Clean the pot, set on sauté mode, add oil, heat it up, add Brussels sprouts and vinegar, toss and cook for 1 minute. Add sugar and pecans, stir, cook for 30 seconds more, divide into appetizer plates and serve. Enjoy!

Nutrition: calories 186, fat 4, fiber 5, carbs 9, protein 3

Chicken Appetizer Salad

Preparation time: 1 hour
Cooking time: 5 minutes
Servings: 2

Ingredients:
- 1 chicken breast, skinless and boneless
- 3 cups water
- 2 garlic cloves, minced
- 1 tablespoon honey
- Salt and black pepper to the taste
- 1 tablespoon mustard
- 2 tablespoons olive oil
- 1 tablespoon balsamic vinegar
- Mixed salad greens
- A handful cherry tomatoes, halved

Directions:
In a bowl, mix 2 cups water with salt to the taste and chicken, toss a bit and keep in a cold place for 1 hour. Add the rest of the water to your instant pot, add the steamer basket, drain chicken and add to the pot, cover, cook on High for 5 minutes. Transfer to a cutting board, cool down, cut into thin strips, add to a bowl and mix with tomatoes and salad greens. In a bowl, mix garlic with salt, pepper, mustard, honey, vinegar and olive oil and whisk well. Drizzle this vinaigrette over chicken salad, toss, divide between appetizer plates and serve. Enjoy!

Nutrition: calories 173, fat 2, fiber 4, carbs 10, protein 6

Octopus Appetizer

Preparation time: 10 minutes
Cooking time: 35 minutes
Servings: 2

Ingredients:
- 1 pound octopus, cleaned, head removed and tentacles separated
- 1/2 pound potatoes
- 1 garlic clove, minced
- A pinch of peppercorns
- 1 bay leaf
- 1 tablespoon parsley, chopped
- 2 tablespoons vinegar
- Salt and black pepper salad
- 1 tablespoon olive oil

Directions:
Put potatoes in your instant pot, add water to cover, cook at High for 15 minutes, transfer them to a cutting board, cool them down, peel, chop and leave them aside in a bowl for now. Put octopus in your instant pot, add water to cover, bay leaf, peppercorns, salt and pepper, stir, cover, cook on High for 20 minutes, drain, chop and add to the bowl with the potatoes. In a bowl, mix olive oil with vinegar, garlic, salt and pepper, whisk well, drizzle over salad, toss, divide it on appetizer plates and serve with parsley sprinkled on top. Enjoy!

Nutrition: calories 261, fat 5, fiber 2, carbs 8, protein 12

Brussels Sprouts and Apples Appetizer

Preparation time: 10 minutes
Cooking time: 6 minutes
Servings: 4

Ingredients:
- 1 green apple, cored and roughly chopped
- 1 pound Brussels sprouts, halved
- 1 cup cranberries, dried
- 2 tablespoons lemon juice
- 2 tablespoons canola oil
- 1 and ½ cups water, for the instant pot

Directions:
Put the water in your instant pot, add steamer basket, add Brussels sprouts, cover, cook on High for 4 minutes, drain and transfer to a bowl. Clean the pot, set it on sauté mode, add oil, heat it up, add Brussels sprouts, stir and cook for 1 minute. Add apple, cranberries and lemon juice, toss, cook for 1 minutes, divide into appetizer plates and serve. Enjoy!

Nutrition: calories 163, fat 3, fiber 4, carbs 6, protein 3

Sweet Brussels Sprouts Appetizer

Preparation time: 10 minutes
Cooking time: 6 minutes
Servings: 4

Ingredients:
- 2 pounds Brussels sprouts, halved
- ¼ cup orange juice
- 1 teaspoon orange zest, grated
- 1 tablespoon butter
- 2 tablespoons maple syrup

Directions:
Set your instant pot on sauté mode, add butter, melt it, add orange juice, orange zest and maple syrup, stir and cook for 1-2 minutes. Add Brussels sprouts, toss, cover and cook on High for 4 minutes. Divide into appetizer plates and serve. Enjoy!

Nutrition: calories 90, fat 2, fiber 3, carbs 12, protein 3

Orange and Beet Appetizer

Preparation time: 10 minutes
Cooking time: 10 minutes
Servings: 2

Ingredients:
- 1 pound beets, halved
- 1 teaspoon orange zest, grated
- 1 orange peel strip
- 1 tablespoons cider vinegar
- 3 tablespoons orange juice
- 1 tablespoon brown sugar
- 1 scallion, chopped
- 1 teaspoon Dijon mustard
- 1 cup arugula

Directions:
In your instant pot, mix orange peel strips with vinegar, orange juice and beets, cover, cook them on High for 7 minutes, transfer to a cutting board, cool them down, peel, chop and put them into a bowl. Discard peel strip from the pot, add mustard and sugar whisk well. Add scallion and orange zest to beets and toss them. Add liquid from the pot and arugula over beets, toss to coat, divide everything on appetizer plates and serve. Enjoy!

Nutrition: calories 173, fat 2, fiber 4, carbs 7, protein 5

Hulled Barley Appetizer

Preparation time: 10 minutes
Cooking time: 20 minutes
Servings: 2

Ingredients:
- ½ cup hulled barley
- 1 cup water
- ½ cup spinach pesto
- 1 green apple, peeled, cored and chopped
- 2 tablespoons celery, chopped
- Salt and white pepper to the taste

Directions:
Put barley, water, salt and pepper in your instant pot, stir, cover, cook at High for 20 minutes, strain and transfer to a bowl, Add celery, apple, spinach pesto, salt and pepper, toss to coat, divide between appetizer plates and serve. Enjoy!

Nutrition: calories 162, fat 1, fiber 3, carbs 6, protein 8

Appetizer Egg Spread

Preparation time: 10 minutes
Cooking time: 5 minutes
Servings: 4

Ingredients:
- 12 eggs
- ½ cup mayonnaise
- Salt to the taste
- A drizzle of olive oil
- 2 green onions, chopped
- 1 cup water, for the instant pot

Directions:
Grease a baking dish with a drizzle of oil and crack eggs in it. Add the water to your instant pot, add trivet inside, add baking dish, cover and cook on High for 5 minutes. Cool eggs down, mash using a potato masher, mix with mayo, green onions and salt and whisk well. Divide into small bowls and serve as an appetizer. Enjoy!

Nutrition: calories 222, fat 3, fiber 7, carbs 10, protein 4

Potatoes and Shrimp Appetizer Salad

Preparation time: 10 minutes
Cooking time: 13 minutes
Servings: 4

Ingredients:
- 2 cups water, for the instant pot
- 2 pounds shrimp, peeled and deveined
- 8 potatoes, cut into quarters
- 4 tablespoons olive oil
- Juice of 1 lemon
- 1 tablespoon watercress

Directions:
Add the water to the pot, add steamer basket, add potatoes inside, cover, cook on High for 10 minutes, transfer them to a bowl and clean the pot. Set the pot in Sauté mode, add oil, heat it up, add shrimp, lemon juice and return potatoes as well, stir, cover and cook on High for 3 minutes. Divide watercress into appetizer bowls, top with shrimp and potato mix, drizzle some of the lemony cooking juice all over and serve as an appetizer. Enjoy!

Nutrition: calories 167, fat 4, fiber 4, carbs 7, protein 20

Wheat Berries Appetizer

Preparation time: 10 minutes
Cooking time: 35 minutes
Servings: 2

Ingredients:
- 1 cup wheat berries
- 1 and ½ tablespoons olive oil
- Salt and black pepper to the taste
- 2 cups water
- ½ tablespoon balsamic vinegar
- ½ cup cherry tomatoes, halved
- 1 green onion, chopped
- 1 ounce feta cheese, crumbled
- 3 tablespoons kalamata olives, pitted and sliced
- 1 tablespoon basil leaves, chopped
- 1 tablespoon parsley leaves, chopped

Directions:
Set your instant pot on Sauté mode, add ½ tablespoon oil, heat it up, add wheat berries, stir, cook for 5 minutes, add water, salt and pepper, cover pot and cook on High for 30 minutes. Drain wheat berries, transfer to a bowl and mix with the rest of the oil, balsamic vinegar, tomatoes, green onion, olives, cheese, basil and parsley. Toss to coat, divide between appetizer plates and serve. Enjoy!

Nutrition: calories 200, fat 4, fiber 5, carbs 8, protein 6

Veggies and Wheat Appetizer Salad

Preparation time: 10 minutes
Cooking time: 15 minutes
Servings: 2

Ingredients:
- 4 tablespoons whole wheat, cracked
- 1 cup water
- 1 tomato, chopped
- 1 potato, cubed
- 3 cauliflower florets, chopped
- A pinch of salt and black pepper
- ¼ teaspoon mustard seeds
- ¼ teaspoon cumin seeds
- ½ teaspoon ginger, grated
- ½ tablespoon chana dal
- 1 garlic clove, minced
- ½ yellow onion, chopped
- 1 curry leaf
- 1 and ½ teaspoon olive oil
- A pinch of garam masala
- 2 teaspoons cilantro, chopped

Directions:
Set your instant pot on Sauté mode, add the oil, heat it up, add cumin, mustard seeds, onion, garlic, chana dal, ginger, garam masala and curry leaf, stir and cook for 3 minutes. Add cauliflower, potatoes and tomatoes, stir and cook for 4 minutes. Add wheat, salt, pepper and water, stir, cover, cook on High for 5 minutes, divide into small bowls, sprinkle cilantro and serve as an appetizer. Enjoy!

Nutrition: calories 173, fat 3, fiber 4, carbs 10, protein 7

Stuffed Bell Peppers Appetizer

Preparation time: 10 minutes
Cooking time: 12 minutes
Servings: 4

Ingredients:
- 4 mixed colored bell peppers, blanched, tops and seeds removed
- 16 ounces beef, ground
- 2 eggs
- 2 yellow onions, chopped
- 20 ounces canned tomato soup

Directions:
In a bowl, mix beef with eggs and onions and stir very well. Stuff bell peppers with this mix and place them in your instant pot. Add tomato soup, cover pot, cook on High for 12 minutes, arrange them on a platter and serve as a delicious appetizer. Enjoy!

Nutrition: calories 185, fat 10, fiber 4, carbs 14, protein 8

Brussels Sprouts and Potatoes Appetizer Salad

Preparation time: 10 minutes
Cooking time: 5 minutes
Servings: 4

Ingredients:
- 1 and ½ pounds Brussels sprouts, washed and trimmed
- 1 cup new potatoes, chopped
- 1 and ½ tablespoons breadcrumbs
- ½ cup chicken stock
- 1 and ½ tablespoons butter

Directions:
Put sprouts and potatoes in your instant pot, add stock, cover and cook on High for 5 minutes. Set the pot in Sauté mode, add butter and breadcrumbs, toss to coat well, divide between plates and serve as an appetizer. Enjoy!

Nutrition: calories 121, fat 3, fiber 6, carbs 16, protein 2

Fresh Bulgur Appetizer

Preparation time: 15 minutes
Cooking time: 12 minutes
Servings: 2

Ingredients:
- Zest from ½ orange, grated
- Juice from 1 orange
- 1 garlic clove, minced
- 1 teaspoons olive oil
- 1 tablespoon ginger, grated
- ½ cup bulgur, rinsed
- ½ tablespoon soy sauce
- 2 tablespoons scallions, chopped
- 2 tablespoons almonds, chopped
- Salt to the taste
- 1 teaspoon brown sugar
- 4 tablespoons water

Directions:
Set your instant pot on Sauté mode, add oil, heat it up, add ginger, garlic, sugar, bulgur, water and orange juice, stir and cook for 1 minutes. Cover pot, cook on High for 5 minutes, transfer to a bowl and leave aside to cool down a bit. Heat up a pan over medium heat, add almonds, stir and toast them for 3 minutes. Add orange zest, salt, soy sauce, scallions and bulgur, stir, cook for 1 minute more, divide into 2 bowls and serve as an appetizer. Enjoy!

Nutrition: calories 128, fat 4, fiber 4, carbs 8, protein 8

Summer Lentils Appetizer

Preparation time: 10 minutes
Cooking time: 8 minutes
Servings: 2

Ingredients:
- 1 cup chicken stock
- ½ cup lentils
- 1 bay leaf
- ¼ teaspoon thyme, dried
- 2 tablespoons red onion, chopped
- 3 tablespoons celery, chopped
- 2 tablespoons red bell pepper, chopped
- 1 tablespoon olive oil
- ½ tablespoon garlic, minced
- ¼ teaspoon oregano, dried
- Juice of ½ lemon
- 1 tablespoon parsley, chopped
- Salt and black pepper to the taste

Directions:
Put lentils in your instant pot, add bay leaf, thyme and stock, cover, cook on High for 8 minutes, drain and transfer lentils to a bowl. Add celery, onion, bell pepper, garlic, parsley, oregano, lemon juice, olive oil, salt and pepper, toss to coat, divide between 2 appetizer plates and serve. Enjoy!

Nutrition: calories 187, fat 3, fiber 4, carbs 7, protein 10

Veggie Dumplings

Preparation time: 10 minutes
Cooking time: 15 minutes
Servings: 6

Ingredients:
- 12 dumpling wrappers
- 1 tablespoon olive oil
- 1 cup shiitake mushrooms, sliced
- ½ cup carrot, chopped
- 2 tablespoons soy sauce
- 1 and ½ cups water, for the instant pot

Directions:
Set your instant pot on sauté mode, add olive oil, heat it up, add mushrooms, stir and cook them for 2 minutes. Add carrots and soy sauce, stir and cook for 2 minutes more. Place wrappers on a working surface, divide mushroom mix on each and seal dumplings using your wet hands. Add the water to your instant pot, add steamer basket, add dumplings inside, cover and cook on Low for 7 minutes. Arrange dumplings on a platter and serve them as an appetizer. Enjoy!

Nutrition: calories 300, fat 4, fiber 7, carbs 18, protein 6

Tomatoes and Garlic Dip

Preparation time: 10 minutes
Cooking time: 15 minutes
Servings: 6

Ingredients:
- ½ cup water
- 32 ounces canned tomatoes, roughly chopped
- A pinch of salt
- 4 garlic cloves, minced
- ¼ teaspoon red pepper flakes, crushed

Directions:
In your instant pot, mix water with tomatoes, salt, pepper flakes and garlic, stir, cover and cook on High for 15 minutes. Divide dip into small bowls and serve as a party dip. Enjoy!

Nutrition: calories 110, fat 1, fiber 1, carbs 4, protein 2

Pork Burritos

Preparation time: 15 minutes
Cooking time: 15 minutes
Servings: 2

Ingredients:
- 4 ounces pork meat, ground
- Salt and black pepper
- ½ teaspoon thyme, dried
- ½ teaspoon sage, dried
- ½ teaspoon fennel seeds
- ½ teaspoon brown sugar
- A pinch of nutmeg, ground
- A pinch of red pepper flakes, crushed
- 1 cup water + ½ tablespoon
- 4 tortilla shells
- 4 eggs
- 2 teaspoons olive oil
- 2 tablespoons milk
- Cheddar cheese, shredded
- Salsa for serving

Directions:
In a bowl, mix pork with salt, pepper, thyme, sage, fennel, pepper flakes, nutmeg, sugar and ½ tablespoon water and stir well. Brush tortilla shells with the olive oil, arrange them on a baking sheet, cover them with tin foil and seal edges. In a heat proof dish, mix eggs with salt, pepper, milk and meat, stir and cover with some tin foil Add 1 cup water to your instant pot, add the steamer basket, place heatproof dish inside, add wrapped tortilla shells on top, cover and cook on High for 15 minutes. Unwrap tortilla shells, stuff them with meat mix, top with salsa and cheddar cheese, arrange on a platter and serve as an appetizer. Enjoy!

Nutrition: calories 264, fat 5, fiber 8, carbs 12, protein 8

Beef Sandwiches

Preparation time: 10 minutes
Cooking time: 40 minutes
Servings: 2

Ingredients:
- ½ tablespoon brown sugar
- 1 pound beef roast, cut into small chunks
- Salt and black pepper to the taste
- ½ teaspoon smoked paprika
- 1 teaspoon garlic powder
- ½ teaspoons mustard powder
- ½ teaspoons onion flakes
- 1 cup beef stock
- 2 teaspoons balsamic vinegar
- ½ tablespoon Worcestershire sauce
- 1 tablespoon butter, melted
- 2 hoagie rolls
- 2 cheddar cheese slices

Directions:
Put the meat in your instant pot, add salt, pepper, paprika, garlic powder, mustard powder, onion flakes, stock, vinegar and Worcestershire sauce, stir well, cover the pot and cook at High for 40 minutes. Transfer meat to a cutting board, shred it using 2 forks and divide between the 2 rolls after you've greased them with the butter. Divide cheese on top of the meat, introduce sandwiches in preheated broiler, broil them for a couple of minutes and serve them as a snack with some of the cooking liquid from the instant pot on the side. Enjoy!

Nutrition: calories 284, fat 6, fiber 2, carbs 8, protein 20

Cashew Spread

Preparation time: 10 minutes
Cooking time: 6 minutes
Servings: 8

Ingredients:
- ½ cup water
- ½ cup cashews, soaked overnight and drained
- 10 ounces chickpeas hummus
- ¼ cup nutritional yeast
- ¼ teaspoon garlic powder

Directions:
In your instant pot, mix cashews and water, stir, cover and cook on High for 6 minutes. Transfer to your blender, add hummus, yeast and garlic powder, pulse really well, divide into bowls and serve as an appetizer spread. Enjoy!

Nutrition: calories 180, fat 2, fiber 2, carbs 4, protein 5

Mushroom Appetizer Salad

Preparation time: 10 minutes
Cooking time: 13 minutes
Servings: 4

Ingredients:
- 7 garlic cloves, minced
- 1 teaspoon olive oil
- 1 cup veggie stock
- 8 ounces mushrooms, halved
- 2 chipotle chilies in adobo sauce

Directions:
Set your instant pot on sauté mode, add oil, heat it up, garlic, stir and cook for 5 minutes. Add chipotle chili peppers, stock and mushroom halves, toss, cover and cook on High for 8 minutes. Divide mushroom salad into small bowls and serve as an appetizer. Enjoy!

Nutrition: calories 201, fat 5, fiber 8, carbs 13, protein 5

Turnips Spread

Preparation time: 10 minutes
Cooking time: 5 minutes
Servings: 2

Ingredients:
- 2 turnips, peeled and chopped
- Salt and black pepper
- ½ yellow onion, chopped
- 2 tablespoons sour cream
- 1/3 cup chicken stock

Directions:
In your instant pot, mix turnips with stock and onion, stir, cover, cook on High for 5 minutes, drain and transfer turnips to your blender. Add sour cream, salt and pepper, pulse really well and serve as a party spread. Enjoy!

Nutrition: calories 100, fat 3, fiber 2, carbs 6, protein 2

Calamari Salad

Preparation time: 10 minutes
Cooking time: 32 minutes
Servings: 2

Ingredients:
- 1 pound calamari, tentacles separated and cut into strips
- Salt and black pepper
- 7 ounces canned tomatoes, chopped
- ½ bunch parsley, chopped
- 1 garlic clove, minced
- 3 tablespoons white wine
- ½ cup water
- 1 anchovy
- 1 tablespoon olive oil
- Juice of ½ lemon
- A pinch of red pepper flakes

Directions:
Set your instant pot on Sauté mode, add oil, pepper flakes, garlic, anchovies and calamari, stir and cook for 9 minutes. Add wine, tomatoes, water, half of the parsley, salt and pepper, stir, cover and cook on High for 25 minutes. Add the rest of the parsley, the lemon juice, salt and pepper, stir, divide into bowls and serve as an appetizer. Enjoy!

Nutrition: calories 200, fat 4, fiber 2, carbs 7, protein 12

Lemony Endives Appetizer

Preparation time: 10 minutes
Cooking time: 13 minutes
Servings: 4

Ingredients:
- 8 endives, trimmed
- 3 tablespoons olive oil
- Juice of ½ lemon
- ½ cup chicken stock
- 2 tablespoons parsley, chopped

Directions:
Set your instant pot on sauté mode, add oil, heat it up, add endives and cook them for 3 minutes. Add lemon juice and stock, stir, cover and cook on High for 10 minutes. Arrange endives on a platter, drizzle some of the cooking juices all over, sprinkle parsley and serve as an appetizer. Enjoy!

Nutrition: calories 120, fat 2, fiber 7, carbs 12, protein 4

Easy Endives Platter

Preparation time: 10 minutes
Cooking time: 7 minutes
Servings: 4

Ingredients:
- 4 endives, trimmed and halved
- Salt to the taste
- A pinch of chili powder
- 1 tablespoon lemon juice
- 1 tablespoon butter

Directions:
Set your instant pot on Sauté mode, add butter, melt it, add endives, salt, chili powder and lemon juice, cover and cook on High for 7 minutes. Arrange endives on a platter, drizzle cooking juice over them and serve as an appetizer. Enjoy!

Nutrition: calories 90, fat 4, fiber 7, carbs 12, protein 3

Cauliflower Salad

Preparation time: 10 minutes
Cooking time: 6 minutes
Servings: 2

Ingredients:
- ½ cauliflower head, florets separated
- ½ pound broccoli head, florets separated
- ½ romanesco cauliflower head, florets separated
- 1 orange, peeled and sliced
- Zest from ½ orange, grated
- Juice from ½ orange
- A pinch of hot pepper flakes
- 2 anchovies
- ½ cup water
- ½ tablespoon capers, chopped
- Salt and black pepper to the taste
- 2 tablespoons olive oil

Directions:
In a bowl, mix orange zest with orange juice, pepper flakes, anchovies, capers salt, pepper and olive oil and whisk well. Add the water to your instant pot, add the steamer basket, add cauliflower and broccoli inside, cover and cook on Low for 6 minutes. Transfer cauliflower and broccoli to a bowl, add orange slices and the vinaigrette you've made earlier, toss to coat, divide between 2 appetizer plates and serve. Enjoy!

Nutrition: calories 200, fat 3, fiber 4, carbs 7, protein 4

Chicken Sandwiches

Preparation time: 10 minutes
Cooking time: 15 minutes
Servings: 2

Ingredients:
- 2 chicken breasts, skinless and boneless
- 3 ounces canned orange juice
- 1 tablespoons lemon juice
- 4 ounces canned peaches and their juice
- ½ teaspoon soy sauce
- 7 ounces canned pineapple, chopped
- 2 teaspoons cornstarch
- 1 tablespoon brown sugar
- 2 hamburger buns
- 2 pineapple slices, grilled

Directions:
In a bowl, mix orange juice with soy sauce, lemon juice, canned pineapples pieces, peaches and sugar, stir well, pour half of this mix into your instant pot, add chicken, then pour the rest of the orange mix, cover and cook on High for 20 minutes Transfer chicken to a cutting board, cool it down, shred and transfer to a bowl. In a bowl, mix cornstarch with 1 tablespoon cooking juice, pour into the pot, return chicken meat as well, set the pot on sauté mode and cook for a couple of minutes. Divide this chicken mix on hamburger buns, top with grilled pineapple pieces and serve as a snack. Enjoy!

Nutrition: calories 200, fat 4, fiber 4, carbs 7, protein 10

Creamy Endives Appetizer Salad

Preparation time: 10 minutes
Cooking time: 18 minutes
Servings: 3

Ingredients:
- 3 big endives, roughly chopped
- ½ yellow onion, chopped
- 2 tablespoons extra virgin olive oil
- 1 cup veggie stock
- 3 tablespoons heavy cream

Directions:
Set your instant pot on Sauté mode, add oil, heat it up, add onion, stir and cook for 4 minutes. Add endives, stir and cook for 4 minutes more. Add stock, stir, cover and cook on High for 10 minutes. Add heavy cream, stir, cook for 1 minute, divide into appetizer bowls and serve. Enjoy!

Nutrition: calories 253, fat 4, fiber 7, carbs 12, protein 15

Zucchini Spread

Preparation time: 10 minutes
Cooking time: 9 minutes
Servings: 6

Ingredients:
- 1 and ½ pounds zucchinis, chopped
- 1 tablespoon olive oil
- 2 garlic cloves, minced
- ½ cup water
- 1 bunch basil, chopped

Directions:
Set your instant pot on Sauté mode, add oil, heat it up, add garlic, stir and cook for 3 minutes. Add zucchini and water, stir, cover and cook on High for 3 minutes. Add basil, blend everything using an immersion blender, set the pot on simmer mode and cook everything for a couple of minutes more. Transfer to a bowl and serve as an appetizer. Enjoy!

Nutrition: calories 120, fat 2, fiber 4, carbs 7, protein 2

Lamb Ribs

Preparation time: 15 minutes
Cooking time: 26 minutes
Servings: 2

Ingredients:
- 4 lamb ribs
- 1 garlic clove, minced
- 1 carrot, chopped
- 6 ounces veggie stock
- 2 rosemary sprigs
- 1 tablespoon olive oil
- Salt and black pepper
- 1 tablespoon white flour

Directions:
Set your instant pot on Sauté mode, add the oil, heat it up, add lamb, garlic, salt and pepper and brown it on all sides. Add flour, stock, rosemary and carrots, stir, cover the pot, cook on High for 20 minutes, arrange ribs on a platter and serve with cooking juices on the side. Enjoy!

Nutrition: calories 213, fat 4, fiber 6, carbs 7, protein 20

Pork Cakes

Preparation time: 10 minutes
Cooking time: 10 minutes
Servings: 2

Ingredients:
- ½ pound ground pork meat
- ½ tablespoon parsley, chopped
- 1 egg
- ½ bread slice, soaked and squeezed
- 1 garlic clove, minced
- Salt and black pepper
- ½ cup beef stock
- A pinch of nutmeg, ground
- 1 and ½ tablespoon flour
- ¼ teaspoon Worcestershire sauce
- ¼ teaspoon sweet paprika
- 1 tablespoon olive oil
- 1 bay leaf
- 2 tablespoons white wine

Directions:
In a bowl, combine meat with bread, egg, salt, pepper, parsley, paprika, garlic and nutmeg and stir well. Add a splash of stock and Worcestershire sauce, stir, shape small cakes out of this mix and dredge them in flour Set your instant pot on Sauté mode, add oil, heat it up, add cakes and brown them on all sides. Add bay leaf, stock and wine, cover the pot and cook at High for 6 minutes. Discard bay leaf, arrange cakes on a platter and serve them as an appetizer. Enjoy!

Nutrition: calories 283, fat 4, fiber 7, carbs 10, protein 14

Instant Pot Dessert Recipes

Cranberries Dessert Bowl

Preparation time: 10 minutes
Cooking time: 30 minutes
Servings: 2

Ingredients:
For the sauce:
- 2 tablespoons orange juice
- 3 tablespoons sugar
- 1 cup cranberries
- A pinch of cinnamon powder

For the bowls:
- 1 cup milk
- 1 egg, whisked
- 2 tablespoons butter, melted
- 3 tablespoons sugar
- Zest from ½ orange, grated
- ½ teaspoon vanilla extract
- ½ bread loaf, cubed
- ½ cup water

Directions:
Set your instant pot on sauté mode, add cranberries, orange juice, a pinch of cinnamon and 3 tablespoons sugar, stir, cook for 5 minutes and transfer to a greased pan. In a bowl, mix butter with milk, 3 tablespoon sugar, egg, vanilla extract, bread cubes and orange zest, stir and pour into greased pan as well. Add the water to your instant pot, add the steamer basket, add pan inside, cover and cook on High for 25 minutes. Divide into dessert bowls and serve as a dessert. Enjoy!

Nutrition: calories 284, fat 4, fiber 5, carbs 10, protein 4

Banana Cake

Preparation time: 10 minutes
Cooking time: 55 minutes
Servings: 2

Ingredients:
- 1 cup water
- ½ cup sugar
- 1 cups flour
- 1 and ½ bananas, peeled and mashed
- 1 egg
- ½ stick butter
- ½ teaspoon baking powder
- ½ teaspoon cinnamon powder
- ½ teaspoon nutmeg, ground

Directions:
In a bowl, mix eggs with butter, sugar, baking powder, cinnamon, nutmeg, bananas and flour, stir and pour into a greased cake pan. Add the water to your instant pot, add the steamer basket, add cake pan inside, cover pot and cook on High for 55 minutes. Leave cake to cool down a bit before serving. Enjoy!

Nutrition: calories 293, fat 7, fiber 3, carbs 8, protein 6

Simple Pumpkin and Yogurt Cake

Preparation time: 10 minutes
Cooking time: 45 minutes
Servings: 12

Ingredients:
- 1 and ½ cups flour
- ½ teaspoon baking powder
- ¾ cup sugar
- ½ cup Greek yogurt
- 8 ounces canned pumpkin puree
- 1 and ½ cups water, for the instant pot

Directions:
In a bowl, mix flour with sugar, baking powder, yogurt and pumpkin puree, whisk well and pour into a greased cake pan. Add the water to your instant pot, add trivet inside, add cake pan, cover and cook on High for 45 minutes. Leave cake to cool down, slice and serve. Enjoy!

Nutrition: calories 201, fat 3, fiber 5, carbs 15, protein 4

Apple Bread

Preparation time: 10 minutes
Cooking time: 1 hour
Servings: 4

Ingredients:
- 1 cup water, for the instant pot
- 1 tablespoon baking powder
- 3 eggs
- 2 and ½ cups white flour
- 1 and ½ cups condensed milk, sweetened
- 3 apples, peeled, cored and chopped

Directions:
In a bowl, mix baking powder with eggs and whisk well. Add milk, flour and apple pieces, whisk well and pour into a greased loaf pan. Add the water to your instant pot, add trivet, add loaf pan inside, cover and cook on High for 1 hour. Leave apple bread to cool down, slice and serve. Enjoy!

Nutrition: calories 211, fat 2, fiber 7, carbs 14, protein 4

Apple Cobbler

Preparation time: 10 minutes
Cooking time: 15 minutes
Servings: 2

Ingredients:
- ½ plum, stone removed and chopped
- ½ pear, cored and chopped
- ½ apple, cored and chopped
- 1 tablespoon honey
- ¼ teaspoon cinnamon powder
- 1 cup water
- 1 and ½ tablespoons coconut oil
- 2 tablespoons pecans, chopped
- 2 tablespoons coconut, shredded
- 1 tablespoon sunflower seeds

Directions:
Put plum, pear and apple in a heatproof dish, add coconut oil, cinnamon and honey and toss. Add the water to your instant pot, add the steamer basket, add heat proof dish inside, cover, cook on High for 10 minutes and transfer fruits to a bowl. In the same baking dish, mix coconut with sunflower seeds and pecans, stir, return dish to your instant pot, cover again and cook on High for 2 minutes more, Sprinkle these over fruits, toss and serve as a dessert. Enjoy!

Nutrition: calories 163, fat 4, fiber 3, carbs 6, protein 7

Pumpkin Granola

Preparation time: 20 minutes
Cooking time: 15 minutes
Servings: 2

Ingredients:
- 1 and ½ cups water
- ½ tablespoon butter
- ½ cup pumpkin puree
- ½ cup steel cut oats
- 2 tablespoons maple syrup
- 1 teaspoon cinnamon powder
- ½ teaspoon pumpkin pie spice

Directions:
Set your instant pot on Sauté mode, add butter, melt it, add oats, stir and cook for 3 minutes. Add pumpkin puree, water, cinnamon, salt, maple syrup and pumpkin spice, stir, cover the pot and cook at High for 10 minutes. Divide into 2 bowls and serve as a dessert. Enjoy!

Nutrition: calories 173, fat 2, fiber 3, carbs 8, protein 12

Easy Sweet Soufflé

Preparation time: 10 minutes
Cooking time: 30 minutes
Servings: 6

Ingredients:
- 1 teaspoon vanilla extract
- ¼ cup sugar
- 8 ounces chocolate, chopped and melted
- 3 egg yolks, beaten
- ¼ teaspoon cream of tartar
- 1 cup water, for the instant pot

Directions:
In a bowl, mix melted chocolate with vanilla, sugar, egg yolks and cream of tartar, whisk really well and divide into greased ramekins. Add the water to your instant pot, add steamer basket, add ramekins, cover and cook on High for 30 minutes. Leave soufflé to cool down just a bit and serve. Enjoy!

Nutrition: calories 190, fat 2, fiber 3, carbs 7, protein 3

Tasty Blackberry Pie

Preparation time: 10 minutes
Cooking time: 35 minutes
Servings: 6

Ingredients:
- 1/3 cup tapioca pearls
- 1 cup sugar
- 4 cups blackberries
- 2 tablespoons butter, soft
- A pie crust
- 1 and ½ cups water, for the instant pot

Directions:
In a bowl, mix tapioca with sugar, blackberries and butter and whisk until sugar melts and pour into pie crust. Add the water to your instant pot, add steamer basket, add pie, cover and cook on High for 35 minutes. Leave pie to cool down, slice, divide between plates and serve. Enjoy!

Nutrition: calories 251, fat 3, fiber 7, carbs 7, protein 8

Rice Pudding

Preparation time: 5 minutes
Cooking time: 17 minutes
Servings: 2

Ingredients:
- ½ cup brown rice
- 3 tablespoons coconut chips
- ½ cup coconut milk
- 1 cup water
- 3 tablespoons maple syrup
- 2 tablespoons raisins
- 2 tablespoons almonds, chopped
- A pinch of cinnamon powder

Directions:
Put the rice in your instant pot, add the water, cover and cook on High for 12 minutes. Add milk, coconut chips, almonds, raisins, salt, cinnamon and maple syrup, stir well, cover the pot and cook at High for 5 minutes. Divide into 2 bowls and serve. Enjoy!

Nutrition: calories 200, fat 3, fiber 4, carbs 6, protein 8

Black Rice Pudding

Preparation time: 10 minutes
Cooking time: 35 minutes
Servings: 2

Ingredients:
- 3 cups water
- 3 tablespoons sugar
- 1 cup black rice
- 1 cinnamon stick
- 2 cardamom pods, crushed
- 1 clove
- 3 tablespoons coconut, grated
- 2 tablespoons mango, chopped

Directions:
Put the rice in your instant pot, add the water, cardamom, clove and cinnamon, cover and cook on Low for 25 minutes Discard cinnamon, clove and cardamom, add coconut, set the pot on sauté mode, cook rice for 10 minutes, divide between 2 plates, divide mango on top and serve. Enjoy!

Nutrition: calories 118, fat 2, fiber 2, carbs 5, protein 5

Millet Pudding

Preparation time: 10 minutes
Cooking time: 10 minutes
Servings: 2

Ingredients:
- 7 ounces milk
- 3 ounces water
- ½ cup millet
- 4 dates, pitted
- Honey for serving

Directions:
Put the millet in your instant pot, add dates, milk and water, stir, cover and cook on High for 10 minutes. Divide into 2 bowls, add honey on top and serve. Enjoy!

Nutrition: calories 200, fat 4, fiber 3, carbs 4, protein 7

Peanut Butter Cups

Preparation time: 10 minutes
Cooking time: 4 minutes
Servings: 12

Ingredients:
- 4 cups milk
- 8 ounces chocolate pudding mix
- 10 ounces cake, already prepared and cubed
- 12 ounces whipped cream
- 16 ounces mini peanut butter cups
- 1 and ½ cups water, for the instant pot

Directions:
In a bowl, mix chocolate pudding mix with milk and whipped cream and whisk. Divide cake cubes in small ramekins, add chocolate mixture and top with peanut butter cups. Add the water to your instant pot, add trivet inside, add ramekins, cover and cook on High for 4 minutes. Leave cups to cool down a bit and serve. Enjoy!

Nutrition: calories 177, fat 2, fiber 3, carbs 6, protein 7

Simple Cake Bars

Preparation time: 10 minutes
Cooking time: 20 minutes
Servings: 12

Ingredients:
- 1 and ½ cups water, for the instant pot
- 1 yellow cake mix
- ½ cup milk
- 1 egg, whisked
- 1 cup baking chips
- 1/3 cup canola oil

Directions:
In a bowl, mix cake mix with milk, eggs, oil and baking chips, stir well, pour into a baking pan and spread well. Add the water to your instant pot, add trivet, add baking pan inside, cover and cook on High for 20 minutes. Leave cake to cool down, cut into medium bars and serve. Enjoy!

Nutrition: calories 276, fat 6, fiber 6, carbs 8, protein 3

Sweet Chia Pudding

Preparation time: 10 minutes
Cooking time: 3 minutes
Servings: 2

Ingredients:
- 4 tablespoons chia seeds
- 1 cup almond milk
- 2 tablespoons almonds
- 2 tablespoons coconut, shredded
- 4 teaspoons sugar

Directions:
Put chia seeds in your instant pot. Add milk, almonds, sugar and coconut flakes, stir, cover and cook at High for 3 minutes. Divide pudding into bowls and serve. Enjoy!

Nutrition: calories 125, fat 3, fiber 4, carbs 6, protein 8

Lemon Marmalade

Preparation time: 10 minutes
Cooking time: 15 minutes
Servings: 2

Ingredients:
- ½ pounds lemons, washed and sliced
- 1 pound sugar
- ¼ tablespoon vinegar

Directions:
Put lemon in your instant pot, cover and cook on High for 10 minutes. Add sugar, cover the pot again and cook at High for 4 more minutes. Pour marmalade into 2 small jars and serve. Enjoy!

Nutrition: calories 73, fat 2, fiber 4, carbs 7, protein 7

White Chocolate Mousse

Preparation time: 10 minutes
Cooking time: 3 minutes
Servings: 6

Ingredients:
- 12 ounces white chocolate, chopped
- 2 cups heavy cream
- 1 tablespoon sugar
- 1 teaspoon vanilla extract
- 1 ounce black chocolate, chopped

Directions:
In your instant pot mix, white and black chocolate with cream, stir, cover and cook on High for 3 minutes. Add sugar and vanilla, stir until sugar melts, divide into bowls and serve cold. Enjoy!

Nutrition: calories 176, fat 4, fiber 4, carbs 12, protein 3

Easy Lemon Pie

Preparation time: 10 minutes
Cooking time: 10 minutes
Servings: 8

Ingredients:
- 1 graham cracker pie crust
- ½ cup sugar
- 8 ounces cream cheese
- 15 ounces canned lemon pie filling
- 8 ounces whipped topping
- 1 and ½ cups water, for the instant pot

Directions:
In a bowl, mix cream cheese with lemon pie filling and sugar, whisk well, spread into pie crust and top with whipped topping. Add the water to your instant pot, add trivet, add pie inside, cover and cook on High for 10 minutes. Leave pie aside to cool down, slice and serve. Enjoy!

Nutrition: calories 233, fat 4, fiber 4, carbs 6, protein 3

Pumpkin Cake

Preparation time: 10 minutes
Cooking time: 45 minutes
Servings: 2

Ingredients:
- ½ cup white flour
- ½ cup whole wheat flour
- ¼ teaspoon baking soda
- ¼ teaspoon pumpkin pie spice
- 3 tablespoons sugar
- 1 banana, mashed
- ¼ teaspoon baking powder
- ½ tablespoon canola oil
- 2 tablespoons Greek yogurt
- 2 ounces canned pumpkin puree
- Cooking spray
- 1-quart water
- 1 egg
- ¼ teaspoon vanilla extract
- 2 tablespoons chocolate chips

Directions:
In a bowl, mix white flour with whole-wheat flour, salt, baking soda and powder and pumpkin spice and stir. Add sugar, oil, banana, yogurt, pumpkin puree, vanilla and egg and stir using a mixer. Add chocolate chips, stir and transfer to a cake pan greased with cooking spray Add the water to your instant pot, add the steamer basket, add cake pan inside, cover and cook on High for 35 minutes. Leave cake to cool down, divide between 2 plates and serve. Enjoy!

Nutrition: calories 200, fat 4, fiber 4, carbs 7, protein 2

Apple Cake

Preparation time: 10 minutes
Cooking time: 1 hour
Servings: 2

Ingredients:
- 1 and ½ cups apples, cored and cubed
- ½ cup sugar
- ½ tablespoon vanilla extract
- 1 egg
- ½ tablespoon apple pie spice
- 1 cup flour
- ½ tablespoon baking powder
- ½ stick butter
- 1 cup water

Directions:
In a bowl mix egg with butter, apple pie spice, sugar, apples, baking powder and flour stir well and pour into a greased cake pan. Add the water to your instant pot, add the steamer basket, add cake pan inside, cover and cook on High for 1 hour. Leave cake pan to cool down a bit, divide between 2 plates and serve. Enjoy!

Nutrition: calories 93, fat 1, fiber 3, carbs 8, protein 6

Special Cookies

Preparation time: 10 minutes
Cooking time: 10 minutes
Servings: 20

Ingredients:
- 17 ounces chocolate cookie mix
- ¼ cup canola oil
- 1 egg
- 1 and ½ cups chocolate covered coffee beans, chopped
- 1 cup macadamia nuts, chopped
- 1 cup water, for the instant pot

Directions:
In a bowl, mix chocolate cookie mix with oil, egg, coffee beans and nuts, whisk well and divide into small cookies. Add the water to your instant pot, add steamer basket, add cookies inside, cover and cook on High for 10 minutes. Leave cookies to cool down and serve them. Enjoy!

Nutrition: calories 200, fat 3, fiber 4, carbs 6, protein 4

Delicious Berry Cobbler

Preparation time: 10 minutes
Cooking time: 35 minutes
Servings: 12

Ingredients:
- 40 ounces canned raspberry filling
- 1 package cake mix
- ½ cup canola oil
- 1 and ¼ cups milk
- Vanilla ice cream for serving
- 1 and ½ cups water, for the instant pot

Directions:
In a bowl, combine cake mix with milk and oil and whisk well. In a pie pan, spread raspberry filling and top and cake mix. Add the water to your instant pot, add steamer basket, add cake pan, cover and cook on High for 35 minutes. Leave cobbler to cool down, add vanilla ice cream on top and serve. Enjoy!

Nutrition: calories 227, fat 4, fiber 7, carbs 8, protein 3

Chocolate Cake

Preparation time: 10 minutes
Cooking time: 6 minutes
Servings: 2

Ingredients:
- 1 egg
- 4 tablespoons sugar
- 2 tablespoons olive oil
- 4 tablespoons milk
- 4 tablespoons flour
- A pinch of salt
- 1 tablespoon cocoa powder
- ½ teaspoon baking powder
- ½ teaspoon orange zest
- 1 cup water

Directions:
In a bowl, mix egg with sugar, oil, milk, flour, salt, cocoa powder, baking powder and orange zest, stir very well and pour into 2 greased ramekins. Add the water to your instant pot, add the steamer basket, add ramekins inside, cover and cook on High for 6 minutes. Serve warm. Enjoy!

Nutrition: calories 200, fat 2, fiber 1, carbs 7, protein 2

Easy Apples and Wine

Preparation time: 10 minutes
Cooking time: 10 minutes
Servings: 2

Ingredients:
- 2 apples, cored
- ½ cup red wine
- 2 tablespoons raisins
- ½ teaspoon cinnamon powder
- 3 tablespoons sugar

Directions:
Put the apples, wine, raisins, sugar and cinnamon in your instant pot, cover and cook on High for 10 minutes. Divide between 2 plates and serve as a dessert. Enjoy!

Nutrition: calories 172, fat 1, fiber 2, carbs 7, protein 1

Simple Ricotta Mousse

Preparation time: 10 minutes
Cooking time: 8 minutes
Servings: 4

Ingredients:
- ¼ cup pecans, chopped
- 2/3 cup maple syrup
- 1 and ¼ cups ricotta cheese
- ½ cup heavy cream
- ½ cup mascarpone cheese

Directions:
In your instant pot mix maple syrup with pecans and ricotta, stir, cover and cook on High for 3 minutes. Add heavy cream and mascarpone, stir, divide into bowls, leave aside to cool down and serve. Enjoy!

Nutrition: calories 182, fat 3, fiber 7, carbs 10, protein 4

Baked Custard

Preparation time: 10 minutes
Cooking time: 15 minutes
Servings: 6

Ingredients:
- 2 cups heavy cream, heated
- 3 eggs
- 2 egg yolks
- ¼ cup Irish cream liqueur, heated
- ¾ cup sugar
- 1 and ½ cups water

Directions:
In a bowl, mix egg yolks with eggs and sugar and whisk until sugar melts. Add cream and liqueur, whisk really well and divide into ramekins. Add the water to your instant pot, add steamer basket, add custard, cover and cook on High for 15 minutes. Leave custards to cool down and serve. Enjoy!

Nutrition: calories 191, fat 3, fiber 8, carbs 9, protein 4

Apricots and Cranberries Pudding

Preparation time: 10 minutes
Cooking time: 35 minutes
Servings: 2

Ingredients:
- 2 ounces dried cranberries, soaked in hot water, drained and chopped
- 1 teaspoon olive oil
- 2 cups water
- 2 ounces apricots, chopped
- ½ cup white flour
- 1 and ½ teaspoons baking powder
- ½ cup sugar
- ½ teaspoon ginger powder
- A pinch of cinnamon powder
- 2 eggs
- 7 tablespoons butter
- 1 small carrot, grated
- 1 and ½ tablespoons maple syrup

Directions:
In a blender, mix flour with baking powder, sugar, cinnamon, ginger, butter, maple syrup, eggs, carrot, cranberries and apricots, pulse well and spread this mix into a pudding mold greased with the oil. Add the water to your instant pot, add the steamer basket, add pudding mix inside, cover and cook on High for 35 minutes. Leave pudding aside to cool down, divide into 2 bowls and serve. Enjoy!

Nutrition: calories 214, fat 3, fiber 3, carbs 8, protein 2

Beans Cake

Preparation time: 10 minutes
Cooking time: 32 minutes
Servings: two

Ingredients:
- ½ cup borlotti beans, soaked and drained
- 2 cups water
- A pinch of almond extract
- 3 tablespoons cocoa powder
- 3 tablespoons sugar
- 1 and ½ tablespoon olive oil
- 1 egg
- 1 teaspoon baking powder
- 2 tablespoons almonds, chopped

Directions:
Put beans and water in your instant pot, cover, cook on High for 12 minutes, drain, reserve ½ cup cooking liquid, transfer to a blender and pulse well. Add cocoa powder, almond extract, baking powder, egg, sugar and oil and pulse again. Transfer mix to a greased heatproof dish and spread well. Add reserved water from cooking the beans to your instant pot, add the steamer basket, add cake mix, cover and cook on High for 20 minutes. Sprinkle almonds on top, divide cake between 2 plates and serve. Enjoy!

Nutrition: calories 172, fat 2, fiber 4, carbs 8, protein 3

Rhubarb and Strawberries Mix

Preparation time: 10 minutes
Cooking time: 6 minutes
Servings: 6

Ingredients:
- 3 cups rhubarb, sliced
- ¼ cup orange juice
- 1/3 cup sugar
- 1 cup whipping cream
- 2 cups strawberries, halved

Directions:
In your instant pot, mix rhubarb with sugar and orange juice, stir, cover and cook on High for 6 minutes. Pulse using an immersion blender, cool down a bit, add strawberries and whipping cream, divide into bowls and serve cold. Enjoy!

Nutrition: calories 222, fat 5, fiber 8, carbs 10, protein 3

Cherry Pie

Preparation time: 10 minutes
Cooking time: 30 minutes
Servings: 16

Ingredients:
- ½ cup butter
- 2o ounces canned cherries
- ½ cup walnuts, chopped
- 1 yellow cake mix
- 2 tablespoons blueberries
- 1 and ½ cups water, for the instant pot

Directions:
In a bowl, combine cake mix with butter, stir until your obtain a crumbly mixture and press it on the bottom of a pie pan. In a separate bowl, mix cherries with blueberries and walnuts, stir and spread over the crust. Add the water to your instant pot, add steamer basket, add pie inside, cover and cook on High for 30 minutes. Leave pie to cool down, slice, divide between plates and serve. Enjoy!

Nutrition: calories 261, fat 3, fiber 7, carbs 12, protein 3

Orange Cream

Preparation time: 1 hour
Cooking time: 15 minutes
Servings: 2

Ingredients:
- 1 cup fresh cream
- ½ teaspoon cinnamon powder
- 3 egg yolks
- 2 tablespoons sugar
- Zest from ½ orange, grated
- A pinch of nutmeg, ground
- 2 cups water

Directions:
Heat up a pan over medium high heat, add cream, cinnamon and orange zest, stir, bring to a boil, take off heat and leave aside for half an hour. In a bowl, mix egg yolks with white sugar, whisk well, add to orange cream, stir well, strain this into 2 ramekins and cover them with tin foil. Add the water to your instant pot, add the steamer basket, add ramekins inside, cover and cook on Low for 10 minutes. Sprinkle nutmeg on top and leave aside for another half an hour before serving. Enjoy!

Nutrition: calories 200, fat 2, fiber 4, carbs 8, protein 5

Pears with Garlic and Jelly

Preparation time: 10 minutes
Cooking time: 10 minutes
Servings: 2

Ingredients:
- 2 pears
- Juice of ½ lemon
- Zest from ½ lemon, grated
- 13 ounces grape juice
- 6 ounces currant jelly
- 1 garlic clove
- 1/3 vanilla bean
- 2 peppercorns
- 1 rosemary sprigs

Directions:
Add currant jelly, grape juice, lemon juice and lemon zest to your instant pot. Add pears, garlic, peppercorns, rosemary and vanilla bean, cover pot and cook on High for 10 minutes. Divide pears between plates and serve with the sauce from the pot. Enjoy!

Nutrition: calories 173, fat 4, fiber 2, carbs 8, protein 10

Stuffed Strawberries

Preparation time: 10 minutes
Cooking time: 2 minutes
Servings: 24

Ingredients:
- 24 big strawberries, stems removed and tops cut off
- ¼ teaspoon almond extract
- 11 ounces cream cheese, soft
- ½ cup sugar
- 1 tablespoon chocolate, grated
- 1 cup water, for the instant pot

Directions:
In a bowl, mix cream cheese with almond extract and sugar, stir until sugar melts and stuff strawberries with this mix. Add the water to your instant pot, add steamer basket, arrange strawberries inside, cover and cook on High for 2 minutes. Divide strawberries on dessert plates and serve them cold. Enjoy!

Nutrition: calories 200, fat 4, fiber 2, carbs 6, protein 3

Glazed Fruits

Preparation time: 10 minutes
Cooking time: 12 minutes
Servings: 6

Ingredients:
- ½ cup honey
- ½ cup balsamic vinegar
- 6 peaches, pitted and halved
- A pinch of salt
- Vanilla ice cream

Directions:
Set the instant pot on sauté mode, add honey and balsamic vinegar, stir and cook for 2 minutes. Add a pinch of salt and peaches, stir, cover and cook on Manual for 10 minutes. Divide into bowls, leave aside to cool down, add vanilla ice cream on top and serve. Enjoy!

Nutrition: calories 169, fat 2, fiber 3, carbs 7, protein 3

Classic Ricotta Cake

Preparation time: 30 minutes
Cooking time: 30 minutes
Servings: 2

Ingredients:
- ½ pound ricotta
- 3 oz. dates
- 1 ounce honey
- 2 eggs
- 1 ounce sugar
- 8 ounces water
- Zest from 1/3 orange, grated
- Juice from 1/3 orange

Directions:
In a bowl, whisk ricotta with eggs and whisk really well. Add honey, vanilla, dates, orange zest and juice, stir, pour into a heatproof cake pan, spread well and cover with tin foil. Add the water to your instant pot, add the steamer basket, add the cake pan, cover and cook on High for 20 minutes. Divide between 2 plates and serve. Enjoy!

Nutrition: calories 200, fat 4, fiber 3, carbs 8, protein 10

Spicy Tomato Jam

Preparation time: 10 minutes
Cooking time: 30 minutes
Servings: 2

Ingredients:
- ½ pounds tomatoes, chopped
- ½ tablespoons lime juice
- 2 tablespoons white sugar
- 2 teaspoons ginger, grated
- ¼ teaspoon cinnamon powder
- A pinch of cumin, ground
- A pinch of cloves, ground
- 1 jalapeno pepper, minced

Directions:
In your instant pot mix tomatoes with sugar, lime juice, ginger, cumin, cinnamon, cloves and jalapeno pepper, stir, cover and cook on High for 30 minutes, divide into 2 bowls and serve. Enjoy!

Nutrition: calories 182, fat 0, fiber 2, carbs 9, protein 1

Peach Jam

Preparation time: 10 minutes
Cooking time: 5 minutes
Servings: 2

Ingredients:
- 2 cups peaches, peeled, stones removed and cubed
- 2 cups sugar
- 2 tablespoons ginger, grated
- ¼ box fruit pectin

Directions:
In your instant pot, mix peaches, ginger, sugar and pectin, stir, set on sauté mode and bring to a simmer. Cover the pot, cook jam on High for 5 minutes, divide into 2 jars and serve. Enjoy!

Nutrition: calories 83, fat 3, fiber 2, carbs 4, protein 3

Lemon Cookies

Preparation time: 10 minutes
Cooking time: 15 minutes
Servings: 30

Ingredients:
- 1 egg, whisked
- 18 ounces lemon cake mix
- 1 cup crisp rice cereal
- ½ cup butter
- 1 teaspoon lemon peel, grated
- 1 cup water, for the instant pot

Directions:
In a bowl, mix the egg with cake mix, rice cereal, butter and lemon peel, whisk well, shape cookies out of this mix and arrange on a baking sheet. Add the water to your instant pot, add trivet, add baking sheet, cover and cook for 15 minutes. Leave cookies to cool down and serve them. Enjoy!

Nutrition: calories 221, fat 3, fiber 3, carbs 6, protein 3

Chocolate Cake

Preparation time: 10 minutes
Cooking time: 6 minutes
Servings: 3

Ingredients:
- 1 egg
- 4 tablespoons sugar
- 4 tablespoons milk
- 4 tablespoons self-raising flour
- 1 tablespoon cocoa powder
- 1 cup water, for the instant pot

Directions:
In a bowl, mix the egg with sugar, milk, flour and cocoa powder, stir very well and pour this into a greased cake pan. Add water to your instant pot, add steamer basket, add cake inside, cover and cook on High for 6 minutes. Serve your cake warm. Enjoy!

Nutrition: calories 261, fat 5, fiber 5, carbs 20, protein 4

Lime Pie

Preparation time: 10 minutes
Cooking time: 15 minutes
Servings: 2

Ingredients:
For the crust:
- ½ tablespoon sugar
- 1 and ½ tablespoons butter, melted
- 3 graham crackers, crumbled

For the filling:
- 2 egg yolks
- 6 ounces condensed milk
- 2 tablespoons key lime juice
- 3 tablespoons sour cream
- Cooking spray
- 1 cup water
- ½ tablespoons key lime zest, grated

Directions:
In a bowl, whisk egg yolks with milk, lime juice, sour cream and lime zest. In another bowl, mix butter with crackers and sugar, stir well and spread on the bottom of a pie pan greased with cooking spray. Add eggs cream and cover the pan with tin foil. Add the water to your instant pot, add the steamer basket, add pie pan inside, cover and cook on High for 15 minutes. Leave pie to cool down completely before dividing between 2 plates and serving. Enjoy!

Nutrition: calories 212, fat 3, fiber 3, carbs 7, protein 8

Peach Compote

Preparation time: 10 minutes
Cooking time: 3 minutes
Servings: 2

Ingredients:
- 3 peaches, stones removed and chopped
- 2 tablespoons sugar
- ¼ teaspoon cinnamon powder
- ¼ teaspoon vanilla extract
- ¼ vanilla bean, scraped
- ½ tablespoons grape nuts cereal

Directions:
Put peaches, sugar, cinnamon, vanilla bean and vanilla extract in your instant pot, cover and cook on High for 3 minutes. Add grape nuts, stir well, divide compote into 2 bowls and serve. Enjoy!

Nutrition: calories 100, fat 0, fiber 2, carbs 3, protein 1

Apples and Wine Sauce

Preparation time: 10 minutes
Cooking time: 10 minutes
Servings: 6

Ingredients:
- 6 apples, cored
- 1 cup red wine
- 1 teaspoon cinnamon powder
- ¼ cup raisins
- ½ cup sugar

Directions:
Put the apples in your instant pot, add wine, cinnamon, raisins and sugar, cover pot and cook on High for 10 minutes. Divide apples on dessert plates and serve warm. Enjoy!

Nutrition: calories 200, fat 3, fiber 7, carbs 34, protein 3

Cream and Cinnamon Puddings

Preparation time: 20 minutes
Cooking time: 15 minutes
Servings: 6

Ingredients:
- 2 cups fresh cream
- 1 teaspoon cinnamon powder
- 6 egg yolks
- 5 tablespoons sugar
- Zest of 1 orange
- 2 cups water, for the instant pot

Directions:
Set the pot on sauté mode, heat it up, add cream, cinnamon and orange zest, stir, cook for a few minutes and leave aside for 20 minutes. In a bowl, mix egg yolks with sugar, whisk well, add to cold cream, whisk well again, strain this mix, divide it into ramekins and cover them with tin foil. Clean the pot, add the water, add steamer basket, add ramekins, cover and cook on Low for 10 minutes. Serve puddings cold. Enjoy!

Nutrition: calories 211, fat 8, fiber 5, carbs 20, protein 10

Carrot Cake

Preparation time: 10 minutes
Cooking time: 30 minutes
Servings: 2

Ingredients:
- 2 ounces flour
- ¼ teaspoon baking powder
- ¼ teaspoon baking soda
- ¼ teaspoon cinnamon powder
- A pinch of nutmeg, ground
- A pinch of allspice
- 1 egg
- 2 cups water
- 1 tablespoon yogurt
- 2 tablespoons sugar
- 2 tablespoons pineapple juice
- 2 tablespoons coconut oil, melted
- 2 tablespoons carrots, grated
- 2 tablespoons pecans, toasted and chopped
- 2 tablespoons coconut flakes
- Cooking spray

Directions:
In a bowl, mix flour with baking soda and baking powder, allspice, cinnamon, nutmeg, egg, yogurt, sugar, pineapple juice, oil, carrots, pecans and coconut flakes, stir and pour into a cake pan greased with cooking spray. Add the water to your instant pot, add the steamer basket, add the cake pan, cover and cook on High for 32 minutes. Divide between 2 plates and serve. Enjoy!

Nutrition: calories 162, fat 2, fiber 3, carbs 7, protein 3

Cheesecake

Preparation time: 15 minutes
Cooking time: 1 hour
Servings: 2

Ingredients:
- 1 tablespoon butter, melted
- 3 tablespoons chocolate graham crackers, crumbled
- 2 tablespoons heavy cream
- 3 tablespoons sugar
- 6 ounces cream cheese, soft
- ½ teaspoon vanilla extract
- 2 tablespoons sour cream
- ½ tablespoon flour
- 1 egg yolk
- 1 eggs
- Cooking spray
- 1 cup water

For the topping:
- 6 caramels
- ½ coconut, shredded
- 2 tablespoons chocolate, chopped

Directions:
In a bowl, mix crackers with butter, stir, spread in the bottom of a pan greased with cooking spray and keep in the freezer for 10 minutes. In another bowl, mix cheese with sugar, heavy cream, vanilla, flour, sour cream, egg yolk and egg, whisk well, pour over crust, spread and cover with tin foil. Add the water to your instant pot, add the steamer basket, add the pan, cover and cook on High for 35 minutes. Meanwhile, spread coconut on a lined baking sheet, introduce in the oven at 300 degrees F and bake for 20 minutes. Put caramels in a heatproof bowl, introduce in the microwave for 2 minutes, mix them with toasted coconut and spread this on your cheesecake. Put chocolate in another heatproof bowl, introduce in your microwave for a few seconds until it melts and drizzle over your cake. Serve cake really cold. Enjoy!

Nutrition: calories 273, fat 3, fiber 1, carbs 10, protein 6

Poached Pears

Preparation time: 10 minutes
Cooking time: 10 minutes
Servings: 6

Ingredients:
- 6 green pears
- 2 teaspoons vanilla extract
- A pinch of cinnamon
- 7 oz. sugar
- 1 cup red wine

Directions:
In your instant pot, mix wine with sugar, vanilla, cinnamon and pears, cover pot and cook on High for 10 minutes. Leaves pears to cool, transfer them to bowls, drizzle wine sauce all over and serve. Enjoy!

Nutrition: calories 172, fat 5, fiber 7, carbs 20, protein 4

Flavored Pears

Preparation time: 10 minutes
Cooking time: 10 minutes
Servings: 4

Ingredients:
- 4 pears
- Juice and zest of 1 lemon
- 26 ounces grape juice
- 11 ounces currant jelly
- 2 rosemary springs

Directions:
Pour currant jelly and grape juice in your instant pot, add lemon zest and juice and stir. Add pears and rosemary springs, cover and cook on High for 10 minutes. Arrange pears on plates and serve them cold with the cooking juice on top. Enjoy!

Nutrition: calories 172, fat 4, fiber 7, carbs 17, protein 12

Chocolate Pudding

Preparation time: 10 minutes
Cooking time: 20 minutes
Servings: 2

Ingredients:
- 3 ounces chocolate, chopped
- 3 tablespoons milk
- 1 cup heavy cream
- 3 egg yolks
- 3 tablespoons brown sugar
- 1 teaspoon vanilla extract
- 1 and ½ cups water
- A pinch of cardamom, ground
- Crème fraiche for serving

Directions:
Put cream and milk in a pot, bring to a simmer over medium heat, take off heat, add chocolate and whisk. In a bowl, mix egg yolks with vanilla, sugar and cardamom, stir, strain, mix with chocolate, transfer to 2 small soufflé dishes and cover with tin foil. Put the water in your instant pot, add the steamer basket, add soufflé dishes, cover pot and cook on Low for 18 minutes. Leave chocolate pudding to cool down completely and serve with crème fraiche on top. Enjoy!

Nutrition: calories 212, fat 2, fiber 4, carbs 6, protein 8

Carrot Pudding and Rum Sauce

Preparation time: 10 minutes
Cooking time: 1 hour and 10 minutes
Servings: 2

Ingredients:
- 1 and ½ cups water
- Cooking spray
- 2 tablespoons brown sugar
- 1 egg
- 2 tablespoons molasses
- 2 tablespoon flour
- A pinch of allspice
- A pinch of cinnamon powder
- A pinch of nutmeg, ground
- ¼ teaspoon baking soda
- 1/3 cup shortening, grated
- 3 tablespoons pecans, chopped
- 3 tablespoons carrots, grated
- 3 tablespoons raisins
- ½ cup bread crumbs

For the sauce:
- 1 and ½ tablespoons butter
- 2 tablespoons brown sugar
- 2 tablespoons heavy cream
- ½ tablespoons rum
- A pinch of cinnamon powder

Directions:
In a bowl, mix molasses with eggs and 2 tablespoons sugar, flour, shortening, carrots, nuts, raisins, bread crumbs, salt, a pinch of cinnamon, allspice, nutmeg and baking soda, stir everything, pour into a pudding pan greased with cooking spray and cover with tin foil. Add the water to your instant pot, add the steamer basket, add pudding inside, cover and cook on High 1 hour. Meanwhile, heat up a pan with the butter for the sauce over medium heat, add 2 tablespoons sugar, stir and cook for 2 minutes. Add cream, rum and a pinch of cinnamon, stir and simmer for 2 minutes more. Divide pudding into 2 bowls, drizzle rum sauce all over and serve.

Nutrition: calories 261, fat 6, fiber 6, carbs 10, protein 8

Dates and Ricotta Cake

Preparation time: 30 minutes
Cooking time: 20 minutes
Servings: 6

Ingredients:
- 1 pound ricotta, softened
- 6 oz. dates, soaked for 15 minutes and drained
- 4 ounces honey softened
- Juice of 2 oranges
- 4 eggs
- 17 ounces water, for the instant pot

Directions:
In a bowl, mix soft ricotta with eggs and whisk well. Add honey, dates, and orange juice, whisk, pour into a cake pan and cover with tin foil. Add water to your instant pot, add steamer basket, add cake pan, cover and cook at High for 20 minutes. Allow cake to cool down, slice and serve. Enjoy!

Nutrition: calories 212, fat 7, fiber 1, carbs 20, protein 9

Lemon and Orange Jam

Preparation time: 10 minutes
Cooking time: 30 minutes
Servings: 8

Ingredients:
- Juice of 2 lemons
- 3 pounds sugar
- 1 pound oranges, halved, pulp separated and peel grated
- 1-pint water
- 1 teaspoon vanilla extract

Directions:
In your instant pot, mix lemon juice with orange juice, vanilla extract, water and peel, cover and cook on High for 15 minutes. Add sugar, set the pot on sauté mode, cook until sugar dissolves, divide into jars and serve cold. Enjoy!

Nutrition: calories 87, fat 1, fiber 0, carbs 13, protein 2

Lemon Pudding

Preparation time: 30 minutes
Cooking time: 10 minutes
Servings: 2

Ingredients:
- ½ cup milk
- Zest from ½ lemon, grated
- 3 egg yolks
- ½ cup fresh cream
- 1 cup water
- 3 tablespoons sugar
- Blackberry syrup for serving

Directions:
Heat up a pan over medium heat, add milk, lemon zest and cream, stir, bring to a boil, take off heat and leave aside for 30 minutes. In a bowl, mix egg yolks with sugar and cream mix, stir well, pour into your 2 greased ramekins and cover with tin foil. Add the water to your instant pot, add the steamer basket, add ramekins, cover and cook on High for 10 minutes. Serve with blackberry syrup on top. Enjoy!

Nutrition: calories 162, fat 2, fiber 2, carbs 8, protein 2

Sweet Corn Pudding

Preparation time: 10 minutes
Cooking time: 30 minutes
Servings: 2

Ingredients:
- 6 ounces canned creamed corn
- 2 cups water
- 1 cup milk
- 1 and ½ tablespoons sugar
- 1 egg, whisked
- 1 tablespoon flour
- ½ tablespoons butter
- Cooking spray

Directions:
Put the water in your instant pot, set on Simmer mode and bring to a boil. In a bowl, mix corn with eggs, milk, butter, salt, flour and sugar, stir well, pour into a heat proof dish greased with cooking spray and cover with tin foil Add the steamer basket into the pot, add the pan, cover and cook on High for 20 minutes. Divide into 2 bowls and serve cold. Enjoy!

Nutrition: calories 162, fat 3, fiber 2, carbs 8, protein 7

Ginger and Peach Marmalade

Preparation time: 10 minutes
Cooking time: 5 minutes
Servings: 6

Ingredients:
- 4 and ½ cups peaches, peeled and cubed
- 6 cups sugar
- 3 tablespoon ginger, grated
- ½ teaspoon vanilla extract
- 1 box fruit pectin

Directions:
Set your instant pot on sauté mode, add peaches, ginger, vanilla extract and pectin, stir, bring to a boil, add sugar, stir, cover and cook on High for 5 minutes. Divide jam into jars and serve. Enjoy!

Nutrition: calories 87, fat 4, fiber 3, carbs 9, protein 2

Winter Cherry Mix

Preparation time: 10 minutes
Cooking time: 5 minutes
Servings: 6

Ingredients:
- 16 ounces cherries, pitted
- 2 tablespoons water
- 2 tablespoons lemon juice
- Sugar to the taste
- 2 tablespoons cornstarch

Directions:
In your instant pot, mix cherries with sugar and lemon juice, stir, cover and cook on High for 3 minutes. In a bowl, mix water with cornstarch, stir well, add to the pot, set the pot on sauté mode, add the rest of the cherries, stir, cook for 2 minutes, divide into bowls and serve cold. Enjoy!

Nutrition: calories 161, fat 4, fiber 2, carbs 8, protein 6

Apricot Jam

Preparation time: 10 minutes
Cooking time: 14 minutes
Servings: 2

Ingredients:
- 1 pound apricots, stones removed and halved
- ½ pound white sugar
- 1 orange, peeled and sliced
- 1 teaspoon orange zest, grated
- ½ tablespoon butter
- ¼ teaspoon almond extract

Directions:
Put apricots in your food processor, pulse really well, transfer to your instant pot, add sugar, orange slices and orange zest, stir, set the pot on sauté mode and boil the jam for 6 minutes. Add butter and almond extract, cover, cook on High for 8 minutes, divide into 2 jars and serve cold Enjoy!

Nutrition: calories 180, fat 0, fiber 3, carbs 3, protein 8

Blueberry Jam

Preparation time: 10 minutes
Cooking time: 11 minutes
Servings: 2

Ingredients:
- ½ pound blueberries
- 1/3 pound sugar
- Zest from ½ lemon, grated
- ½ tablespoon butter
- A pinch of cinnamon powder

Directions:
Put the blueberries in your blender, pulse them well, strain, transfer to your instant pot, add sugar, lemon zest and cinnamon, stir, cover and simmer on sauté mode for 3 minutes. Add butter, stir, cover the pot and cook on High for 8 minutes. Transfer to a jar and serve. Enjoy!

Nutrition: calories 211, fat 3, fiber 3, carbs 6, protein 6

Peach and Cinnamon Compote

Preparation time: 10 minutes
Cooking time: 5 minutes
Servings: 6

Ingredients:
- 8 peaches, chopped
- 6 tablespoons sugar
- 1 teaspoon cinnamon, ground
- 1 teaspoon vanilla extract
- 2 tablespoons grape nuts cereal

Directions:
Put peaches in your instant pot, add sugar, cinnamon and vanilla extract, stir well, cover pot and cook on High for 5 minutes. Add grape nuts, stir, divide into bowls and serve cold Enjoy!

Nutrition: calories 121, fat 4, fiber 2, carbs 17, protein 4

Ginger Cookies Cheesecake

Preparation time: 15 minutes
Cooking time: 15 minutes
Servings: 6

Ingredients:
- 2 cups water, for the instant pot
- 2 teaspoons butter, melted
- ½ cup ginger cookies, crumbled
- 16 ounces cream cheese, soft
- 2 eggs
- ½ cup sugar

Directions:
Grease a cake pan with the butter, add cookie crumbs and spread them evenly. In a bowl, beat cream cheese with a mixer. Add eggs and sugar and stir very well. Add the water to your instant pot, add steamer basket, add cake pan inside, cover and cook on High for 15 minutes. Keep cheesecake in the fridge for a few hours before serving it. Enjoy!

Nutrition: calories 394, fat 12, fiber 3, carbs 20, protein 6

Bread Pudding

Preparation time: 10 minutes
Cooking time: 20 minutes
Servings: 4

Ingredients:
- 2 egg yolks
- 1 and ½ cups brioche cubed
- 1 cup half and half
- ¼ teaspoon vanilla extract
- ½ cup sugar
- 1 tablespoon butter, soft
- ½ cup cranberries
- 2 cups water
- 3 tablespoons raisins
- Zest from 1 lime, grated

Directions:
In a bowl mix, egg yolks with half and half, cubed brioche, vanilla extract, sugar, cranberries, raisins and lime zest, stir, pour into a baking dish greased with the butter and leave aside for 10 minutes. Add the water to your instant pot, add the steamer basket, add the dish, cover and cook on High for 20 minutes. Serve this cold. Enjoy!

Nutrition: calories 162, fat 6, fiber 7, carbs 9, protein 8

Cranberry Bread Pudding

Preparation time: 10 minutes
Cooking time: 15 minutes
Servings: 2

Ingredients:
- 2 egg yolks
- 1 and ½ cups bread, cubed
- 1 cup heavy cream
- Zest from ½ orange, grated
- Juice from ½ orange
- 2 teaspoons vanilla extract
- ½ cup sugar
- 2 cups water
- 1 tablespoon butter
- ½ cup cranberries

Directions:
In a bowl, mix egg yolks with bread, heavy cream, orange zest and juice, vanilla extract, sugar, butter and cranberries, stir and pour into a baking dish. Add the water to your instant pot, add the steamer basket, add baking dish, cover pot and cook on High for 15 minutes. Divide between 2 plates and serve cold. Enjoy!

Nutrition: calories 189, fat 3, fiber 1, carbs 4, protein 7

Strawberry and Chia Marmalade

Preparation time: 10 minutes
Cooking time: 4 minutes
Servings: 6

Ingredients:
- 2 tablespoons chia seeds
- 4 tablespoons sugar
- 2 pounds strawberries, halved
- ½ teaspoon vanilla extract
- Zest of 1 lemon, grated

Directions:
In your instant pot, mix sugar with strawberries, vanilla extract, lemon zest and chia seeds, stir, cover and cook on High for 4 minutes. Stir again, divide into cups and serve cold Enjoy!

Nutrition: calories 110, fat 2, fiber 2, carbs 2, protein 3

Lemon and Maple Syrup Pudding

Preparation time: 10 minutes
Cooking time: 5 minutes
Servings: 7

Ingredients:
- 3 cups milk
- Juice of 2 lemons
- Lemon zest from 2 lemons, grated
- ½ cup maple syrup
- 2 tablespoons gelatin
- 1 cup water, for the instant pot

Directions:
In your blender, mix milk with lemon juice, lemon zest, maple syrup and gelatin, pulse really well and divide into ramekins. Add the water to your instant pot, add steamer basket, add ramekins inside, cover and cook on High for 5 minutes. Serve puddings cold. Enjoy!

Nutrition: calories 151, fat 3, fiber 2, carbs 18, protein 3

Apples and Pears Salad

Preparation time: 10 minutes
Cooking time: 15 minutes
Servings: 2

Ingredients:
- 1 quart water
- 1 tablespoon sugar
- ½ pound mixed apples, pears and cranberries
- 3 star anise
- A pinch of cloves, ground
- 1 cinnamon sticks
- Zest from ½ orange, grated
- Zest from ½ lemon, grated

Directions:
Put the water, sugar, apples, pears, cranberries, star anise, cinnamon, orange and lemon zest and cloves in your instant pot, cover and cook on High for 15 minutes. Discard cinnamon stick. Divide salad into 2 bowls and serve cold. Enjoy!

Nutrition: calories 83, fat 0, fiber 0, carbs 0, protein 2

Apples and Red Grape Juice

Preparation time: 10 minutes
Cooking time: 10 minutes
Servings: 2

Ingredients:
- 2 apples
- ½ cup natural red grape juice
- 2 tablespoons raisins
- 1 teaspoon cinnamon powder
- ½ tablespoons sugar

Directions:
Put the apples in your instant pot, add grape juice, raisins, cinnamon and stevia, toss a bit, cover and cook on High for 10 minutes. Divide into 2 bowls and serve. Enjoy!

Nutrition: calories 110, fat 1, fiber 1, carbs 3, protein 4

Simple Banana Cake

Preparation time: 10 minutes
Cooking time: 1 hour
Servings: 4

Ingredients:
- 1 cup water, for the instant pot
- 1 and ½ cups sugar
- 2 cups flour
- 4 bananas, peeled and mashed
- 1 teaspoon cinnamon powder
- 1 teaspoon nutmeg powder

Directions:
In a bowl, mix sugar with flour, bananas, cinnamon and nutmeg, stir, pour into a greased cake pan and cover with tin foil. Add the water to your instant pot, add steamer basket, add cake pan, cover and cook on High for 1 hour. Slice, divide between plates and serve cold. Enjoy!

Nutrition: calories 300, fat 10, fiber 4, carbs 45, protein 4

Pineapple Pudding

Preparation time: 10 minutes
Cooking time: 5 minutes
Servings: 8

Ingredients:
- 1 tablespoon avocado oil
- 1 cup rice
- 14 ounces milk
- Sugar to the taste
- 8 ounces canned pineapple, chopped

Directions:
In your instant pot, mix oil, milk and rice, stir, cover and cook on High for 3 minutes. Add sugar and pineapple, stir, cover and cook on High for 2 minutes more. Divide into dessert bowls and serve. Enjoy!

Nutrition: calories 154, fat 4, fiber 1, carbs 14, protein 4

Strawberry Shortcakes

Preparation time: 20 minutes
Cooking time: 25 minutes
Servings: 2

Ingredients:
- Cooking spray
- 3 tablespoons sugar
- 1 cup white flour
- 1 cup water
- ½ teaspoon baking powder
- ¼ teaspoon baking soda
- 3 tablespoons butter
- ½ cup buttermilk
- 1 egg, whisked
- 1 and ½ tablespoons sugar
- 1 cups strawberries, sliced
- ½ tablespoon rum
- ½ tablespoon mint, chopped
- ½ teaspoon lime zest, grated

Directions:
In a bowl, mix flour with 2 tablespoons sugar, baking powder and baking soda and stir. In another bowl, mix buttermilk with egg, stir, add to flour mixture and whisk everything. Spoon this dough into 2 jars greased with cooking spray and cover with tin foil. Add the water to your instant pot, add the steamer basket inside, add jars, cover pot and cook on High for 25 minutes. Meanwhile, in a bowl, mix strawberries with 1 tablespoon sugar, rum, mint and lime zest and toss to coat Divide strawberry mix on shortcakes and serve. Enjoy!

Caramel Pudding

Preparation time: 20 minutes
Cooking time: 20 minutes
Servings: 2

Ingredients:
- Cooking spray
- ½ teaspoon baking powder
- ½ cup white flour
- 2 tablespoons white sugar
- ¼ teaspoon cinnamon
- 2 tablespoons butter
- 4 tablespoons milk
- 3 tablespoons pecans chopped
- 1 and ½ cups water
- 3 tablespoons raisins
- 3 tablespoons orange zest, grated
- 3 tablespoons brown sugar
- 3 tablespoons orange juice
- Caramel topping

Directions:
In a bowl, mix flour with white sugar, baking powder and cinnamon and stir. Add half of butter and milk and stir again well. Add pecans and raisins, stir and pour into a pudding pan greased with cooking spray. Heat up a small pan over medium high heat, add ½ cup water, orange juice, orange zest, the rest of the butter and the brown sugar, stir, bring to a boil for 2 minutes and pour over pudding. Add 1 cup water to your instant pot, add the steamer basket, add pudding pan inside, cover and cook on High for 20 minutes. Divide into 2 bowls and serve with caramel topping on top. Enjoy!

Nutrition: calories 194, fat 3, fiber 2, carbs 6, protein 7

Coconut Cream and Cinnamon Pudding

Preparation time: 10 minutes
Cooking time: 10 minutes
Servings: 6

Ingredients:
- 2 cups coconut cream
- 1 teaspoon cinnamon powder
- 6 tablespoons flour
- 5 tablespoons sugar
- Zest of 1 lemon, grated
- 2 cups water, for the instant pot

Directions:
Set your instant pot on sauté mode, add coconut cream, cinnamon and orange zest, stir, simmer for a couple of minutes, transfer to a bowl and leave aside. Add flour and sugar, stir well and divide this into ramekins. Add the water to your instant pot, add steamer basket, add ramekins, cover pot, cook on Low for 10 minutes and serve cold. Enjoy!

Nutrition: calories 170, fat 5, fiber 2, carbs 8, protein 10

Coconut Pancake

Preparation time: 10 minutes
Cooking time: 40 minutes
Servings: 4

Ingredients:
- 2 cups self-raising flour
- 2 tablespoons sugar
- 2 eggs
- 1 and ½ cups coconut milk
- A drizzle of olive oil

Directions:
In a bowl, mix eggs with sugar, milk and flour and whisk until you obtain a batter. Grease your instant pot with the oil, add the batter, spread into the pot, cover and cook on Low for 40 minutes. Slice pancake, divide between plates and serve cold. Enjoy!

Nutrition: calories 162, fat 3, fiber 2, carbs 7, protein 3

Black Tea Cake

Preparation time: 10 minutes
Cooking time: 30 minutes
Servings: 2

Ingredients:
- 2 tablespoons black tea powder
- ½ cup milk
- 1 tablespoon butter
- 1 cup sugar
- 2 eggs
- 1 teaspoons vanilla extract
- 3 tablespoons coconut oil
- 2 cups flour
- ¼ teaspoon baking soda
- 2 cups water
- 1 teaspoon baking powder

For the cream:
- 1 and ½ tablespoons honey
- 1 and ½ cups sugar
- ¼ cup butter, soft

Directions:
Put the milk and tea in a pot, warm it up over medium heat, take off the stove and leave aside to cool down. In a bowl, mix 1 tablespoon butter with 1 cup sugar, eggs, oil, vanilla extract, baking powder, baking soda and 2 cups flour, stir everything really well and pour into a greased pan. Add the water to your instant pot, add the steamer basket, add the cake pan, cover and cook on High for 30 minutes. Meanwhile, in a bowl, mix honey with 1 and ½ cups sugar and ¼ cup butter and whisk well. Spread this over cake, leave aside to cool down, divide between 2 plates and serve. Enjoy!

Nutrition: calories 150, fat 4, fiber 4, carbs 6, protein 2

Green Tea Pudding

Preparation time: 10 minutes
Cooking time: 5 minutes
Servings: 2

Ingredients:
- 7 ounces milk
- 1 tablespoon green tea powder
- 7 ounces heavy cream
- 1 and ½ tablespoons sugar
- ½ teaspoon honey

Directions:
In your instant pot, mix milk with green tea powder, heavy cream, sugar and honey, stir, cover and cook on High for 3 minutes. Divide into 2 cups and serve cold. Enjoy!

Nutrition: calories 110, fat 2, fiber 2, carbs 3, protein 6

Easy Plum Jam

Preparation time: 20 minutes
Cooking time: 8 minutes
Servings: 12

Ingredients:
- 3 pounds plums, stones removed and roughly chopped
- 2 tablespoons lemon juice
- 2 pounds sugar
- 1 teaspoon vanilla extract
- 3 ounces water

Directions:
In your instant pot, mix plums with sugar and vanilla extract, stir and leave aside for 20 minutes. Add lemon juice and water, stir, cover and cook on High for 8 minutes. Divide into bowls and serve cold. Enjoy!

Nutrition: calories 191, fat 3, fiber 4, carb 12, protein 4

Blueberry and Coconut Sweet Bowls

Preparation time: 10 minutes
Cooking time: 6 minutes
Servings: 1

Ingredients:
- 1 cup coconut milk
- 1 cup coconut, unsweetened and flaked
- 1 cup vanilla yogurt
- 1 cup blueberries
- 2 teaspoons sugar
- 1 and ½ cups water, for the instant pot

Directions:
In a heatproof dish, combine milk with coconut, yogurt, blueberries and sugar, stir well and cover with tin foil. Put the water in your instant pot, add trivet, add dish, cover and cook on High for 6 minutes. Divide into bowls and serve cold. Enjoy!

Nutrition: calories 142, fat 2, fiber 3, carbs 4, protein 6

Lemon Curd

Preparation time: 10 minutes
Cooking time: 10 minutes
Servings: 2

Ingredients:
- 2 cups blueberries
- ¼ cup lemon juice
- 2/3 cup sugar
- 2 teaspoons lemon zest, grated
- 4 tablespoons butter, softened
- 3 egg yolks, whisked
- 1 and ½ cups water

Directions:
Set your instant pot on sauté mode, add lemon juice and blueberries, stir and simmer for 2 minutes. Strain into a bowl, mash, mix with sugar, butter, lemon zest and egg yolks, whisk well and pour into a ramekin. Add the water to your instant pot, add the steamer basket, add the ramekin inside, cover pot and cook on High for 6 minutes. Serve this cold. Enjoy!

Nutrition: calories 140, fat 3, fiber 3, carbs 6, protein 8

Apples and Honey

Preparation time: 10 minutes
Cooking time: 20 minutes
Servings: 2

Ingredients:
- 2 big apples, cored
- 1 tablespoon raisins
- ½ tablespoon cinnamon, ground
- 2 tablespoons honey
- 1 and ½ cups water

Directions:
Stuff apples with raisins, sprinkle cinnamon and drizzle honey all over. Add the water to your instant pot, add the steamer basket, add apples, cover pot and cook on High for 10 minutes. Divide apples on 2 plates and serve. Enjoy!

Nutrition: calories 160, fat 2, fiber 3, carbs 4, protein 5

Strawberries Dessert

Preparation time: 5 minutes
Cooking time: 10 minutes
Servings: 2

Ingredients:
- 1/3 cup rolled oats
- 2 tablespoon strawberries, chopped
- 2 cups water
- 2/3 cup whole milk
- 2 teaspoons white sugar

Directions:
Put the water in your instant pot, add strawberries, oats, milk and sugar, stir, cover and cook on High for 10 minutes. Divide into 2 bowls and serve. Enjoy!

Nutrition: calories 160, fat 2, fiber 2, carbs 12, protein 8

Coconut and Avocado Pudding

Preparation time: 2 hours
Cooking time: 2 minutes
Servings: 3

Ingredients:
- ½ cup avocado oil
- 4 tablespoons sugar
- 1 tablespoon cocoa powder
- 14 ounces canned coconut milk
- 1 avocado, pitted, peeled and chopped

Directions:
In a bowl, mix oil with cocoa powder and half of the sugar, stir well, transfer to a lined container, keep in the fridge for 1 hour and chop into small pieces. In your instant pot, mix coconut milk with avocado and the rest of the sugar, blend using an immersion blender, cover pot and cook on High for 2 minutes. Add chocolate chips, stir, divide pudding into bowls and keep in the fridge until you serve it. Enjoy!

Nutrition: calories 140, fat 3, fiber 2, carbs 3, protein 4

Cocoa and Milk Pudding

Preparation time: 50 minutes
Cooking time: 3 minutes
Servings: 4

Ingredients:
- 1 and ½ cups water, for the instant pot+ 2 tablespoons
- 2 tablespoons gelatin
- 4 tablespoons sugar
- 4 tablespoons cocoa powder
- 2 cups coconut milk, hot
- ½ teaspoon cinnamon powder

Directions:
In a bowl, mix milk with sugar, cinnamon and cocoa powder and stir well. In a bowl, mix gelatin with 2 tablespoons water, stir well, add to cocoa mix, stir and divide into ramekins. Add the water to your instant pot, add the steamer basket, add ramekins inside, cover and cook on High for 4 minutes. Serve puddings cold. Enjoy!

Nutrition: calories 120, fat 2, fiber 1, carbs 4, protein 3

Peaches and Cream

Preparation time: 10 minutes
Cooking time: 3 minutes
Servings: 2

Ingredients:
- 2 peaches, stones removed and chopped
- 1 cup whole milk
- 2 teaspoons sugar
- 1 cup steel cut oats
- ½ vanilla bean
- 2 cups water

Directions:
Put the peaches in your instant pot, add milk, oats, vanilla bean and water, stir, cover and cook on High for 3 minutes. Divide into 2 bowls and serve. Enjoy!

Nutritional value: 130, fat 1, fiber 2, carbs 6, protein 3

Stuffed Peaches

Preparation time: 10 minutes
Cooking time: 4 minutes
Servings: 2

Ingredients:
- 2 peaches, tops cut off and insides removed
- 2 tablespoons flour
- 2 tablespoons maple syrup
- 2 tablespoons butter
- ½ teaspoon cinnamon powder
- ½ teaspoon almond extract
- 1 cup water

Directions:
In a bowl, mix flour with maple syrup, butter, cinnamon and almond extract, stir well and stuff peaches with this mix. Add the water to your instant pot, add the steamer basket, add peaches inside, cover and cook on High for 4 minutes. Arrange peaches on 2 plates and serve. Enjoy!

Nutrition: calories 140, fat 2, fiber 2, carbs 8, protein 3

Cocoa and Walnuts Sweet Cream

Preparation time: 10 minutes
Cooking time: 2 minutes
Servings: 6

Ingredients:
- 2 ounces avocado oil
- 4 tablespoons cocoa powder
- 1 teaspoon vanilla extract
- 1 cup walnuts, chopped
- 4 tablespoons sugar

Directions:
In your instant pot, mix oil with cocoa, vanilla, walnuts and sugar, blend using an immersion blender, cover pot and cook on High for 2 minutes. Divide into small bowls and keep in the fridge until you serve it. Enjoy!

Nutrition: calories 120, fat 4, fiber 3, carbs 9, protein 2

Cream Cheese Pudding

Preparation time: 10 minutes
Cooking time: 20 minutes
Servings: 2

Ingredients:
- 1 and ½ teaspoons caramel extract
- 2 ounces cream cheese
- 2 eggs
- 1 and ½ tablespoons sugar
- ¼ teaspoon vanilla extract
- 1 cup water, for the instant pot

Directions:
In your blender, mix cream cheese with eggs, caramel extract, vanilla extract and sugar, pulse well and divide into greased ramekins. Add the water to your instant pot, add steamer basket, add ramekins inside, cover and cook on High for 20 minutes. Serve your puddings cold. Enjoy!

Nutrition: calories 174, fat 7, fiber 1, carbs 2, protein 4

Cranberry and Pear Cake

Preparation time: 10 minutes
Cooking time: 35 minutes
Servings: 2

Ingredients:
- 1 cup flour
- ¼ teaspoon baking powder
- ¼ teaspoon baking soda
- ¼ teaspoon cardamom, ground
- 4 tablespoons milk
- 3 tablespoons maple syrup
- 1 tablespoon flax seeds
- 1 tablespoon vegetable oil
- ½ cup pear, cored and chopped
- 4 tablespoons cranberries, chopped
- 1 and ½ cups water

Directions:
In a bowl, mix flour with baking soda and powder, cardamom, milk, flax seeds, maple syrup and oil and stir well. Add chopped pear and cranberries, stir and pour into a greased cake pan. Add the water to your instant pot, add the steamer basket, add cake pan, cover pot and cook on High for 35 minutes. Divide between 2 dessert plates and serve. Enjoy!

Nutrition: calories 140, fat 3, fiber 2, carbs 9, protein 3

Chocolate Fondue

Preparation time: 5 minutes
Cooking time: 2 minutes
Servings: 2

Ingredients:
- 2 cups water
- 1.5 ounces dark chocolate, cut into chunks
- 1.5 ounces coconut milk
- ½ teaspoon Amaretto liquor

Directions:
In a ramekin, mix chocolate pieces with coconut milk and liquor. Add the water to your instant pot, add the steamer basket, add ramekin, cover and cook on High for 2 minutes. Stir chocolate mix well and serve. Enjoy!

Nutrition: calories 180, fat 2, fiber 3, carbs 7, protein 3

Egg and Coconut Cream

Preparation time: 20 minutes
Cooking time: 10 minutes
Servings: 6

Ingredients:
- 2 cups coconut cream, hot
- 1 teaspoon cinnamon powder
- 6 egg yolks
- 5 tablespoons sugar
- Zest of 1 lemon, grated
- 2 cups water, for the instant pot

Directions:
In a bowl, mix cream with cinnamon and orange zest, stir and leave aside to cool down Add egg yolks and sugar, stir well, strain and divide this into ramekins. Add the water to your instant pot, add steamer basket, add ramekins, cover pot and cook on Low for 10 minutes. Serve cold. Enjoy!

Nutrition: calories 190, fat 4, fiber 2, carbs 12, protein 11

Blueberries and Strawberries Compote

Preparation time: 10 minutes
Cooking time: 7 minutes
Servings: 8

Ingredients:
- 1 cup blueberries
- 2 cups strawberries, chopped
- 2 tablespoons lemon juice
- White sugar to the taste
- 1 tablespoon water

Directions:
In your instant pot, mix blueberries with strawberries, lemon juice, sugar and water, stir, cover, cook on High for 7 minutes, divide into cups and serve cold. Enjoy!

Nutrition: calories 170, fat 2, fiber 3, carbs 12, protein 2

Pear and Maple Dessert

Preparation time: 10 minutes
Cooking time: 10 minutes
Servings: 2

Ingredients:
- 1 pear, cored and chopped
- ½ teaspoon maple extract
- 2 cups milk
- ½ cup steel cut oats
- ½ teaspoon vanilla extract
- 1 tablespoon stevia
- ¼ cup walnuts, chopped for serving

Directions:
In your instant pot, mix pear with maple extract, milk, oats, vanilla extract, sugar and walnuts, stir, cover and cook on High for 10 minutes. Divide into 2 bowls and serve. Enjoy!

Nutrition: calories 150, fat 1, fiber 2, carbs 4, protein 4

Cherry Bowls

Preparation time: 10 minutes
Cooking time: 10 minutes
Servings: 2

Ingredients:
- 1 cup milk
- 1 cup water+ 1 tablespoon
- ½ cup steel cut oats
- 1 tablespoon cocoa powder
- 1 cup cherries, pitted + 3 tablespoons
- 2 tablespoons maple syrup
- ½ teaspoon almond extract

Directions:
Put the milk in your instant pot, add 1 cup water, oats, cocoa powder, 3 tablespoons cherries, maple syrup and half of the almond extract, stir, cover and cook on High for 10 minutes. Meanwhile, in a pot, mix 1 tablespoon water with 3 tablespoons cherries and the rest of the almond extract, stir and simmer for a few minutes over medium high heat. Divide cherries mix into 2 bowls, drizzle the sauce all over and serve. Enjoy!

Nutrition: calories 120, fat 1, fiber 2, carbs 4, protein 4

Sweet Zucchini Bread

Preparation time: 10 minutes
Cooking time: 20 minutes
Servings: 6

Ingredients:
- 1 cup milk
- 3 eggs, whisked
- 4 tablespoons sugar
- 2 cups zucchini, grated
- 2 and ½ cups self-raising flour
- 2 cups water, for the instant pot

Directions:
In a bowl, mix milk with eggs, sugar, flour and zucchini, whisk well and pour into a loaf pan. Add the water to your instant pot, add steamer basket, add cake pan, cover and cook on High for 20 minutes. Slice and serve cold as a dessert. Enjoy!

Nutrition: calories 200, fat 3, fiber 6, carbs 12, protein 3

Poached Figs

Preparation time: 10 minutes
Cooking time: 4 minutes
Servings: 4

Ingredients:
- 1 cup grape juice
- 1 pound figs
- ½ cup pine nuts, toasted
- 4 tablespoons brown sugar
- ¼ teaspoon vanilla extract

Directions:
In your instant pot, mix grape juice with figs and sugar, cover pot and cook on High for 4 minutes. Divide this into bowls, sprinkle pine nuts on top and serve cold. Enjoy!

Nutrition: calories 140, fat 0, fiber 2, carbs 10, protein 3

Cold Pineapple and Cherries Mix

Preparation time: 10 minutes
Cooking time: 10 minutes
Servings: 10

Ingredients:
- 3 cups canned pineapple chunks, drained
- 3 cups canned cherries, drained
- 3 cups natural applesauce
- 2 tablespoons sugar
- 1 teaspoon cinnamon powder

Directions:
Put pineapples, cherries, applesauce, cinnamon and sugar in your instant pot, cover and cook on High for 10 minutes. Divide into dessert bowls and keep in the fridge until you serve. Enjoy!

Nutrition: calories 140, fat 0, fiber 2, carbs 2, protein 1

Fall Plums Mix

Preparation time: 10 minutes
Cooking time: 6 minutes
Servings: 4

Ingredients:
- 12 plums, stones removed and halved
- 1 tablespoon cornstarch
- 2 cup sugar
- 1 teaspoon vanilla extract
- 6 tablespoons water

Directions:
In your instant pot, mix plums with sugar, cornstarch, vanilla and water, stir, cover and cook on High for 6 minutes. Divide into bowls and serve cold. Enjoy!

Nutrition: calories 150, fat 2, fiber 1, carbs 6, protein 5

Sweet Blueberry Butter

Preparation time: 10 minutes
Cooking time: 10 minutes
Servings: 2

Ingredients:
- 1 cup blueberries puree
- ½ teaspoons cinnamon powder
- Zest from 1/3 lemon, grated
- 2 tablespoons sugar
- A pinch of nutmeg, ground
- ¼ teaspoon ginger, ground

Directions:
In your instant pot, mix blueberries with cinnamon, lemon zest, sugar, nutmeg and ginger, stir, cover and cook on High for 10 minutes. Divide into jars and serve cold. Enjoy!

Nutrition: calories 133, fat 1, fiber 2, carbs 4, protein 6

Sweet Quinoa Dessert

Preparation time: 10 minutes
Cooking time: 20 minutes
Servings: 2

Ingredients:
- ½ cup apricots, dried and chopped
- ½ cup red quinoa
- ¼ cup steel cut oats
- 1 tablespoon sugar
- ¼ teaspoon vanilla bean paste
- ¼ cup hazelnuts, toasted and chopped
- 3 cups water

Directions:
In your instant pot, mix quinoa with apricots, oats, sugar, vanilla paste, hazelnuts and water, stir, cover and cook on High for 20 minutes. Divide into 2 bowls and serve. Enjoy!

Nutrition: calories 151, fat 3, fiber 5, carbs 6, protein 5

Sweet Baked Plums

Preparation time: 10 minutes
Cooking time: 6 minutes
Servings: 2

Ingredients:
- 6 plums, stones removed and halved
- 1 cup sugar
- ½ teaspoon cinnamon powder
- 3 tablespoons water
- ½ tablespoon cornstarch

Directions:
In your instant pot, mix plums with sugar, cinnamon, water and cornstarch, stir, cover and cook on High for 6 minutes. Divide into 2 bowls and serve cold. Enjoy!

Nutrition: calories 140, fat 2, fiber 1, carbs 3, protein 4

Pumpkin and Coconut Sweet Mix

Preparation time: 10 minutes
Cooking time: 14 minutes
Servings: 6

Ingredients:
- 2 cups water
- 1 tablespoon butter, melted
- 1 cup pumpkin puree
- 1 cup coconut flakes
- 3 tablespoons sugar

Directions:
Set your instant pot on sauté mode, add butter, heat up, add coconut flakes, pumpkin, water and sugar stir, cover and cook on High for 14 minutes. Divide into bowls and serve cold. Enjoy!

Nutrition: calories 202, fat 2, fiber 4, carbs 8, protein 3

Apricot Marmalade

Preparation time: 10 minutes
Cooking time: 15 minutes
Servings: 4

Ingredients:
- 2 pounds apricots, stones removed and halved
- 1 pound sugar
- 2 oranges, peeled and sliced
- 1 tablespoon butter
- ½ teaspoon vanilla extract

Directions:
Put apricots in your food processor, pulse, set the instant pot on sauté mode, add apricots mix to the pot, also add sugar and orange slices, stir and boil the jam for 6 minutes. Add butter and vanilla extract, cover, cook on High for 8 minutes, divide into jars and serve cold. Enjoy!

Nutrition: calories 200, fat 0, fiber 2, carbs 7, protein 3

Milk and Cream Pudding

Preparation time: 10 minutes
Cooking time: 5 minutes
Servings: 4

Ingredients:
- 14 ounces milk
- 2 tablespoons matcha powder
- 14 ounces heavy cream
- 3 tablespoons sugar
- 1 teaspoon honey

Directions:
In your instant pot, mix milk with green tea powder, heavy cream, sugar and honey, stir, cover and cook on High for 5 minutes. Divide into dessert cups and keep in the fridge until you serve it. Enjoy!

Nutrition: calories 220, fat 1, fiber 2, carbs 5, protein 2

Fall Pear Cake

Preparation time: 10 minutes
Cooking time: 35 minutes
Servings: 4

Ingredients:
- 2 cups self-raising flour
- 8 tablespoons milk
- 5 tablespoons maple syrup
- 2 tablespoons vegetable oil
- 1 cup pear, cored and chopped
- 1 and ½ cups water, for the instant pot

Directions:
In a bowl, mix flour with milk, maple syrup, oil and pear, stir and pour into a greased cake pan. Add the water to your instant pot, add the steamer basket, add cake pan, cover and cook on High for 35 minutes. Leave cake to cool down, slice and serve. Enjoy!

Nutrition: calories 150, fat 2, fiber 2, carbs 10, protein 2

Recipe Index

A

Acorn Squash Side Dish, 131
Appetizer Egg Spread, 204
Apple Bread, 217
Apple Butter, 39
Apple Cake, 224
Apple Cobbler, 218
Apple Steel Cut Oats, 19
Apples and Honey, 252
Apples and Pears Salad, 246
Apples and Red Grape Juice, 246
Apples and Wine Sauce, 235
Apricot Jam, 242
Apricot Marmalade, 262
Apricots and Cranberries Pudding, 228
Arborio Rice Side Salad, 151
Artichokes and Citrus Sauce, 97
Artichokes Side Dish, 127
Artichokes Spread, 197
Asian Wings, 172
Avocado Spread, 57

B

Baby Back Ribs Appetizer, 171
Baby Carrots Snack, 166
Baked Custard, 227
Baked Sweet Potatoes, 116
Banana Cake, 216
BBQ Chicken Wings, 169
BBQ Square Ribs, 174
Bean Casserole, 96
Beans and Avocado Salsa, 142
Beans and Chorizo, 124
Beans Cake, 228
Beans Chili, 98
Beef and Artichokes, 82
Beef Curry, 82
Beef Dip, 167
Beef Meatballs, 169
Beef Sandwiches, 209
Beef Stew, 66
Beef Stew, 71
Beet and Cabbage Mix, 132
Beet Appetizer Salad, 183
Beet Soup, 87
Beets Cakes, 193
Beets Side Dish, 130
Beets Spread, 55
Bell Peppers and Sausages, 148
Bell Peppers Stir Fry, 146
Black Bean Soup, 72
Black Bean Soup, 89

Black Beans Patties, 189
Black Rice Pudding, 220
Black Tea Cake, 250
Blue Cheese Dip, 184
Blueberries and Strawberries Compote, 257
Blueberry and Coconut Sweet Bowls, 251
Blueberry Breakfast Bowl, 25
Blueberry Breakfast Delight, 32
Blueberry Jam, 242
Boiled Peanuts, 173
Bok Choy and Rice, 152
Braised Collard Greens, 129
Braised Endives, 150
Bread Pudding, 35
Bread Pudding, 244
Breakfast Apple Dish, 42
Breakfast Apple Dumplings, 60
Breakfast Arugula Salad, 45
Breakfast Bacon Potatoes, 32
Breakfast Banana Bread, 30
Breakfast Banana Bread, 33
Breakfast Cheese Spread, 58
Breakfast Chestnut Butter, 62
Breakfast Chickpeas Spread, 58
Breakfast Cobbler, 41
Breakfast Couscous Salad, 62
Breakfast Egg Salad, 50
Breakfast Meat Soufflé, 18
Breakfast Orange Marmalade, 52
Breakfast Rice and Chickpeas Medley, 43
Breakfast Rice Pudding, 27
Breakfast Rice Pudding, 38
Breakfast Tortillas, 29
Broccoli and Bacon Appetizer Salad, 198
Broccoli and Cheese Soup, 93
Broccoli and Garlic, 132
Broccoli Appetizer Salad, 196
Broccoli Pasta, 116
Brown Rice Mix, 42
Brown Rice Salad, 155
Brussels Sprouts and Apples Appetizer, 202
Brussels Sprouts and Broccoli Appetizer Salad, 200
Brussels Sprouts and Chestnuts, 139
Brussels Sprouts and Potato Bowls, 47
Brussels Sprouts and Potatoes Appetizer Salad, 206
Brussels Sprouts Side Salad, 137
Buckwheat Porridge, 28
Buckwheat Porridge, 37

C

Cabbage and Cream, 128
Cabbage Rolls, 187

Cabbage Side Dish, 122
Cajun Sausage Mix, 99
Calamari Salad, 211
Calamari Stew, 109
Cantaloupe Soup, 95
Caramel Pudding, 248
Carrot Breakfast Salad, 61
Carrot Cake, 236
Carrot Pudding and Rum Sauce, 238
Carrots and Kale, 128
Cashew Spread, 210
Cauliflower and Barley Bowls, 49
Cauliflower and Grapes, 139
Cauliflower Dip, 195
Cauliflower Salad, 105
Cauliflower Salad, 213
Celeriac Breakfast Mix, 51
Cheesecake, 236
Cheesy Broccoli Appetizer Salad, 198
Cheesy Cauliflower Bowls, 53
Cherry Bowls, 258
Cherry Pie, 229
Chestnut Mushrooms, 135
Chicken and Fennel Soup, 88
Chicken and Kale Soup, 88
Chicken and Potatoes Mix, 99
Chicken and Red Cabbage Soup, 90
Chicken and Salsa, 111
Chicken and Tomatillo Salsa, 80
Chicken and Veggie Soup, 86
Chicken Appetizer Salad, 201
Chicken Curry, 66
Chicken Dip, 184
Chicken Sandwiches, 213
Chicken with Dates, 80
Chicken Wrap, 76
Chickpea Curry, 74
Chickpeas Appetizer, 191
Chickpeas Cakes, 113
Chili Dip, 185
Chili Mahi Mahi, 79
Chinese Fish, 106
Chinese Mustard Greens, 131
Chinese Style Peanuts, 170
Chocolate Bread Pudding, 36
Chocolate Cake, 226
Chocolate Cake, 233
Chocolate Fondue, 256
Chocolate Oatmeal, 17
Chocolate Pudding, 238
Chunky Warm Salsa, 186
Clams Appetizer, 181
Classic Ricotta Cake, 232
Cocktail Boiled Peanuts, 168

Cocoa and Milk Pudding, 253
Cocoa and Walnuts Sweet Cream, 255
Coconut and Avocado Pudding, 253
Coconut Cabbage, 161
Coconut Cream and Cinnamon Pudding, 249
Coconut Pancake, 249
Coconut Quinoa, 76
Cod and Beer, 104
Cod and Orange Sauce, 81
Cold Pineapple and Cherries Mix, 260
Collard Greens and Bacon, 152
Collard Greens and Peas, 129
Collard Greens Stew, 105
Comforting Chicken Dish, 73
Corn Dip, 185
Corn on the Cob, 163
Cornmeal Porridge, 27
Cornmeal Porridge, 40
Couscous and Mint, 63
Crab Spread, 180
Cranberries Dessert Bowl, 216
Cranberry and Pear Cake, 256
Cranberry Beans Salad, 45
Cranberry Bread Pudding, 244
Cranberry Side Dish, 140
Cream and Cinnamon Puddings, 235
Cream Cheese Pudding, 255
Cream of Spinach, 95
Creamy Broccoli Appetizer, 196
Creamy Corn, 134
Creamy Endives Appetizer Salad, 214
Creamy Spinach, 125
Creamy Squash Bowl, 59
Crispy Chicken, 68
Crispy Chicken, 173
Crunchy Brussels Sprouts Salad, 200
Cumin Dip, 186

D
Dates and Ricotta Cake, 239
Delicious and Simple Octopus, 85
Delicious Berry Cobbler, 225
Delicious Egg Bake, 16
Delicious Green Beans and Blue Cheese, 123
Delicious Meatloaf, 94
Delicious Mushrooms Side Dish, 136
Delicious Onion Soup, 90
Delicious Ribs, 69
Delicious Shiitake Mushrooms Mix, 137

E
Easy Apples and Wine, 226
Easy Breakfast Butter, 60
Easy Endives Platter, 212
Easy Lemon Pie, 223
Easy Mac and Cheese, 67

Easy Plum Jam, 251
Easy Sweet Soufflé, 219
Easy Tortillas, 199
Easy Turkey Mix, 101
Egg and Coconut Cream, 257
Egg Muffins, 35
Eggplant and Cashews Mix, 156
Eggs and Bacon Breakfast Risotto, 23
Espresso Oatmeal, 38
Espresso Steel Cut Oats, 17

F
Fall Pear Cake, 263
Fall Plums Mix, 260
Fast Breakfast Oatmeal, 24
Fast Salmon, 75
Fast Shrimp Scampi, 83
Fennel and Shallots, 158
Fennel Cream, 103
Fish and Orange Sauce, 114
Fish Balls, 166
Fish Soup, 79
Flavored Parmesan Mushrooms, 143
Flavored Pasta, 96
Flavored Pears, 237
French Eggs, 23
French Toast, 20
Fresh Bulgur Appetizer, 207
Fresh Peach Jam, 52

G
Garlic Beets Salad, 160
Garlic Green Beans, 126
Ginger and Peach Marmalade, 241
Ginger Cookies Cheesecake, 243
Glazed Fruits, 231
Grated Carrot Appetizer Salad, 176
Greek Meatballs, 168
Green Beans and Bacon, 140
Green Beans and Cranberries Side Dish, 123
Green Beans Fries, 145
Green Beans Salad, 176
Green Beans Stew, 111
Green Cabbage and Tomatoes Side Dish, 156
Green Olive Pate, 190
Green Tea Pudding, 250

H
Ham and Cheese Dip, 178
Ham And Egg Casserole, 16
Haricots Verts Side Salad, 121
Honey Chicken Appetizer, 177
Hot Wings, 177
Hulled Barley Appetizer, 203

I
Italian Dip, 179
Italian Eggplant Breakfast Mix, 59
Italian Eggplants Bowls, 49
Italian Mussels, 181

J
Jambalaya, 102
Juicy Roast, 67

K
Kale and Carrots Salad, 192
Kale and Wild Rice Appetizer Salad, 194
Kale Sauté, 126
Kidney Beans and Corn Side Dish, 155

L
Lamb Casserole, 100
Lamb Ribs, 215
Lemon and Maple Syrup Pudding, 245
Lemon and Olive Chicken, 78
Lemon and Orange Jam, 239
Lemon Cookies, 233
Lemon Curd, 252
Lemon Lamb Chops, 115
Lemon Marmalade, 222
Lemon Pepper Salmon, 77
Lemon Pudding, 240
Lemony Endives Appetizer, 212
Lentils Patties, 189
Light Lemon Dip, 188
Lime Pie, 234

M
Mango Salsa, 193
Mango Side Salad, 160
Mashed Potatoes, 136
Mediterranean Cod, 112
Mexican Breakfast, 20
Mexican Corn on the Cob, 174
Mexican Zucchini Side Dish, 144
Milk and Cream Pudding, 263
Millet and Oats Porridge, 31
Millet Porridge, 56
Millet Pudding, 220
Minestrone Soup, 91
Minty Carrots, 117
Minty Kale Salad, 194
Mixed Veggies, 145
Mixed Veggies Side Dish, 148
Mushroom Appetizer Salad, 210
Mushroom Cakes, 191
Mushroom Dip, 195
Mushrooms and Asparagus, 138
Mussels and White Wine Sauce, 87
Mussels Appetizer, 179
Mussels Bowls, 97

O
Octopus Appetizer, 201
Onion Cream, 89

Onion Dip, 183
Onion, Celery and Bread Side Dish, 138
Orange and Beet Appetizer, 203
Orange Cream, 230

P

Parmesan Zucchini Fries, 141
Parsnip and Quinoa Breakfast Mix, 48
Pasta and Spinach, 98
Pasta Appetizer Salad, 175
Pasta with Salmon and Pesto, 110
Pea and Ham Soup, 100
Pea Rice, 158
Peach and Cinnamon Compote, 243
Peach Breakfast, 34
Peach Compote, 234
Peach Jam, 232
Peaches and Cream, 254
Peaches Oatmeal, 19
Peanut Butter Cups, 221
Pear and Maple Dessert, 258
Pearl Onions Side Dish, 121
Pears with Garlic and Jelly, 230
Pineapple and Peas Breakfast Curry, 47
Pineapple Pudding, 247
Pinto Bean Dip, 188
Pinto Beans Breakfast Salad, 57
Poached Fennel, 157
Poached Figs, 259
Poached Pears, 237
Pomegranate Oatmeal, 53
Pork and Lemon Sauce, 103
Pork and Pineapple Delight, 84
Pork Burritos, 209
Pork Cakes, 215
Pork Chops and Tomato Sauce, 73
Pork Roast, 84
Pork Tenderloin and Pomegranate Sauce, 115
Potato and Salmon Breakfast, 64
Potato and Spinach Hash, 33
Potato Soup, 93
Potato Soup, 94
Potato Wedges, 167
Potatoes and Shrimp Appetizer Salad, 204
Pumpkin and Coconut Sweet Mix, 262
Pumpkin Cake, 224
Pumpkin Granola, 218
Pumpkin Oatmeal, 28

Q

Quinoa and Tomatoes Breakfast Mix, 43
Quinoa Bowls, 25
Quinoa Breakfast, 26
Quinoa Salad, 44
Quinoa with Sausages, 56

R

Radishes Side Salad, 159
Red Onions and Apples Mix, 133
Red Pepper Dip, 197
Red Pepper Soup, 92
Refried Beans, 118
Rhubarb and Strawberries Mix, 229
Rhubarb Breakfast Spread, 65
Rice and Beans, 70
Rice and Black Beans Breakfast Dish, 46
Rice and Edamame, 157
Rice Pudding, 220
Rice with Fennel, 161
Rich Breakfast Potatoes, 54
Rich Chicken Salad, 107
Roasted Hummus, 175

S

Salmon and Chili Sauce, 108
Salmon and Risotto, 106
Salmon and Veggies, 110
Salmon Casserole, 108
Salmon with Lemon, 104
Sautéed Escarole, 165
Scallion Spread, 180
Shrimp and Tomatoes Appetizer Mix, 190
Shrimp Boil, 83
Simple Banana Cake, 247
Simple BBQ Ribs, 102
Simple Beef Dish, 74
Simple Bok Choy Side Dish, 150
Simple Burrito Casserole, 22
Simple Buttery Potatoes, 143
Simple Cake Bars, 221
Simple Cauliflower Rice, 118
Simple Chicken Fall Stew, 101
Simple Chili, 69
Simple Collard Greens Side Dish, 154
Simple Corn Side Dish, 147
Simple Frittata, 21
Simple Fruit Cobbler, 36
Simple Lamb Ribs and Sauce, 109
Simple Potato Salad, 48
Simple Pumpkin and Yogurt Cake, 217
Simple Quince Jam, 63
Simple Red Pepper Hummus, 172
Simple Ricotta Mousse, 227
Simple Roasted Potatoes, 120
Simple Scotch Eggs, 24
Simple Shredded Chicken, 71
Simple Shrimp, 81
Simple Spinach Side Dish, 153
Southern Peanuts, 170
Spaghetti Squash Delight, 127
Spanish Frittata, 22
Spanish Rice, 124

Special Breakfast Beans, 44
Special Cookies, 225
Special Pancake, 29
Special Ranch Spread, 182
Spicy Chicken Wings, 107
Spicy Collard Greens, 154
Spicy Salmon, 112
Spicy Tomato Jam, 232
Spicy Zucchini, 142
Spinach and Squash Mix, 164
Spinach Pasta, 113
Squash and Apple Mash, 153
Squash and Apple Soup, 86
Squash Porridge, 30
Squash Porridge, 37
Squash Risotto, 122
Steamed Leeks, 163
Steamed Tilapia, 77
Stir Fried Okra, 165
Strawberries Dessert, 252
Strawberry and Chia Marmalade, 245
Strawberry and Rhubarb Breakfast Compote, 65
Strawberry Jam, 50
Strawberry Quinoa Bowl, 40
Strawberry Shortcakes, 248
Stuffed Bell Peppers Appetizer, 206
Stuffed Chicken Breasts, 171
Stuffed Peaches, 254
Stuffed Strawberries, 231
Summer Lentils Appetizer, 207
Sweet and Sour Side Salad, 119
Sweet Baked Plums, 261
Sweet Blueberry Butter, 261
Sweet Brussels Sprouts, 120
Sweet Brussels Sprouts Appetizer, 202
Sweet Chia Pudding, 222
Sweet Corn Pudding, 240
Sweet Pearl Onion Mix, 149
Sweet Potato Hash, 31
Sweet Potato Puree, 130
Sweet Potato Side Salad, 162
Sweet Potatoes Casserole, 54
Sweet Potatoes Mash, 162
Sweet Quinoa Dessert, 261
Sweet Zucchini Bread, 259
Swiss Chard Salad, 55
Swiss Chard Soup, 91

T

Tapioca Pudding, 61
Tasty and Easy Shrimp, 114

Tasty Beef and Broccoli, 75
Tasty Black Bean Salsa, 182
Tasty Blackberry Pie, 219
Tasty Breakfast Cake, 26
Tasty Carrots and Walnuts Salad, 119
Tasty Carrots Mix, 117
Tasty Maple Acorn Squash Dish, 133
Tasty Mushrooms and Rosemary, 135
Tasty Pho, 72
Tasty Quiche, 18
Tasty Rice and Quinoa, 134
Tasty Spinach and Salami, 125
Tasty Tikka Masala, 78
Tasty Turkey Meatballs, 70
Tasty Vidalia Onions Mix, 141
Teriyaki Scallops, 85
Tofu and Sweet Potato Mix, 41
Tofu Appetizer, 187
Tomatoes and Burrata Side Salad, 151
Tomatoes and Corn Side Salad, 149
Tomatoes and Garlic Dip, 208
Tomatoes Appetizer Salad, 192
Tomatoes Side Salad, 147
Turkey Breast Breakfast Mix, 51
Turkey Soup, 92
Turnip Mash, 159
Turnips and Chili Pepper Side Dish, 164
Turnips Spread, 211
Vegetarian Lentils Soup, 68

V

Veggie and Couscous Breakfast, 64
Veggie Breakfast Casserole, 34
Veggie Dumplings, 208
Veggie Quiche, 39
Veggies and Wheat Appetizer Salad, 205

W

Watercress Appetizer Salad, 178
Western Omelette, 21
Wheat Berries Appetizer, 205
White Beans Dip, 199
White Chocolate Mousse, 223
Wild Rice Breakfast Salad, 46
Winter Cherry Mix, 241

Y

Yellow Squash and Zucchini, 146

Z

Zucchini and Mushrooms, 144
Zucchini Spread, 214

Copyright 2018 by Shon Brooks All rights reserved.

All rights Reserved. No part of this publication or the information in it may be quoted from or reproduced in any form by means such as printing, scanning, photocopying or otherwise without prior written permission of the copyright holder.

Disclaimer and Terms of Use: Effort has been made to ensure that the information in this book is accurate and complete, however, the author and the publisher do not warrant the accuracy of the information, text and graphics contained within the book due to the rapidly changing nature of science, research, known and unknown facts and internet. The Author and the publisher do not hold any responsibility for errors, omissions or contrary interpretation of the subject matter herein. This book is presented solely for motivational and informational purposes only.

Made in the USA
Lexington, KY
14 July 2018